The Origins of the Borough of Wallingford

Archaeological and historical perspectives

Edited by

K. S. B. Keats-Rohan
D. R. Roffe

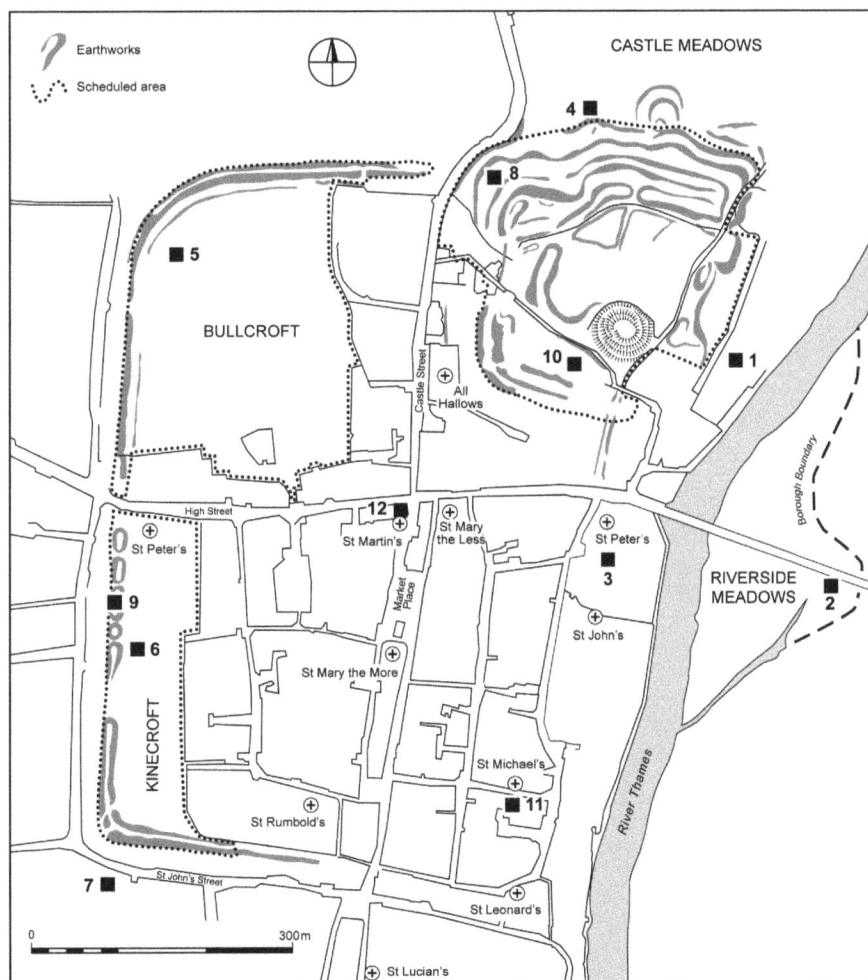

BAR British Series 494
2009

Published in 2016 by
BAR Publishing, Oxford

BAR British Series 494

The Origins of the Borough of Wallingford

ISBN 978 1 4073 0537 0

BAR Publishing is the trading name of British Archaeological Reports (Oxford) Ltd.
British Archaeological Reports was first incorporated in 1974 to publish the BAR
Series, International and British. In 1992 Hadrian Books Ltd became part of the BAR
group. This volume was originally published by Archaeopress in conjunction with
British Archaeological Reports (Oxford) Ltd / Hadrian Books Ltd, the Series principal
publisher, in 2009. This present volume is published by BAR Publishing, 2016.

Printed in England

BAR
PUBLISHING

BAR titles are available from:

BAR Publishing
122 Banbury Rd, Oxford, OX2 7BP, UK
EMAIL   info@barpublishing.com
PHONE   +44 (0)1865 310431
FAX   +44 (0)1865 316916
www.barpublishing.com

CONTENTS

FIGURES

FOREWORD

The importance of Wallingford's well-defined defensive earthworks and ditches has long been recognized. Its familiar rectilinear features, and road pattern, disturbed by the later imposition of a Norman castle in the north-east and a priory in the north-west, were interpreted for several centuries as survivals of a Roman town, with a closely argued case being made by the Victorian owner and occupier of the castle site, John Kirby Hedges. He engaged in much historical investigation, employing researchers to transcribe documents in the Public Record Office. His privately published two-volume work was the first serious attempt to compile a full history of the town and while there are many inaccuracies and misinterpretations, it has nevertheless proved a useful starting point for more thorough documentary work. The full recognition of Wallingford's Saxon significance emerged as Anglo-Saxon archaeology gained greater recognition as an academic discipline from the 1950s. Excavations by Nicholas Brooks in the 1960s were published only as a short interim report but clearly supported a Saxon dating of parts of the defences as did other smaller excavations such as the cutting through the Saxon defences in 1971.

The archaeological implications of potential development in the town were highlighted in a publication by Caroline Simpson for the newly formed Oxford Archaeological Unit in 1973. This led directly to a public meeting in November 1973, convened by OAU's first director, Tom Hassall, at which The Wallingford Historical and Archaeological Society (TWHAS) was founded. The new society took on a specific brief to keep watch over the town's historic legacy, a function which it continues to fulfil. The Wallingford Museum, opened in 1981, was a development from TWHAS, with a role of presenting the town's history to the public. TWHAS has run a continuing research programme for exhibitions since its inception and in the past 10 years has made a more significant contribution by collecting together *Sources for Wallingford History*, a large body of printed transcripts, abstracts, extracts and references from primary and secondary sources from the 12th to 20th centuries. There is also a searchable people index with over 70,000 entries. The rich body of Wallingford Borough medieval records, located in the Berkshire Record Office, include a wide variety of 12th – 15th century documents providing considerable scope for further research.

Though many small archaeological investigations have been made within the town in the last 35 years, it is only with the present Wallingford *Burh* to Borough Project that Wallingford has become the subject of an in-depth archaeological study. The Project recognized that the town still has many large undeveloped open spaces, which give it a unique archaeological potential. It also appreciated the value of the research done by TWHAS whose members were happy to share their findings. The organization of the *Origins of Wallingford* conference in May 2008 was a contribution to the Project by TWHAS to enable a formal coming together of academic expertise on Wallingford's past for the first time and to provide a platform for broader based questions on early urban development.

The papers collected here embody the discussions that ensued. Six were presented in the conference; that given by David Hill has been omitted since its substance has been published elsewhere. A further paper comparing Wallingford with Bedford by Matt Edgeworth (originally read to a meeting of the CBA in Wallingford in April 2008) has been added to the collection. Together, they represent interestingly disparate disciplinary approaches and it should be borne in mind that they reflect the coming together of expertise in the initial stages of this project. They are a fascinating convergence of archaeological and historical scholarship which it is hoped will raise questions that will stimulate further consideration of the fundamental question of the origins and development of medieval towns.

Judy Dewey, August 2009
Curator of Wallingford Museum

ACKNOWLEDGEMENTS

This book is largely the product of a day conference held on 31 May 2008, The Origins of Wallingford: A Reassessment. We should like first and foremost to thank the many members of The Wallingford Historical and Archaeological Society who gave such full and enthusiastic support to mounting what was the Society's first large-scale conference, attended by some 120 people. Secondly, sincere thanks to our hosts for the event, the Wallingford Methodist Church, who provided an outstanding venue in the heart of Wallingford itself. Stuart Dewey, President of TWHAS, gave the opening address and, together with Ron Calcutt, provided the technical backup for each of the presentations. Special thanks are due to Paul Smith, Oxfordshire County Archaeologist, who ably chaired papers throughout the day and gave an excellent summing up at the end.

The editors are grateful to our publishers BAR for accepting and publishing this work, to our contributors for the range and quality of their contributions, and to those who have provided specialist input in the form of illustrations, such as Stuart Dewey, Mike Rouillard and June Strong, and to our typesetter John Saunders, who gamely agreed to turn a complex project around in a very short time. We also thank David Hemming for the contributions to the Wallingford Bibliography printed here, many of which came from his invaluable website, http://sites.google.com/site/wallingfordhistorygateway/.

Finally, a special tribute is due to Judy Dewey, who, always ably assisted by husband Stuart, has brought a new dimension to the role of local historian. Without their tireless work TWHAS and the allied Wallingford Museum would not have come into existence. The new awareness that these ventures created have certainly helped to preserve much of Wallingford's heritage from inappropriate development. A born communicator, Judy is much in demand as a course and single event lecturer. Her encyclopaedic knowledge of the town and its history has been generously shared with all contributors to this volume, and has helped to save the editors from a number of *faux pas*. For any that remain, the editors take full responsibility.

Katharine Keats-Rohan and David Roffe
2009

NOTES ON CONTRIBUTORS

Paul Booth

Paul Booth is a senior project manager at Oxford Archaeology where he has been for nearly 20 years, having previously worked for Warwickshire Museum. He has wide-ranging interests in Roman Britain, from rural settlement and 'small towns' to pottery production and use. Current preoccupations include aspects of Romano-British religion, burials and cemeteries.

Neil Christie

Neil Christie is currently Reader in Archaeology at the University of Leicester and Co-Director of the Wallingford *Burh* to Borough Research Project. His principal research interests have focussed on the history and archaeology of Italy and the Western Mediterranean *c.* 300–1000 AD, examining in particular the transition period from Roman to medieval and the evolution of settlement patterns. A major survey of the period (*An Archaeology of Italy, AD 300–850*) was published in 2006. Core themes in this research include the evolution of towns and the role of defence. An additional research field relates to castle origins and urban growth, with Italy again the main zone of interest.

Oliver Creighton

Oliver Creighton, Senior Lecturer at the University of Exeter and Co-Director of the Wallingford *Burh* to Borough Research Project, is a landscape archaeologist and medievalist who specialises in the study of medieval castles, towns and elite landscapes. He has a long-term research interest in the study of medieval castles within their broader landscape and social context and has published a major monograph on the subject, *Castles and Landscapes* (2002, 2nd edition 2005). Oliver has also published a concise guide to the subject with R. A. Higham, *Medieval Castles* (2003). He continues to pursue new approaches to the study of castles, with particular emphasis on their social and symbolic roles and their place in the European medieval landscape. He has a particular research interest in the impact of status and authority on past landscapes.

Judy Dewey

After graduating from the University of Durham, where she specialised in Anglo-Saxon history, Judy Dewey taught in London before moving to Wallingford in 1972 as Head of History at Didcot Girls' School. She has since spent many years as a part-time lecturer in Local History for the Department of External Studies at the University of Oxford and for the WEA. She has been researching Wallingford's history for 35 years and, with her husband Stuart, was co-founder of The Wallingford Historical and Archaeological Society and later of Wallingford Museum, of which she is honorary Curator. Together they publish local history books as Pie Powder Press, including a number of their own works. Judy's particular interests lie in the Saxon and medieval

town, the Civil War period and the overall progression of the town's development.

Matt Edgeworth

Following his PhD (1992) in Archaeology and Anthropology at the University of Durham, Matt Edgeworth worked as Project Officer and Site Director for a number of commercial archaeology units, including Albion Archaeology, Cambrian Archaeological Projects and Birmingham University Archaeological Fieldwork Unit. He has carried out several urban surveys and directed urban excavations in Bedford, Rugby, Manchester, Wednesbury, Birmingham and elsewhere. Prior to joining the Wallingford *Burh* to Borough Project at Leicester University as Research Associate/Project Director, much of his work on landscapes of Anglo-Saxon and Viking defence was grounded in detailed study of the archaeology of Bedfordshire, especially in the county town of Bedford, and the countryside around Tempsford on the River Great Ouse.

Helena Hamerow

Based at the Institute of Archaeology, University of Oxford, Professor Hamerow's research interests are the archaeology of north-west Europe from AD 400–1000, all aspects of early medieval rural settlements and economy, and the archaeology of Anglo-Saxon England. She has recently completed work on the *Novum Inventorium Sepulchrale* (web.arch.ox.ac.uk/archives/inventorium), an on-line database of Anglo-Saxon graves and grave-goods from Kent. As well as working on the Wallingford *Burh* to Borough Project, she is currently a co-director of the School of Archaeology's excavations at the Roman small town at Dorchester-on-Thames; of particular interest to this project is examining evidence for the Roman to post-Roman transition in the 5th and 6th centuries, and for the 7th century, when it became the centre of the first bishopric of Wessex.

Katharine Keats-Rohan

Katharine Keats-Rohan is a medievalist with research interests in north-west France from the 9th to 11th centuries, currently focused on the abbey of Mont-Saint-Michel and monastic necrologies, and the Norman Conquest of England. She is particularly interested in the use and development of prosopography as a research method and is founder director of the Unit for Prosopographical Research at Linacre College, Oxford and General Editor of its Prosopographica et Genealogica imprint, which has published 12 volumes since 1997. A Fellow of the European Humanities Research Centre at Oxford since 1997, she is currently employed on a prosopographical project, Who Were the Nuns?, at Queen Mary, University of London.

David Roffe

David Roffe is an historian who has worked widely in archaeological units and more recently as a research fellow in the University of Sheffield, where he was co-director, with Professor Edmund King, of the Sheffield Hundred Rolls Project. His research interests include the Danelaw, landscape history, church history, and insanity in the Middle Ages. Much of his work, however, has focused on the inquest as an instrument of government. His main area of study has been Domesday Book. He has published extensively on different aspects of the record, including two important monographs, *Domesday The Inquest and the Book* (2000) and *Decoding Domesday* (2007) and has edited five volumes in the Alecto County Edition of the Domesday text.

INTRODUCTION

David Roffe

Wallingford today is a largely unspoilt town with a quality and pace of life that contrasts with that of many of its busy neighbours. It is a quintessentially English town, albeit one that is not on the tourist trail (it is a discovery yet to be made). Like many small towns in England and beyond, it has had to adjust to the globalized economy of the modern world. It has, nevertheless, retained something of its character as a market town. Throughout the ages, towns like this have thrived as local and often regional centres. Their markets were the point of exchange for their rural hinterland and in return they provided the services of craftsmen and industrialists for the wider community. Towns worked hard for their living. Wallingford still does so. It offers a variety of shops with numerous local tradesmen and serves the surrounding villages. Unlike some of its regional neighbours however – notably Oxford and Reading – Wallingford has not experienced massive growth and many of its inhabitants look further afield for additional goods, services and employment.

It has not always been so. At the start of its recorded history, Wallingford had already assumed a regional role. In the late 9th century King Alfred of Wessex constructed a *burh* that was conceived as part of a kingdom-wide system of defence. Judging from its large assessment, which was equalled only by that of Winchester, Wallingford was a key site in the defence of Wessex against the Danes. By 1086 it had become the county town of Berkshire and the location of one of the most important royal castles in southern England. In the 12th and 13th centuries the castle was an important garrison and one of the favoured residences of the king, while the town flourished as a centre of trade and industry.

The 14th century, by contrast, saw a change in pace. The castle was still a royal residence, but its military role was diminished. At the same time, the growth of Oxford and Reading began to draw trade away from Wallingford and by the late 16th century Abingdon had become the county town. It is tempting to see the later Middle Ages as the start of Wallingford's decline. This, however, would be to misrepresent its history. In common with many other towns of the period, it experienced a contraction in its population. Churches became redundant and parishes were amalgamated. Nevertheless, it adapted to the new circumstances and emerged as a market town. By the 17th century it had developed a malting industry and successfully traded down the Thames to London. Its horizons were essentially local into the 19th century when its iron industry served the agricultural hinterland, but major industrialization was left to its larger neighbours. Wallingford remained a market town.

Why Wallingford did not develop like its regional neighbours is an interesting question that remains to be answered. The fact has, however, provided an all but unique opportunity for the archaeologist and the historian to understand its earlier history. Perhaps serendipitously, a mass of borough archives survives from the Middle Ages and beyond. From the 19th century onwards local historians have made good use of these sources. Early accounts of the borough are largely antiquarian collections of extracts from sources. More recent studies, under the aegis of The Wallingford Historical and Archaeological Society (TWHAS), have begun to analyse the topography, society, and economy of Wallingford. More widely, Wallingford has been less well known. It has figured in discussions of the Burghal Hidage. Otherwise, it has contributed little to the debate on the origins of towns.

In its late medieval and early modern documentary cover Wallingford is not unlike many other towns and cities, but it has an exceptionally rich and as yet largely untapped wealth of 13th century material. What also distinguishes it is the preservation of the physical fabric of the earlier town. The earthworks of its defences are upstanding for much of their circuit and can be easily traced where they have been built upon to the south. The castle in the north-east quadrant of the town was razed in 1652, but, apart from the building and later demolition of two large houses and a farm on the site with some associated garden landscaping, the multi-period earthworks have remained relatively undisturbed into the modern day. So have the large intramural open spaces that are Kinecroft and Bullcroft to the west. Its street pattern is largely unchanged from the early 17th century and almost certainly represents that of the medieval town. Finally, there are numerous buildings that preserve early fabric.

A better site for the investigation of urban origins could not be found. And yet there has been no concerted campaign of archaeological investigation as there has in major urban centres like Winchester, York, and Lincoln, and even smaller market towns like Stamford. From the 1960s to the early 1980s research in places such as these was driven by state-funded rescue archaeology in advance of large-scale inner-city redevelopment. Thereafter, archaeology has been developer funded under the remit of PPG16 (Department of the Environment, now Communities and Local Government, Planning Policy Guidance 16: Archaeology and Planning). Wholesale redevelopment in Wallingford was averted so there were consequently few excavations under either regime. On the castle site a research project cut across the north-west outer rampart and development plans led to substantial work in the middle bailey. Elsewhere there was a cut through the Kinecroft banks and TWHAS did a rescue dig on St Michael's churchyard. Subsequent developer-funded archaeology has, as elsewhere, been fairly limited in scope. The only relatively large excavation, and then limited in purpose, has been of the cemetery of St Martin's church on the Waitrose site in 2006.

It was this background that prompted a team of archaeologists from the universities of Exeter, Leicester, and Oxford to launch the Wallingford *Burh* to Borough Research Project in 2003. With full funding from 2008–10, an innovative programme of investigation has commenced, in cooperation with TWHAS, that aims to study the origins and growth of the town into the 13th century. An initial survey of the surviving earthworks has already been undertaken and there is on-going geophysical survey of key areas. Excavation is an integral part of the programme. Trenches were opened on the Kinecroft, Bullcroft and Castle Meadows in 2008 and in the castle's inner bailey and Wallingford School playing fields in 2009, along with a further trench on the Kinecroft. More widely, test pitting, so-called 'garden archaeology' which was pioneered in rural contexts, has been brought to an urban context for the first time to assess the distribution of deposits. At the time of writing 10 have already been excavated and as many as 100 are envisaged in the course of the project.

In 2008 TWHAS organized a conference to bring together academic expertise on the early history of Wallingford to inform a strategy of research. What discussion there has been of the early town has assumed a conventional development similar to that postulated for other Burghal Hidage *burhs*. It is asserted that it was founded anew by King Alfred the Great and laid out to a standard grid pattern aligned on a new crossing of the river where the bridge was then or subsequently built. The castle was inserted into this planned town after the Conquest and settlement expanded with the subsequent development of a suburb outside the south gate. By contrast, recent topographical and historical research undertaken by TWHAS has suggested a more nuanced picture. The papers presented here outline the present thinking on the origins and growth of Wallingford in the light of that new work.

Paul Booth opens with an over-view of the pre-*burh* archaeology of the town and its immediate vicinity. Evidence for permanent settlement and continuous exploitation in the area dates from the Neolithic period. It is not until the later Bronze Age and early Iron Age, however, that there are any firm indications of how society was organized. By the middle Iron Age there is evidence that the Wallingford area was extensively settled with a marked hierarchical structure, although there is less evidence for the gravel terraces in the immediate vicinity of the borough. Numerous finds have come to light from the Roman period and it is likely that there was a secondary settlement to the west of the river crossing, but no concrete evidence for its existence has come to light. In Dorchester, across the Thames three miles to the north, there is evidence for continuity into the 5th and 6th centuries.

In Wallingford itself, by contrast, the site of early Saxon occupation has yet to be located. However, the discovery of its burial ground, lying partly under St John's School on St John's Road, confirmed its existence, most likely in the same general vicinity. Helena Hamerow reports on a current reappraisal of this highly intriguing mixed inhumation/cremation cemetery, dating from the mid 5th century into the late 6th. She comments that the cemetery was large for the area with an estimated 150 burials. There were two high status burials, but above all it is characterized by the high proportion of females and infants. How this site fits into the early development of Wallingford remains mysterious; its wider interpretation must await further research.

Some of the earliest evidence for the first Saxon settlements in Wallingford is sought by Judy Dewey in the topography of the area and the emerging parish boundaries of the town. Early place-names and natural boundaries are considered, leading to an analysis of the significance of the later parish boundaries. She recognises that the re-establishment of Christianity in the area in the 7th century was closely associated with the power and patronage of kings, bishops, and lords, and the lands of churches often reflect the fact. Parish boundaries, then, are potentially an important source for the early history of settlement. In practice, however, they are usually difficult to interpret. Although they are often treated as immutable physical features of the landscape, in reality they delineated social institutions that responded to changing needs. The modern parish is a palimpsest of many centuries of usually undocumented acts and decisions. The analysis of Wallingford's parishes presents particularly acute problems of this kind. In the 12th century there were 11 churches in the borough with more or less full parochial rights. By the 16th century there were only four. In the interim, churches had fallen into decay and become redundant and their parishes joined to neighbours. The earliest fully recorded boundaries, dating from the 17th century, represent an amalgam, but the medieval town documents allow pin-pointing of some properties within parishes.

Starting with the earliest sources, Judy Dewey unpicks the evidence for each church and attempts to reconstruct the earlier parishes. The result inevitably remains a palimpsest – here remarkably close to a twelfth-century one – but it enables a comparison of foundations. A contrast becomes apparent between churches with lands in the fields and beyond and those that are purely urban. The latter are apparently directly related to the borough, and their parishes are in some cases appreciably later than those of the former. Dewey concludes that the churches with large parishes – here St Leonard, possibly sited in an early oval-shaped enclosure, and St Lucian in the south of the town, together with All Saints in the north east – mark the nuclei of pre-burghal settlements.

Surviving documents go some way to providing a tenurial context for these nuclei. Undoubtedly the most important source for the early history of Wallingford is the Domesday survey of the borough. It is one of the longest and fullest accounts of a town to be found in the record. David Roffe provides a new edition and translation of the text and uses its data to reconstruct the topography, society, and economy of the borough in the mid 11th century. This analysis allows an examination of a yet earlier source for Wallingford. In a re-appraisal of a pre-Conquest memorandum written in English, Roffe identifies three churches 'outside the port' belonging to Brightwell to the west of Wallingford as St Leonard, St Lucian, and St Rumbold and argues that, in territorial terms, they were part of the pre-*burh* estate. The construction of the borough in the late 9th century saw a shift of focus, if not necessarily settlement, from this estate to the bridge. Apart from topography, there is no evidence for how the All Saints area related to Brightwell in the mid 9th century, but it is likely that it marked a high status royal site from this time. The northwest quadrant of the borough was similarly high status, being the site of a collegiate church, possibly episcopal, founded in the early 10th century. The town developed to the south of High Street. By the time of the Domesday inquest it was already of considerable size. At least eight of the 11 medieval churches were in existence and there is evidence that its four wards were already established.

From the start of its history, the *burh* had a regional role. According to the late ninth- or early tenth-century Burghal Hidage, there were 2400 hides assigned to it for its defence. As late as 1086 many tenements in Wallingford belonged to rural manors in the surrounding area. Their distribution suggests that the early territory of the borough extended from west Berkshire across the Thames into the Oxfordshire Chilterns east of the River Thame. In the 11th century, Wallingford was no less a centre of power in the middle Thames valley. Katharine Keats-Rohan explores the constitution of the honour of Wallingford and its pre-Conquest antecedents and relates them to the needs of the crown in the defence of the area. Perhaps surprisingly, the honour apparently reflects the earliest territorial organization of the area rather than that of the period of its formation: the bulk of the fees are in south-eastern Oxfordshire rather than Berkshire. Above all, what emerges is that the successive kings kept a tight hold on the honour and the borough. It is not surprising to find, then, that its society was dominated by *ministri*, that is, royal officers and servants.

Royal authority is, of course, most visibly represented in Wallingford by the surviving castle earthworks that take up a quarter of the whole area of the borough. It is, however, no less manifest in the impressive defences. These, the physical fabric of the town and the spaces they define, are explored by Oliver Creighton, Neil Christie, Matt Edgeworth, and Helena Hamerow for clues to the origins and growth of Wallingford. The characterization of the area enclosed by the rampart and ditch is complex. The defences are attributed to King Alfred's campaign of *burh* construction of the late 9th century and, indeed, the two cuts across the bank on the castle site and Kinecroft have provided late Saxon dating evidence. Nevertheless, it is not impossible that the circuit is multi-period. Within there appear to have been distinct zones. Where the castle site and the priory seem to have always been high status, the rest of the town was given over to diverse activities. Bullcroft and Kinecroft to the west always seem to have been open spaces apart from a short-lived development of the late 11th or early 12th century. The developed area was predominantly to the south east, although the medieval churches may represent aristocratic residences associated with gateways.

Much of early urban history has concentrated on the origins of towns and in consequence there has been a tendency to assume that there is a single point of foundation, construction, and, more widely, urbanization. This notion manifests itself no more so than in the notion that intramural grids and burgage plots are evidence of primary planning and that suburbs attest secondary development. These are the stock-in-trade assumptions of the urban plan analysis. Matt Edgeworth challenges such simplistic approaches to urban history in a wide-ranging review of the underlying topography of Wallingford. His starting point is a comparison of the town with Bedford. There conventional analysis had identified the early borough sitting neatly within its rectilinear defensive circuit. However, all that was upset by the recent discovery of an earlier ditch under the east-west axial road. What has been perceived until now as an integrated and irreducible whole is shown in fact to be an evolution from an earlier plan and an earlier settlement.

Applying these observations to Wallingford, Edgeworth raises some interesting possibilities, even though they do not necessarily provide answers. He suggests that, although there is no evidence for earlier defences, it is not unlikely that they are yet to be discovered. The diversion of the southern rampart east of south gate to include St Leonard's church suggests, at least, an earlier nucleus rather than a later suburb. What is abundantly clear is that the existing circuit is a dynamic monument, that is, it has survived only because it has remained functional. Not the least of its important roles throughout the ages has been the supply of water. How the network of streets within developed has yet to be determined, but earlier streets, both burghal and pre-burghal, can be detected by careful topographical analysis.

The picture of the early history of Wallingford that emerges from these papers is very different from the received view of the development of the borough. Much of the analysis presented here is inchoate and many of the conclusions tentative. Nevertheless, various problems have been highlighted, many for the first time, that suggest priorities for on-going research beyond the normal aims and objectives of urban studies. The identification of the south gate area as a potentially early, pre-burghal, nucleus is a major advance. With its connections with the estate of Brightwell to the east, it holds out the possibility of providing a context for the Anglo-Saxon cemetery off St John's Road for the first time. Now that it is clear that the area is not a late suburb, different archaeological targets present themselves. Clearly, the church of St Leonard is important, but equally sensitive is St Lucian. So, too, is the boundary of the possibly early enclosure. Although none of these sites is likely to become available for conventional archaeological investigation, garden archaeology holds out a prospect of recovering valuable evidence.

The upstanding defences are, of course, a focus of continuing interest. An investigation of the southern section east of the south gate may provide data on the relationship between the early nucleus and the later *burh*, but opportunities will be limited in this built-up area. Elsewhere any data on construction and chronology of the bank and ditch would be welcome: there is still so little dating evidence. No earlier defences have been identified within the borough. Formal plan analysis may be useful here, but, as in Bedford, it is unlikely to be fruitful in the absence of new archaeological evidence.

The castle is also the subject of on-going investigation. Its form and development are becoming increasingly clear from the earthworks survey and excavation. Further archival research will add to the picture. Earlier features may be more elusive. Although the site has in the main been put down to pasture since the 17th century, it was intensely used in the 600 years of its history as a fortress. It must be suspected, then, that the discovery of any substantial pre-Conquest remains will be serendipitous. However, some areas may be more sensitive than others. The royal free chapel of St Nicholas is of particular interest. Although it is said to have been founded by Miles Crispin shortly after 1086, there are characteristics of its foundation that suggest that it was of pre-Conquest origin. Its environs must be a candidate for the putative Anglo-Saxon royal palace. Equally likely, though, is the site of All Saints church on Castle Street.

Holy Trinity church is also of great interest. Its location is known only approximately: it was somewhere close to the street frontage on the northern side of High Street west. Further documentary research holds out a good chance of pinning it down site or at least its monastic successor. If Holy Trinity was an early tenth-century episcopal foundation, then it is likely that it lay within its own precinct. It is conceivable that this encompassed the whole area of the Bullcroft. Inherited by the priory, the open space may owe its lack of development to this its early specialized function. However, its agricultural use, as evidenced by survey and excavation, may militate against such an interpretation. Judging from the modest scale of the later priory, the foundation was on a smaller scale than those of the royal and episcopal churches of, for example, Gloucester and Chester. Some traces of a precinct boundary may be apparent to the southern end of Bullcroft.

The chronology of planning present different challenges. There is, at present, no detailed information on the boundaries of plots. Continuity from the 10th century into the modern period has frequently been demonstrated by excavation in other places, but this is not to say that all burgage plots in all towns must originate in a single act of planning dating from the foundation of the borough. Pre-Conquest records of urban properties often suggest that primary units of ownership were blocks of land somewhat larger than the standard burgage plot. Such gradations in chronology are not easily amenable to archaeological investigation unless, perhaps, in large-scale open excavation. There is no prospect of such in Wallingford. Detailed topographical analysis of early maps may suggest possibilities, but documentary research is more likely to provide insights into the process.

Much of the early documentation for Wallingford is in this respect uninformative or ambiguous: the earliest references are to 'houses', '*hagas*', or 'messuages'. A handful of entries in the Domesday account of the borough,

however, refer to acres on which there were multiple properties. David Roffe suggests that these properties may be earlier units of ownership. If comparable to urban sokes and liberties elsewhere, as suggested, they may well be identifiable in the later record of urban privileges. No manorial courts within the borough have as yet come to light, but references to the assizes of bread and ale and private views of frankpledge may equally be signs of early tenements. TWHAS has already embarked on an extensive deeds survey: a majority of the properties in the town can now be traced back into the 16th and 17th centuries. Many can be further identified in medieval documents. With continuing research in this area, the record of quitrents and the like may provide further insights on the early organization of land.

This volume concentrates on the early history of Wallingford. Just as the possible continuities with the pre-*burh* landscape have been emphasized, so must it be recognized that this history is a part of an on-going story. Broader issues remain to be addressed. There can be no doubt that Wallingford was *par excellence* a royal foundation and continued into the 14th century as a royal town. What, then, was its relationships with the king? And how did those relations impact upon its society and economy? It may well be that up to about 1300 it had always been a garrison town with a command economy. The borough, it is true, had all the varieties of occupation that are associated with towns, but it never seems to have developed anything other than service industries. It existed first for the palace and then for the castle. Once royal interest and patronage was withdrawn, the town found itself in search of a role. Ultimately that role proved to be a more modest market town. How it emerged from the glory days of Wallingford will form the subject of the next stage in the exploration of the history of the town.

Much remains to be done if the early history of Wallingford is to be more fully understood and it is to be fitted into its broader context. The seven papers collected here, drawn as they are from different approaches to urban history, outline the potential. In the past archaeology has been characterized by condescending historians as the handmaiden of history. Archaeologists have not always rejected that role. Nowadays, that is a relationship no longer admitted. Nevertheless, archaeologists and historians still all too often maintain a wary stand-off across a categorical divide. If more proof were needed, Wallingford shows the value of critical cooperation. History, archaeology, topographical analysis, and the various other disciplines that are brought to bear on the history of towns all have their limitations. Together, however, the sum of the whole is greater than the parts. This remains the way forward for the history of medieval towns.

THE ARCHAEOLOGY OF THE WALLINGFORD AREA
BEFORE THE ANGLO-SAXON BURH

Paul Booth

Abstract

Evidence for prehistoric activity in the general area of
Wallingford extends as far back as the late Upper
Palaeolithic. Monument building is a feature of the area
from the early-middle Neolithic and was maintained into
the early Bronze Age, at least. Evidence for associated settlement is very scarce before the middle Bronze Age, when
field systems begin to appear in the area. Wallingford was
an important focus for ritual deposition of metalwork in the
Thames in the late Bronze Age. Iron Age settlement patterns
are dominated initially by hill forts such as Castle Hill, but
other types of sites also occur and by the later Iron Age,
when Dyke Hills Dorchester is the probable regional focus,
settlement, mostly in individual farmsteads, will have been
widespread along the valley, though local examples are only
known from small scale work. The same is generally true
of the Roman period. The principal north-south (Silchester
to Alchester) road passes to the west of Wallingford and the
Thames itself seems to have been of little strategic significance, though presumably important for local transport. A
spread of finds in the town may suggest the presence of a
minor nucleated settlement here at the west end of a river
crossing, but firm evidence is lacking. The local settlement
pattern probably included both villas and other settlement
types, but the cemetery at Coldharbour Farm need not necessarily have related to a villa. At the end of the Roman
period the Wallingford area was probably linked to the local
power base at Dorchester on Thames.

Keywords

Prehistoric; Roman; early Anglo-Saxon; Thames Valley;
Wallingford; archaeology.

Introduction

This review presents a summary of prehistoric, Roman and
early Anglo-Saxon settlement evidence from the
Wallingford area by way of background to the detailed discussions of aspects of the Saxon and medieval town which
follow. It is not intended to provide a comprehensive
account of all the available evidence, but it attempts to identify what seem to be the main characteristics of the evidence
for successive periods, with its principal emphasis on an
area within a 5km radius of Wallingford, although with reference to more distant sites within the region where this
seems appropriate. The geographical scope of the discussion is broadened for the Roman period, on the basis that
the regional Roman settlement context is important for
understanding developments in the early post-Roman
period and thus, ultimately, aspects of the genesis of the

burh itself. The archaeology of Oxfordshire and the Upper
Thames Valley has been relatively well served by works of
synthesis (e.g. Hingley and Miles 1984; Briggs *et al.* 1986;
Blair 1994; Barclay *et al.* 1996; Miles 1997; Salway 1999;
Hamerow 1999; Henig and Booth 2000) and this summary
benefits from all of these. The most recent consideration of
the wider regional context of the valley itself can be found
in the volumes of the *Thames Through Time* series (Booth *et
al.* 2007; Lambrick forthcoming a; Oxford Archaeology in
preparation)

Prehistoric

The stretch of the Thames Valley around Wallingford pro-
duces evidence for activity from the Mesolithic period
onwards and, if one goes as far south as Goring, from the
late Upper Palaeolithic (Barton 1995), in the form of flint
scatters. As usual at this time, however, none of this material
can be linked directly to distinct archaeological features, let
alone to recognizable locations of settlement. In contrast,
significant monument complexes developed in the area in
the early to middle Neolithic. Central to most of these,
although not necessarily primary components of their
development, were cursus monuments, conveniently summarized in the context of a report on the example at
Drayton, near Abingdon (Barclay *et al.* 2003, 225–232).
The most extensively examined of the local examples was
at Dorchester, where the cursus incorporated or partly
overlay several earlier features, at least one of which may
have been a mortuary enclosure (Whittle *et al.* 1992, 148–
9). This association of earlier features with, or their inclusion by, cursus monuments is also apparently seen at
Benson and the bank barrow at North Stoke, respectively
only *c.* 2km and 4km from Wallingford. The significance of
the cursus monuments, in particular, has been discussed
recently in the Drayton report (Barclay *et al.* 2003). The evidence for burial monuments in this period is less clear, but
they presumably also formed an important component of
the ceremonial landscapes most clearly indicated by the
cursus monuments.

Neolithic settlement evidence is always less common
than that for ceremonial activity, and the Upper Thames
Valley is no exception to this rule. Indications of settlement,
in the form of pits, postholes, gullies and possible post-built
roundhouses perhaps of earlier Neolithic date, from St
Helen's Avenue, Benson are therefore particularly significant in regional terms (Pine and Ford 2003, 135–137, 172–
5). Other evidence that may be indicative of settlement
includes a cluster of early Neolithic pits recently examined
at South Stoke (Timby *et al.* 2005, 228–231), while a
middle Neolithic (Peterborough Ware) pit was found in
Wallingford itself at the Lower School in 1997 (Richmond

2005). Slighter evidence of late Neolithic activity is again present at Benson, but this period is still most clearly represented in the area by ceremonial monuments, in the form of ring ditches and related features. Particularly significant complexes are known at Dorchester and North Stoke (for the latter e.g. Case 1982) and further downriver at, for example, Gatehampton Farm, Goring (Allen 1995, 2–5), while a double ring ditch of Neolithic date was partly examined in 1959 (Moorey 1982) just north of Bradfords Brook, less than 1km south west of Wallingford. These features indicate the continuation of traditions of monument building, this time in a funerary context, into the early Bronze Age at least. Evidence for this activity still survives, of course, in upstanding earthwork form on the nearby Berkshire Downs.

Other activity of the later Neolithic and early Bronze Ages is implied by the presence of pottery from the Grim's Ditch just south east of Wallingford (Cromarty et al. 2006, 162–3). Unusually, a short length of trackway recently examined at Crowmarsh Gifford may have been of early Bronze Age date, though this is not certain (Ford et al. 2006, 202–4); such features are more commonly of middle Bronze Age and later date. Clearly-defined settlement-related evidence of the early Bronze Age in this period thus remains rare, as is usual in this region.

The middle Bronze Age saw very significant changes in the archaeological record, presumably reflecting changes in the organization of society. Field systems, which are identified in the region for the first time, for example at Didcot (Ruben and Ford 1992) and Appleford (Booth and Simmonds forthcoming), formed a basis for settled agricultural communities, generally thought to have been principally concerned with pasturing cattle. Features of this type are now widely known in parts of southern Britain (Yates 1999; 2007). The change in emphasis in the exploitation of the landscape is demonstrated particularly clearly at Dorchester, where a double ditched field system cut across the earlier monument complex, although this example may have been of late Bronze Age rather than middle Bronze Age date (Whittle et al. 1992, 159). At Bradfords Brook, Cholsey, one of the sites excavated on the line of the Wallingford Bypass south west of the town in 1992, the primary use of a waterhole was dated by radiocarbon to the middle Bronze Age (Cromarty et al. 2006, 203, 223) and a partially articulated cow skeleton from Wallingford Upper School is also dated by radiocarbon to the middle Bronze Age (Bradley and Armitage 2002). It is possible that elements of a field system at Bradfords Brook also originated at this time, but the majority of the material derived from these features suggests a late Bronze Age date. This also seems to be the date of field systems at sites such as Mount Farm, Dorchester, where ditches were aligned on a round barrow of early Bronze Age date (Lambrick 1992, 88–89; Lambrick forthcoming b). Middle and/or late Bronze Age field systems again replaced, or perhaps supplemented, monumental landscapes (indicated by aerial evidence for ring ditches) near Long Wittenham, an area which has seen one of the few systematic studies of landscape development in the region (Baker 2002, 20–22). More locally, evidence of late Bronze Age agriculture and possible settlement in

the form of pits and postholes was found beneath Grim's Ditch just south east of Wallingford (Cromarty et al. 2006, 163–167).

An aspect of late Bronze activity for which the Wallingford area is particularly important is that of deposition of metalwork in the Thames. Some finds of such material have been known for a long time, but an indication of the character of the structural context within which this activity might have occurred is provided by the results of successive small scale examinations of an eyot just south of the town at Whitecross Farm (Thomas et al. 1986), now on the west bank of the Thames. The most recent and most extensive of these excavations were carried out in 1992 in advance of the construction of the Wallingford Bypass south of the town. The report on this work (Cromarty et al. 2006) is another contribution of fundamental importance for understanding many aspects of the prehistoric archaeology of the Wallingford area. The eyot itself was narrow and had a palisade on its western side, while timber structures within the channel separating this side from the right bank of the river may have formed a jetty or a more continuous feature of some kind. The apparent removal of the palisade was followed by a phase of occupation and deposition of midden material into the edge of the infilling channel. While an earlier origin is possible, it is likely that most, if not all, of this activity can be assigned to the late Bronze Age. Indications of buildings are scarce (principally a consequence of the small scale of excavation) but the environmental and faunal evidence indicate some domestic activity as well as pasturing of animals on the eyot, at least from time to time. The character of some of the associated finds suggests the importance of a ritual component within the range of activities practised, and the likelihood that the site was a focus of high status activity, perhaps on a periodic basis, is generally accepted.

It is possible that some aspects of the use of the landscape in the Iron Age also involved discontinuities on a scale comparable to that seen between the early and middle Bronze Ages. This is not a consistent picture, however. The most obvious focus of activity in the area in the early Iron Age is at Castle Hill, Little Wittenham, where the hillfort succeeded a late Bronze Age (presumably defensive) enclosure (Allen et al. forthcoming). The relationship between the main phases of enclosure is not completely clear, but their superimposition cannot have been fortuitous and a probable midden site just west of Castle Hill may have seen continued deposition from the late Bronze Age into the early Iron Age period (Hingley 1980), reinforcing the close association of successive defences (and contrasting with the evidence from Wallingford itself, where there is no suggestion that the Whitecross Farm site continued in use into the early Iron Age). The less well known early Iron Age hillfort at Blewburton is only a little further distant (some 6km away) to the south west. The only hillfort on the east side of the Goring gap seems to have been the poorly-known example at Whitchurch Hill, but this lay 11km south of Wallingford and its focus was clearly towards the south and the Middle Thames rather than to the Oxfordshire side of the Chilterns.

Unenclosed settlements of early Iron Age date are also

well attested, however, though not necessarily known at present in the immediate vicinity of Wallingford. The evidence from Bradfords Brook, though admittedly limited, suggests that Iron Age activity succeeded the better-evidenced late Bronze Age settlement and broad continuity of settlement patterns from that period into the Iron Age is likely in at least some cases. This can be seen, for example, at two sites on the Chalgrove-East Ilsley gas pipeline: Site 22 just west of Brightwell cum Sotwell, 4km west of Wallingford), and Site 11 just north of Benson, again roughly 4km distant (Network 2004; Wilson forthcoming). Away from hillfort locations, settlement sites in this period were usually unenclosed. This may have been true of a probable site at Ewe Farm, Newington, some 6km north of Wallingford. The single (unpublished) feature certainly known here, however, is a remarkable but enigmatic oven or kiln structure, partly stone-built, associated with pottery of transitional late Bronze Age-early Iron Age character.

By the middle Iron Age we may envisage that the Thames Valley in the Wallingford area was quite extensively settled. Evidence from aerial photographs indicates settlement on the gravel terraces that is of broadly later prehistoric or later prehistoric/Romano-British character, although the gravel terraces in the immediate vicinity of Wallingford have been neither as extensively revealing of cropmarks nor subject to the same intensive pressures of extraction (with related archaeological activity) as some other nearby areas, such as around Dorchester, so there is not so much excavation evidence to work with. Nevertheless, there are some data from excavation, including work on a number of pipelines across the area. The most nearly adjacent evidence includes material of Iron Age date from the Wallingford Historical and Archaeological Society (TWHAS) excavation at Coldharbour Farm, Crowmarsh (Clarke 1997) and from a rectangular enclosure on the west side of the river immediately south of the town at Bradfords Brook (Moorey 1982 – the publication incorrectly describes this site as being at Newnham Murren). The Chalgrove-East Ilsley pipeline sites already mentioned both produced middle as well as early Iron Age evidence, although this was much more pronounced at Site 11, north of Benson, where possible enclosure features, gullies associated with probable roundhouses and large numbers of pits were all located. Another group of middle Iron Age pits was examined on the Newbury Reinforcement pipeline at South Stoke; but here there were no clear traces of enclosure type features (Timby et al. 2005, 210–216), while a similar situation prevailed at Halfpenny Lane, Moulsford, examined in the course of work on an earlier pipeline (Ford 1990, 26–7).

Field walking evidence is also useful for the Iron Age and the Roman period, important work having been done in the North Stoke area by Steve Ford (Ford and Hazell 1989). This work demonstrates both continuity and discontinuity of settlement location; the most significant site in this area having remained in use from the Iron Age into the Roman period, while the less extensive settlements examined apparently did not show the same continuity of occupation. On some of the excavated sites in the area, however, sequences do extend from the middle (or even early) Iron Age through into the Roman period, even if activity of suc-

cessive phases is not directly superimposed. Such a sequence of development was detected at Moulsford Road North on the Cleeve to Didcot pipeline (Ford 1990, 30–31), while at nearby Halfpenny Lane, in contrast, there was a gap in the occupation sequence between the middle Iron Age and later Roman phases (Ford 1990, 9–11).

Precise characterization of the later prehistoric settlement of the area remains somewhat unclear owing to a relative lack of extensive excavation. It is likely, however, that a general Upper Thames Valley trend towards an increased level of enclosure of settlements in the middle to late Iron Age was followed here. Typically, settlements probably took the form of individual farmsteads, but the extent of the spread of surface finds at the main North Stoke complex suggests the aggregation of several such units. Agriculture was mixed, with the production of spelt wheat and barley important alongside the rearing of the principal domestic animals – cattle, sheep and pig – showing a continued trend towards agricultural diversification away from what may have been a marked concentration on cattle rearing in the middle Bronze Age.

In the late Iron Age and early Roman periods we have the first clear indications of the impact of wider concerns upon the agricultural communities of the area, although this is not to suggest that these communities were isolated in earlier periods (the location of our area at the interface of two major Iron Age ceramic style areas, of the Upper Thames Valley and Wessex, for example, suggests that this was a zone of some cultural interaction and diversity). The extent of the spheres of control of the early Iron Age hillforts, if that is an appropriate way of looking at them, is, however, very unclear. The later Iron Age, by contrast, saw the development in the Thames Valley of a smaller number of key sites defined by substantial earthworks, characterized as 'enclosed oppida' (Allen 2000, 22–26), located at confluences of the Thames and its tributaries, the nearest one of which is the well-known (but not well-understood) Dyke Hills complex at Dorchester, at the confluence of the Thames and the Thame. Settlement within this site, known only from the air (e.g. Cook and Rowley 1985, 17), appears superficially to be of rather amorphous middle Iron Age character rather than incorporating elements of a more organized layout sometimes associated with sites of this general character, for example at Silchester (Fulford and Timby 2000, 8–37). Although they undoubtedly incorporate high status elements, the precise functions of these sites remain unclear, though a role in mediating exchange, probably near the peripheries of territories of developing polities, is likely to have been one.

The potentially circular nature of arguments defining Iron Age (and subsequently Roman) tribal territories on the basis of the distributions of late Iron Age coinages is well known (e.g. Sellwood 1984). Nevertheless, it is likely that our area lies broadly at a point where the interests of tribes later defined as the Catuvellauni, Dobunni and Atrebates all met, and it is quite possible that our stretch of the Thames served in some way to define these interests (e.g. Salway 1999, 3–6; Booth et al. 2007, 365–367). Rather vague terminology is used deliberately as it is uncertain how far the concept of closely defined 'territories' was established at this time. That such a concept was beginning to develop at the very end of the Iron Age may, however, be suggested by the presence of one of the most distinctive local features, the linear earthwork of the Grim's Ditch south east of Wallingford. As far as the dating evidence from a couple of sections will allow precision (Hinchliffe 1975; Cromarty *et al.* 2006, 189, 199), this feature can be assigned to the late Iron Age (as defined in ceramic terms), a situation which is exactly paralleled further north by evidence from Aves Ditch, west of Bicester, a closely comparable feature albeit in a rather different topographical context (Sauer 2005a). While due caution is necessary in interpreting these structures, we may speculatively assign them to a phase of westward expansion by the Catuvellauni (centred in Hertfordshire) in the period shortly before the Roman Conquest of AD 43. Why, given that this was a context of short duration, these monuments then survived as long-term landscape features is uncertain, but their essentially peripheral nature may have something to do with it.

Roman

The immediate impact of the Roman conquest in the Wallingford area was presumably to render the Grim's Ditch irrelevant. In regional strategic terms the impact was manifested in the construction of a probable legionary fortress at Alchester to the north (Sauer 2005b) and in the use of this part of the valley as a strategic route connecting Alchester with Silchester and ultimately with the south coast. The fortress was probably in existence as early as AD 44 (Sauer 2005b, 102). Formalization of the north-south road line will have followed, but exactly how soon is uncertain; for example the straight north-south stretch across Otmoor south of Alchester, admittedly probably a relatively late development, may not have been in place before the end of the 1st century AD (Chambers 1986; see also Cheetham 1995 for this area). Nearer to Wallingford the eventual route, quite possibly established at an early post-Conquest date, ran through Mackney and Brightwell-cum-Sotwell some 2km west of the town (Malpas 1987), but since the direct projection of this alignment to Dorchester would have involved a very difficult river crossing below Castle Hill at the junction of the Thames and the Thame, the road diverted to the north east, heading for a crossing of the Thames between Shillingford and Dorchester. Whether this was the site of a ford or a bridge is unknown, but the result was that the principal road access to Dorchester was from the south east rather than the south. It should be noted, however, that evidence has very recently been presented for the existence of another north-south road in this stretch of the Thames valley, lying east of the river and running between Pangbourne and Benson (Sharpe and Carter 2008).

The wider context of Roman exploitation of the Thames Valley is of some interest. In strategic terms the Thames Valley and in particular the river itself seems to have been of little overall importance, although the latter may have been well used at a local level. The principal Roman lines of communication from London to the west were roads which passed north and south of the valley and were directly joined by only one major route – the Alchester-Silchester road just discussed above (Booth *et al.* 2007, 36–37; Allen *et al.* 1995, 139–45). Reflecting this lack of emphasis, there is a notable absence of Roman nucleated settlement along the Thames Valley itself, the only significant 'small towns' in the entire stretch between Cirencester and London lying at the two road crossing points of Staines and Dorchester, a fact which underlines the importance of the latter site.

Within this framework, what are we to make of settlement in the Wallingford area? The 'small town' of Dorchester may have served as more than just a local focus, although the probable military phase here seems to belong to the period after the Boudican revolt of AD 60–61 and at present there is scant evidence for the development of the town in the later 1st and early 2nd centuries AD. Nevertheless, it acquired a defensive circuit, perhaps by the later 2nd century, and this implies at least a local administrative function for the town, underlined by the well known inscription of the *beneficiarius consularis* Marcus Varius Severus, probably of early 3rd century date (for summaries of Dorchester with fuller references see e.g. Rowley 1985; Burnham and Wacher 1990, 117–122; Henig and Booth 2000, 58–63).

The rural settlement pattern is best understood within the Thames valley, the wider picture being less clear. Between Dorchester and Abingdon, where the evidence is generally good, settlement has been defined as of mixed character, including villas, each presumably the centre of an estate of some kind, and non-villa settlements, mostly located in enclosures associated with trackway systems. The evidence for the valley downstream from Dorchester is less clear, but it is likely that a similar general pattern prevailed. Direct evidence for villas is more elusive in this area, however, though there is one (known only from the air) at South Stoke, just 4km south of Wallingford (St Joseph 1965), and it is possible that the relatively high status lead-lined coffin burial from Crowmarsh indicates the presence of another villa even closer to Wallingford itself, while the villa site at Gatehampton Farm, Goring, is some 10km south. On the right side of the river, the nearest identifiable Romanized structure known lies 5km north west of Wallingford, on the south side of the Wittenham Clumps (Rhodes 1948; Wessex Archaeology 2004). The exact character of this building, which lay within a rectilinear enclosure, is uncertain, however, and it was not definitely a villa house, although associated material includes tesserae and painted wall plaster. Structural evidence of this kind is relatively rare, and points up a distinct and problematic characteristic of the non-villa sites, which is a widespread absence of archaeologically-detectable evidence for buildings, even when the presence of domestic activity is indicated by a range of other types of evidence; there appears to have been a significant change in the character of domestic architecture in the region in the late Iron Age-early Roman period compared to the middle Iron Age, when domestic buildings are readily identified (Allen *et al.* 1984; Henig and Booth 2000, 82).

In more general terms, it may be reasonable to ask if there were local differences in rural settlement patterns on opposite banks of the Thames. If the left bank opposite Wallingford was liberally scattered with Roman settlements, as seems probable, although few of them have been examined on more than a small scale, was the situation on the right bank any different? It is not likely, but it is a question to be addressed rather than something to be taken for granted. The variable character of the landscape also has an influence on the nature of the evidence available for settlement and other activity, so that on the downs to the south west of Wallingford there are extensive traces of field systems, most of which were probably of Roman date (Rhodes 1950; Ford *et al.* 1988). Many of these survived in earthwork form into the 20th century, as at the classic site of Streatley Warren, some 9km south south west of Wallingford (e.g. Henig and Booth 2000, 101), now sadly degraded. The type of settlement to which such field systems related remains uncertain, but, on the evidence of work further west (Gaffney and Tingle 1989), might have included small villas as well as enclosed farmsteads.

In terms of the connections between villas and non-villa farmsteads a fundamental problem, effectively insoluble with archaeological evidence, is that of the nature of land holding and tenurial relationships. One fairly superficial view is that the villas which are known in the area appear to have been mostly quite modest structures (although they could be associated with considerable wealth, as indicated by the gold hoard from near a villa at Didcot) and it is therefore unlikely that these would have formed the centres of very substantial estates. This might mean that a significant proportion of agricultural land in the area was held by what we might term 'small farmers' based in non-villa settlements. In any case what we do know of landholding in this period in general terms suggests that a modern perception of coherent estate territories may be quite inappropriate. At present, therefore, the relationships between villa and non-villa settlements remain unknown.

Another facet of rural settlement might be indicated by sites which appear to be larger than individual farmstead units. Was there, for example, any particular significance in the difference between the latter and the larger settlement indicated by fieldwalking at North Stoke? Were minor agglomerated settlements, such as might be suggested by the extent of this scatter, a distinctive feature of the region? On present evidence they appear scarce, but a possible analogy could be the sort of 'village green' or trackway junction settlement that developed at Appleford (Hinchliffe and Thomas 1980). Such settlements seem to be a development of the middle Roman period in this region and indeed elsewhere (Taylor 2007, 113).

For Wallingford itself, as is well known, a crucial question is to determine the importance, if any, of the ford at this time. If this was a viable crossing point of the river in the Saxon period there is no *a priori* reason why it should not have been useable by the Romano-Britons. It does not necessarily follow from this, however, that such a crossing would have had a significant settlement associated with it, for example at its western end. Such an occurrence is possible, but there are few known sites from the region that might serve as examples. One such is the substantial nucleated settlement at Gill Mill in the lower Windrush valley, but this is associated with a river of very different character from the Thames at Wallingford. At present, direct evidence for such a settlement from Wallingford itself is lacking; although

there are relatively numerous individual findspots of Roman material from within the town, none of these can be convincingly linked to a defined settlement site at the moment. It is worth mentioning that a large antiquarian collection, built up by W. R. Davies, is associated with Wallingford. This collection, dispersed by sale *c.* 1893, included *inter alia* a significant group of Iron Age coins and very large numbers of Roman ones (Cromarty *et al.* 2006, 235), but it has never been clear that these came from Wallingford itself, rather than (at best) the surrounding area (see e.g. Bean 2000, 269 for the difficulties associated with the Iron Age coins). Some of the brooches from the Davies collection are still extant in Reading Museum, but some of these are quite unusual and are indeed most unlikely to have been found locally (Jill Greenaway pers. comm.). The value of this particular collection as a source for late Iron Age and Roman Wallingford is, unfortunately, questionable at best.

Provisionally, therefore, we should see the area covered by the modern town as an integral part of a fairly intensively-utilized rural landscape occupied by scattered farmsteads, probably linked by trackways, with the possibility (as yet speculative) that a larger cluster of farmsteads could have coalesced somewhere west of the river crossing. It may only be the piecemeal nature of the recorded finds that currently prevents them being understood in more coherent terms.

For the Iron Age and early Roman periods almost nothing is known of the burial practices of the inhabitant of such settlements, but by the later Roman period, and particularly the 4th century, settlements were routinely associated with small cemeteries principally, and often exclusively, of inhumation burials. The site excavated by TWHAS at Crowmarsh (Clarke 1996; 1997) is a good example of such a cemetery and fits well into a regional pattern (Booth 2001). Larger cemeteries were associated with nucleated sites such as Dorchester, and indeed the late Roman cemeteries just outside the town, which contained many hundreds of burials, although only a relatively small percentage of these have been excavated, are particularly important in regional terms (Durham and Rowley 1972; Harman *et al.* 1978; Chambers 1987, see further below p. 12). Other components of the rural landscape would have included religious sites. It is just possible that the Roman building at Wittenham Clumps (see above, p. 8) was of this character. If not, the best known rural example of a site of this type was almost 10km distant to the south west on the downs at Lowbury Hill where, however, there was no obvious temple structure as such within the shrine enclosure (Atkinson 1916; Fulford and Rippon 1994). These sites were components of an essentially agricultural landscape, but it is worth remembering that Dorchester lay at the southern end of the pottery production complex of the Oxford industry (Young 1977), with kilns certainly as close as Allen's Pit (Harden 1936, 83–94), only some 6km from Wallingford, and perhaps even closer, immediately adjacent to Dorchester itself (Frere 1984, 128–9, 167–9). As one of the largest, if not the largest single pottery industry in late Roman Britain, its impact may have been felt by communities further afield than the production sites themselves, perhaps particularly in relation to procurement of firewood to fuel the kilns.

One area in which our understanding of this landscape is deficient is in terms of its chronological development. At some sites there may have been extended sequences of occupation from a relatively early time in the Iron Age. A more common sequence of development in this region, however, is that sites which were occupied in the late Iron Age, some of which newly established at that time, saw continued settlement through at least to the early 2nd century. At some sites, such as Jubilee Villa, Benson (Pine 2005) or Moulsford Road North on the Cleeve-Didcot pipeline (Ford 1990, 29–31), occupation then ceased, although in some other cases it may have recommenced relatively close by. The reasons for this widespread, but not universal, hiatus in the settlement sequence have been and remain the subject of much speculation (e.g. Lambrick 1992, 83–84; Henig and Booth 2000, 106–110; Booth *et al.* 2007, 43, 50, 52). Broadly speaking, however, sites occupied from the middle of the 2nd century continued in occupation well into the 4th if not right up to the end of the Roman period (this was not necessarily the case further up the Thames Valley in Gloucestershire, however). Equally, the development of small nucleated rural settlements may be characteristic of the later Roman period. But these are generalizations; the evidence from sites in the immediate vicinity of Wallingford is not sufficient to allow deatiled site narratives to be developed here.

Roman to Anglo-Saxon

What is clear, however, is that the Dorchester area just to the north is a focus of unusually concentrated activity at the very end of the Roman period, at least in terms of the definition of such activity using conventional dating media. This is just one of a number of characteristics that make Dorchester an absolutely key site for developing understanding of the early stages of the transition from Roman Britain to Anglo-Saxon England. The evidence includes very late Roman structures from within the walled town, the likelihood of continued use of the major, possibly Christian, cemeteries to the north and the occurrence of smaller numbers of accompanied burials, in particular an individual from close to the Minchin Recreation Ground buried with a curious mixture of late Roman and early Anglo-Saxon jewellery and a man and a woman from Dyke Hills, he buried with late Roman military style belt fittings and she with a late Romano-British belt buckle and brooches, the latter of continental type and probably early 5th century date (Kirk and Leeds 1952/53). This is familiar and well-rehearsed territory. What is less clear is the extent to which the unusual concentrations of late Roman material from Dorchester and, more importantly, the activity that they represent, extended into the surrounding area. If, as seems likely, Dorchester was an important local, if not regional, power centre in the early 5th century, whatever the basis on which it was maintained, the sort of artefactual material that might be associated with sustaining this centre need not necessarily have been widely distributed in the surrounding countryside, even if its inhabitants fell within the orbit of this centre. As it happens, however, at least two examples of the characteristic late Roman belt buckles of the general type associated with the female burial from Dyke Hills, Dorchester, have

been recovered from the Wallingford area, although the precise provenances of these metal-detected objects is not known (Laycock and Marshall 2005). These, plus a further example from Fenny Stratford (Bucks) have been defined as the 'Wallingford group subtype' of these buckles (Laycock and Marshall 2005). If this grouping, possibly implying quite local manufacture, has any validity it may suggest a focus of late Roman activity even more local than that at Dorchester, though quite likely linked to it. It seems certain that the rural Romano-British population around Wallingford would have been aware of the Dorchester power centre, and may have been attached to it in some way, but in what form these communities survived after its demise is quite unknown. Our material culture props fail us at this point. When they remerge, in the later 5th century, they are of a completely different character.

There is scattered evidence across the area for early Saxon settlement. One of the first such settlements to be identified in England was the site at Sutton Courtenay, located in gravel quarrying about 12km west north west of Wallingford (Leeds 1923; 1927; 1947; see now Hamerow *et al.* 2007), while one of the largest excavated in the region (in 1983–1985) lies at Barrow Hills, Radley, a similar distance north west of Wallingford (Chambers and McAdam 2007). This site comprised both the sunken featured buildings (SFBs, some 45 examples) which are particularly characteristic of such settlements, and also 22 larger posthole structures. These key sites are just part of the reason why the stretch of the Thames valley between Abingdon and Dorchester is seen as having 'the highest concentration of known early Saxon sites in the whole [upper and middle Thames] area' (Booth *et al.* 2007, 91). This concentration includes not only farmsteads but also potentially higher status settlements indicated by hall building complexes at Sutton Courtenay (Hamerow *et al.* 2007) and Long Wittenham (Booth *et al.* 2007, 91, 95), although at Sutton Courtenay, at least, these buildings are thought likely to have been established in the 7th century rather than earlier and therefore to have been later than many, but not necessarily all, of the structures examined by Leeds (Hamerow *et al.* 2007, 187). Elsewhere, early Saxon structural evidence is largely confined to SFBs, probably because excavated settlement samples are mostly relatively small and these distinctive structures are more easily identified than posthole buildings. A single SFB from within the Roman walls at Dorchester may have been of slightly unusual form (Frere 1962, 123–125; see also Tipper 2004, 82) and there are further possible examples, two each from Beech House Hotel and the Old Castle Inn (Rowley and Brown 1981, 10, 12; Bradley 1978, 23), while a further sunken structure adjacent to the Abbey is much larger than usual and probably represents a different kind of building (Keevill 2003, 355–357). Three structures excavated at St Helen's Avenue, Benson, however, demonstrate a fairly typical range of variation in form (Pine and Ford 2003, 141–144). A small rectilinear enclosure from the same site is more unusual since the reuse of late Roman linear boundaries, rather than establishment of new ones, is the pattern most typically seen in the area at this time, as for example at Barton Court Farm (Miles 1986, 17–18) and Wally Corner, Berinsfield (Boyle *et al.* 1995, 24). In some cases settlement evidence is indicated by surface finds and the North Stoke survey was again important in this respect (Ford and Hazell 1989; 1990). One of the key results of this work was the demonstration that the early Saxon settlement pattern in this area was more restricted than the Roman one, the distribution of settlement of the later period being confined to a 'low-lying/terrace edge setting' on the right bank of the Thames, whereas Roman period sites in the same area had extended further east onto the more mixed soils of the Chiltern slopes (Ford and Hazell 1989, 18).

Despite the importance of the settlements known in the region, here, as elsewhere, early Saxon activity is indicated as much if not more so by cemetery evidence as by that for settlement. The cemeteries reflect the location of settlements, but their associated, although not necessarily closely adjacent, settlement sites are often not known, the cemeteries with their distinctive grave goods being more readily drawn to the attention of archaeologists of previous generations. Thus at Wallingford itself the location of settlement associated with the cemetery in the south-west part of the town (see Hamerow below, p. 14) is uncertain. Again the Dorchester area is of prime importance, with cemeteries to the west, for example at Didcot and Long Wittenham and the largest recently excavated cemetery in the area, at Wally Corner, Berinsfield, with 100 inhumation graves containing 114 burials, plus four cremation burials (Boyle *et al.* 1995, 1–197) just to the north east (for a convenient summary of cemetery distribution in the region based on earlier work see Booth *et al.* 2007, 418–429). Several of these sites are important for the early evidence that they contain. Berinsfield, for example, includes several graves dated to the 5th rather than the 6th century, as well as a significant number assigned to a late 5th-mid 6th century range (Boyle *et al.* 1995, 126–7), nor is this evidence unique in the area (Boyle *et al.* 1995, 142).

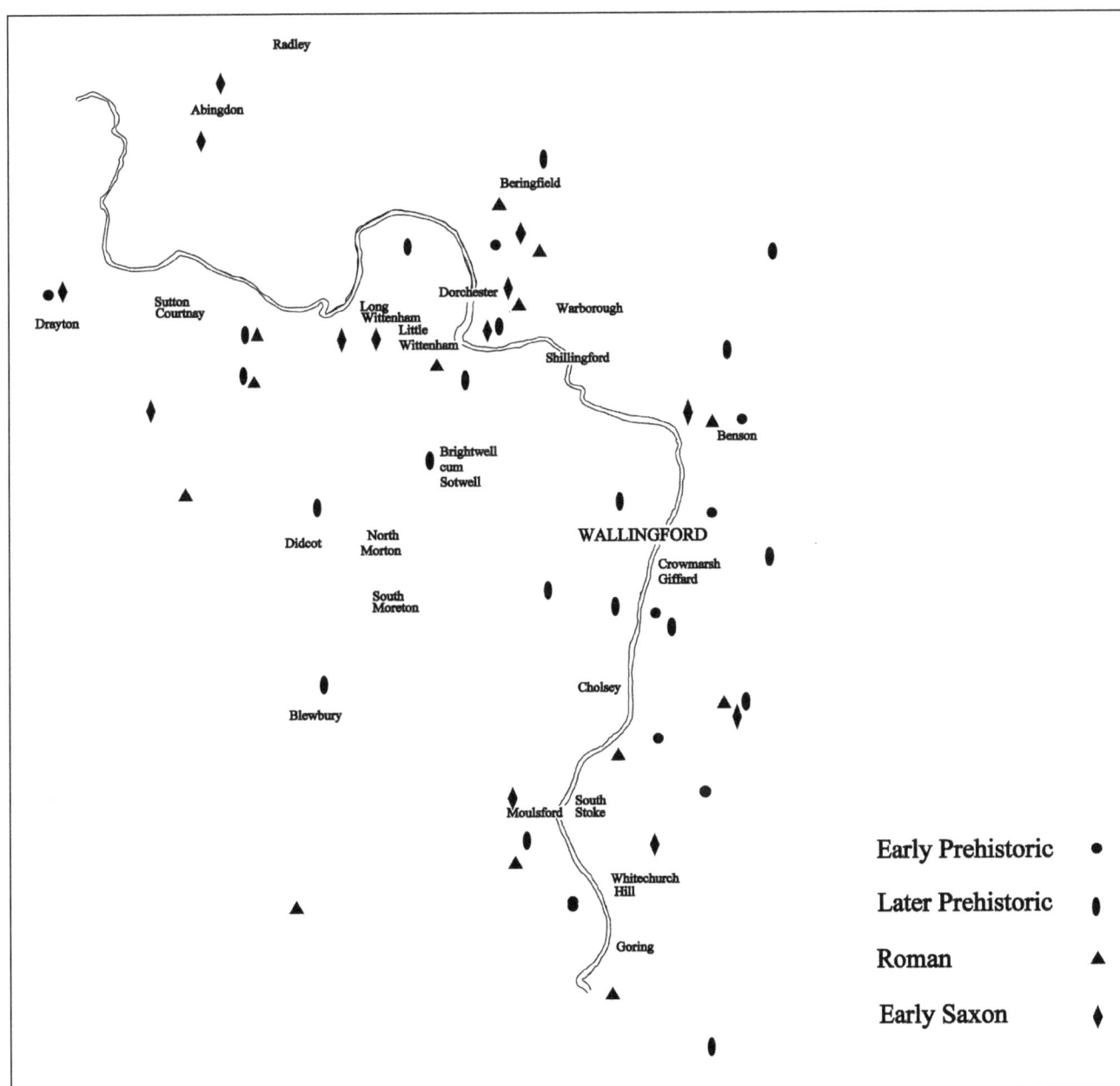

Figure 2.1 Location and dating of sites mentioned in the text (illustration by June Strong)

The chronology of early Saxon settlement and cemeteries in the Dorchester area, as is well known, is particularly important because of the evidence there for the maintenance of at least a local polity into the 5th century (see above, p. 10), with extensive debate focussing on the early 5th century burials discovered both north and south of the Roman town. This is not the place to reprise the debate that has surrounded the questions of the date, ethnicity and, more particularly, the wider significance of these burials. More important is the fact that some of the burials from the nearby 'late Roman' cemetery at Queenford Farm have been dated by radiocarbon to the 5th, if not the 6th, century AD (Chambers 1987, 58). Taken at face value these dates suggest the coexistence of communities burying their dead in radically different ways and, potentially, the survival of a Romano-British population perhaps into the 6th century. Such a suggestion would not be at all radical in a more westerly geographical setting, but in an area of known early Saxon settlement may appear problematic. For this reason a current programme of re-dating, including skeletons from both Queenford Farm and Berinsfield, is particularly important and its results are awaited with interest.

The point has been laboured because of its potential significance for understanding key aspects of the transition from late Roman Britain to early Anglo-Saxon England. The region may be unusually well placed to provide key evidence for the co-existence of British and Saxon communities, in line with one possible model of the development of society at this time. However this may be, key questions remain, relating particularly to the processes which result in the demise of Romano-British material culture and its apparently total replacement in the course of the 5th century by material of typical 'Anglo-Saxon' character. These and other issues require much further work.

Acknowledgement

I am grateful to the organizers of the original day conference and the editors of this volume for the opportunity to contribute to both. Thanks are owed to colleagues in Oxford Archaeology and other organizations who have discussed their work and in some cases kindly allowed reference to results in advance of publication, and also to the Oxfordshire Historic Environment Record for provision of information. None of the above are responsible for the shortcomings of this summary, which remain mine alone.

THE EARLY ANGLO-SAXON CEMETERY AT WALLINGFORD

Helena Hamerow with *Susan Westlake*

Abstract

This paper reviews the evidence for the early Anglo-Saxon cemetery partly excavated in the first half of the 20th century at St John's Road, Wallingford. A re-evaluation of the original records and grave goods indicates that the burials ranged in date from at least the mid fifth to late sixth centuries, and included two fairly richly equipped inhumations as well as a remarkably high proportion of infant and child burials.

Keywords

Pagan Saxon; Berkshire; Wallingford; cemetery.

The Anglo-Saxon cemetery near St John's Road, Wallingford, which lies just beyond the south-west corner of the ramparts of the late Saxon *burh*, has been investigated sporadically for more than a century. Piecing together its rather chequered past is therefore a significant undertaking, and the first part of this paper is an attempt to do just that. The second half examines some of the more notable features of the cemetery, and considers some of the questions that future work may, with luck, resolve.

The first burials were discovered in 1894 when, according to a note in the local newspaper, three or more graves were exposed. In 1910, during the construction of the Council School, ten or eleven inhumations were discovered, although again no details were recorded. Around the same time, some Saxon pottery was reported to have come from property to the east of the school, land owned by a Mr Snow. Most of this information, indeed most of what we know of the cemetery to date, comes from a report published in 1938 by E. T. Leeds the great pioneer of Anglo-Saxon archaeology, who was at that time Keeper of Antiquities in the Ashmolean Museum. Efforts to bring the recording of this important site up to date began in 2004, since when nearly all the finds from the Leeds excavations have been drawn and/or photographed, and as complete an inventory as possible of the finds has been compiled.

During building work on Mr Snow's land in 1924, workmen discovered a grave which Leeds subsequently called Grave 1. At this time, the curator of the local museum, Mr Hutchinson, became involved. The records are vague, but it appears that in 1925, Mr Snow discovered two more graves. These appear to have been excavated by Dr Watts, a member of the Berkshire Archaeological Society, with the help of several others including Captain C. Musgrave, a physical anthropologist at the Natural History Museum of the University of Oxford.

A further grave was uncovered in 1929. In 1932, the Gospel Hall was erected and two more graves were found, about which no details are known. Around this time, a cre-

mation was also uncovered. Around 1936, Musgrave and Leeds became fully involved in the excavation of the cemetery, and the recording improved dramatically. Between 1936 and 1938, a further eleven inhumations were excavated along with five cremations. Leeds and Musgrave carefully recorded these burials and in 1938 Leeds published his report in the *Berkshire Archaeology Journal*. His account of the burials, while admirable for the time, is far from adequate by modern standards and appears to have relied upon the earlier newspaper reports by Mr Hutchinson and information provided by Mr Snow to piece together information about the earlier investigations.

Following Leeds' report, no further publication regarding the cemetery appeared apart from a brief note by Donald Harden in 1940 which simply states that 'some more interments' had been uncovered in the grounds of the Pavilion. There do, however, exist several hand-written notes and photographs of later discoveries in the Ashmolean archives (The E.T. Leeds Archive, Ashmolean Museum, Oxford). It appears that a further ten burials were found at the site and, although details for some of these are vague, others are better recorded, notably by Musgrave.

As will be apparent, a considerable cast of characters was involved in the excavation of the Wallingford cemetery, and a good deal of detective work has been required to piece together its complex history. Indeed, in the course of researching the Leeds Archive in the Ashmolean, a letter was found which mentions two previously unrecorded cremations, excavated between 1937–1940. A note by an unknown writer was also found which describes the discovery of yet a further cremation and two further graves in 1939 and 1940 (The E.T. Leeds Archive, Ashmolean Museum, Oxford).

The latest chapter in the site's history occurred in 2004, when Thames Valley Archaeological Services (TVAS) excavated a small evaluation trench just to the east of the main school buildings (Anthony and Ford 2006). They uncovered several archaeological features, notably an Anglo-Saxon urned cremation. The urn contained, as might be expected, highly fragmented, burnt bone. Three teeth were present, allowing the age at death to be estimated at around six months. Intriguingly, from soil directly beneath the urn, further human remains were found, but these were *unburnt* and well preserved. The remains were again probably those of an infant. If these two sets of remains derive from the same individual, it is notable not only that they were deposited in very different ways, but also that one was cremated and the other not. It seems more likely that these represent two different individuals. The excavation also revealed a well-preserved infant inhumation. Although this could be later medieval in date, it is possible, given its context, that it in fact belongs to the Anglo-Saxon cemetery.

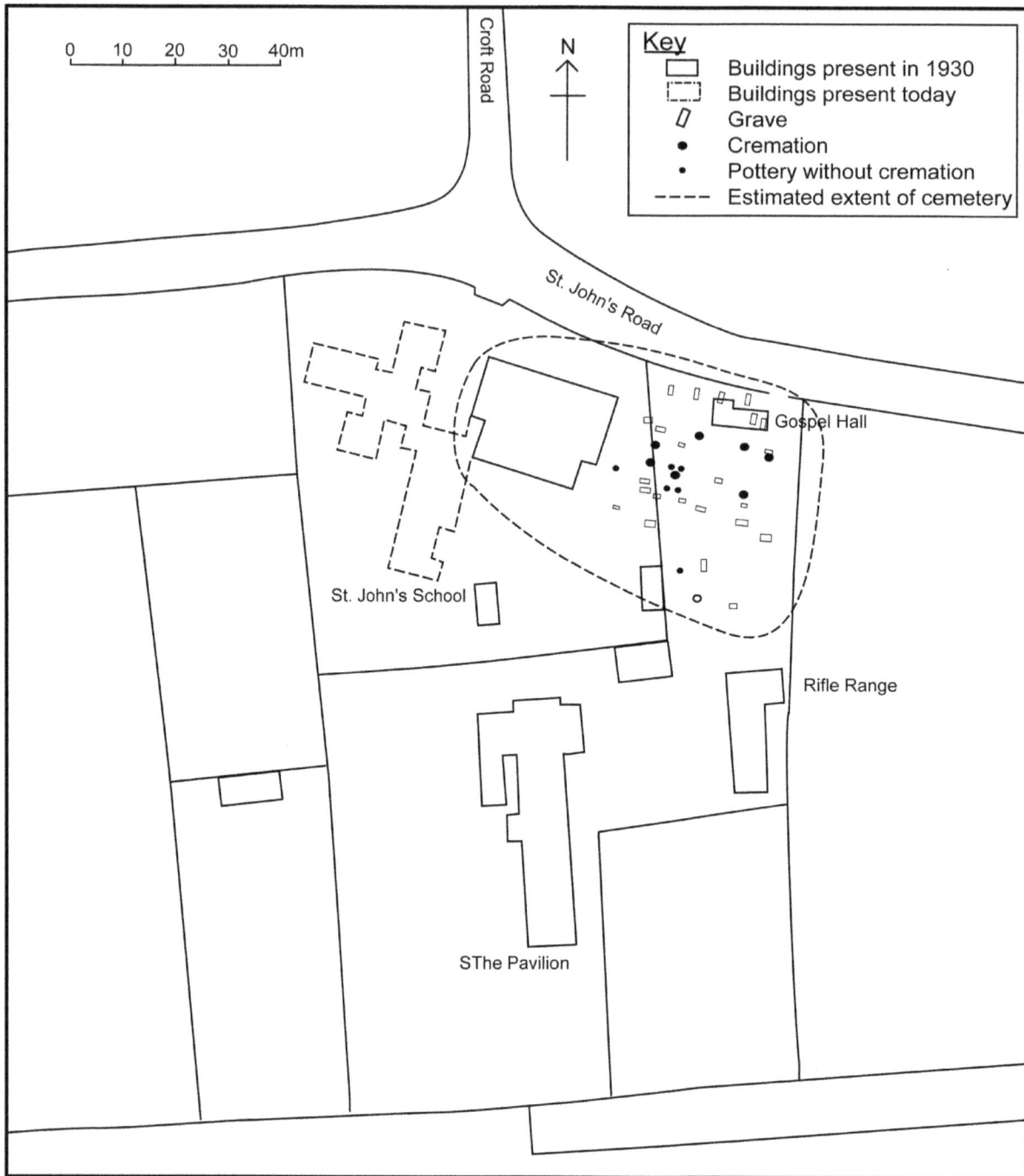

Figure 3.1 The Anglo-Saxon cemetery at St John's Road, Wallingford (S. Westlake).

To summarize, as of 2005, a total of 26 inhumations had been recorded, with around 14 more from before 1924, making a total of around 40 inhumations (Figure 3.1). What percentage of the total cemetery are these burials likely to represent? Early Anglo-Saxon cemeteries in this region do not tend to be very large – perhaps around 100–150 burials at most – so a reasonable guess is that the 26 recorded inhumations represent around a quarter of the whole cemetery. That is a reasonable sample, but we must remember that it is still only a sample.

Of the 26 recorded inhumations, only 11 could be sexed. Of these, according to Musgrave, two were male and nine female. (It had been hoped to re-examine the skeletal material which was deposited in the Natural History Museum, but only four skulls from Wallingford which cannot be

attributed to particular graves, could be located in 2005. I am grateful to Rob Kruszyinski of the Natural History Museum, London, for this information). This skewed gender balance is not particularly unusual in Anglo-Saxon cemeteries of the 5th to 7th centuries, particularly when identification is based largely or exclusively on grave goods, simply because women were more likely to be buried with distinctly 'gendered' grave goods than were men. At least nine urned cremations were also found. This is a relatively high proportion of cremations for this region, although given the limitations of the sample it is difficult to know whether this is significant.

The age distribution – specifically the high proportion of sub-adults found in the cemetery – is, however, most remarkable. The average number of infant and child burials

14

Figure 3.2 Brooches from Grave 15.

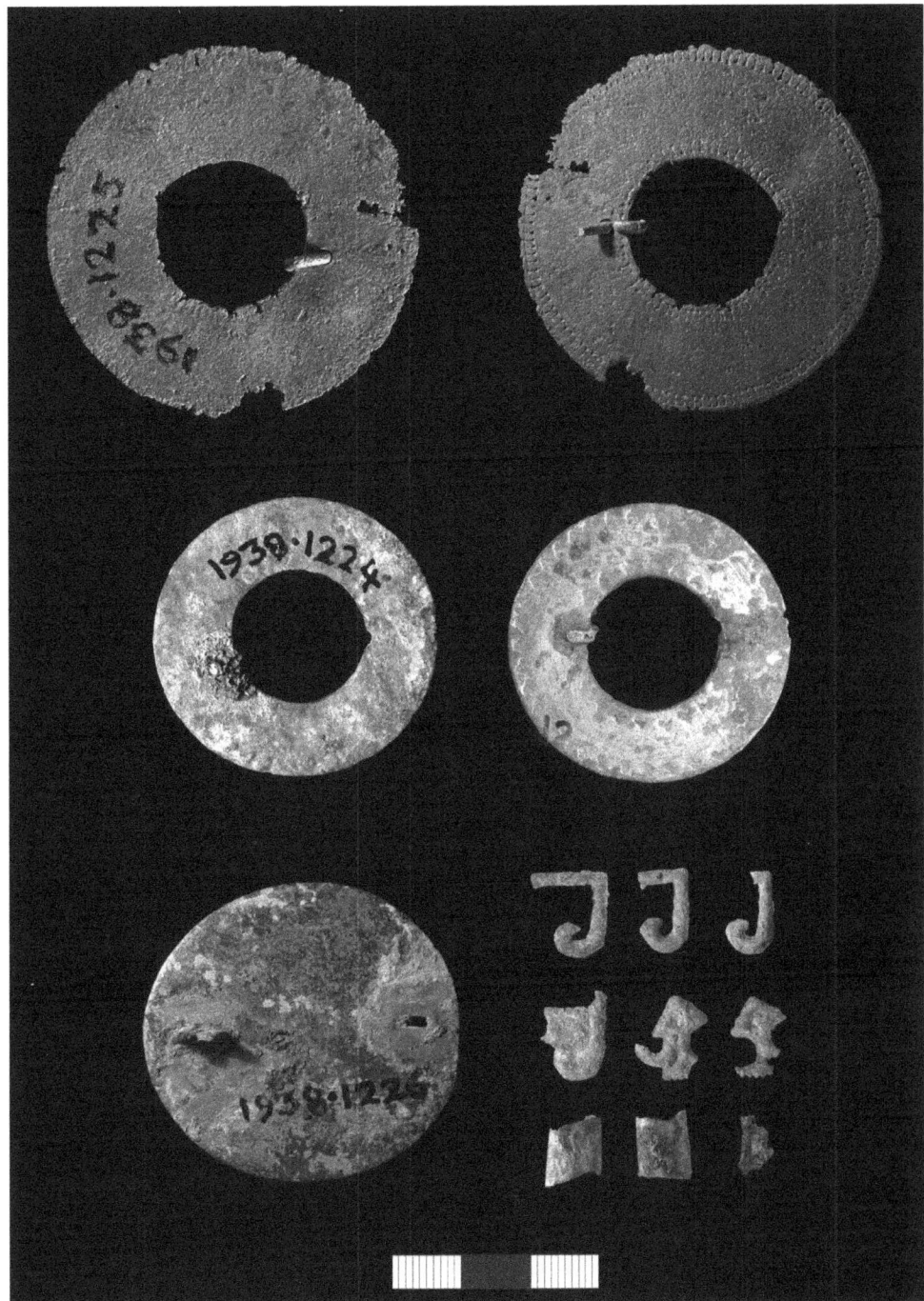

in early Anglo-Saxon cemeteries is around 6% (Crawford 1999). Of the 13 individuals to whom Musgrave attributed an age, six are described as adult, and seven as infants or children. The TVAS excavation also uncovered at least one, and possibly as many as three, further infant burials from the site (see above). This is an extraordinarily high figure and is probably the highest proportion of infant and child graves of any early Anglo-Saxon cemetery in England (S. Crawford pers. comm.). It is of course possible that the excavated part of the cemetery was a special zone in which primarily children were buried, and that were we to have the entire cemetery, the proportion would be lower. Such zoning would itself, however, be highly unusual.

To establish the date range during which the cemetery was in use, we must rely almost entirely on typological analysis of the grave goods, although in fact the majority of the grave assemblages cannot be closely dated. The earliest assemblage is that from Grave 15, a richly attired female who was buried with no fewer than four brooches: two very finely made, tinned 'annular' brooches and two applied disc brooches, of which just the back-plates and a few fragments of the decorative foils survive (Figure 3.2). These fragments were recognized by Tania Dickinson as deriving from a 'floriate cross' design, closely paralleled by an example from the cemetery at Long Wittenham and dated to the 5th century (Dickinson 1976; Evison 1978). The lady in Grave 15 also wore a pin which probably secured some kind of cloak or outer garment. It appears to be unique, but is closely related to a kind of very late Roman form dated by German scholars to the 5th century (Böhme 1974; Ross

15

Figure 3.3 Cruciform mounts/brooches from Grave 12.

1991). Her necklace consisted almost entirely of dark blue annular beads, another indicator of a fifth-century date (Brugmann 2004; Hirst 1985). There is no reason why Grave 15 could not date as early as the middle of the 5th century.

Most of the datable graves, however, are either late 5th or 6th century in date. TVAS obtained a radiocarbon date for the urned cremation which they excavated of between AD 427–540, at a 95% probability level (Anthony and Ford 2006). This fits well with the dating arrived at by a typological assessment of the grave goods. The two latest graves are Graves 1 and 12, both of which date to the second half of the 6th century. Grave 12 contained two enigmatic cruciform objects whose arms are decorated with Style I facemasks. The style of decoration indicates that they were probably made after c. AD 550. Given that they were re-used (see below), they may have been deposited many years after they were made.

Given the fragmentary state of our knowledge of the St John's Road cemetery, it would be spurious to draw any firm conclusions regarding the status and identity of the individuals buried in it. The two cruciform mounts with Style I facemask arms from Grave 12 are, however, amongst the most intriguing indicators of status (Figure 3.3). They are in fact horse-harness fittings which have been re-worked as a pair of brooches. These belong to a growing corpus of horse equipment found reused as dress ornaments in female burials (Grave 12 also contained a necklace and Musgrave identified it as that of a female) (Fern 2005). The comparative rarity of horse equipment, which, when found intact, is invariably associated with high-status males, suggests that these would have been highly prized objects which conveyed considerable status to the wearer.

The burials of certain individuals – notably those in Graves 12 and 15 – stand out, but it would be wrong to view the cemetery as exceptionally rich for the region. Indeed, research into the cemetery's regional context is still at an early stage. The location of the associated Anglo-Saxon settlement is also entirely a matter for speculation, although chances are that it lies somewhere in the vicinity of the cemetery.

There are, of course, other important questions that arise in relation to the pre-*burh* Anglo-Saxon occupation at Wallingford. H. M. Chadwick was the first scholar, over a century ago, to put forward the theory that *burhs* were constructed in places which were already collection points for tribute. Indeed it may be that it was the collection and storage of tribute that was, in the first instance, being protected by the *burh*. We might, therefore, expect to find traces of a pre-*burh* royal or otherwise high status estate (see Roffe below, p. 42) and it is somewhat surprising that so far, so little middle Saxon metalwork and coinage has been recovered from the immediate environs of Wallingford. Indeed, apart from a single penny of Offa, there seems to be an almost complete blank. It is a blank that the Wallingford Project may help to fill.

Acknowledgements

The background work on the inventory and research into the history of the excavations was undertaken by Susan Westlake whose efforts provided a solid foundation for this study. The staff of the Ashmolean Museum – above all Alison Roberts and Arthur MacGregor – have been enormously helpful in providing access to the finds and excavation record. I am also grateful to Judith Dewey of Wallingford Museum for providing access to the material held there and to Thames Valley Archaeological Services for allowing me to see their report in advance of publication.

THE ORIGINS OF WALLINGFORD: TOPOGRAPHY, BOUNDARIES AND PARISHES

Judy Dewey

Abstract

Parish boundaries are often ancient features of the landscape that have a great potential for elucidating the origins
and development of communities. However, they are not
without their problems of interpretation and, in an urban
context, these can be acute. In the 12th century Wallingford
had eleven parish churches but by the 17th century the total
had shrunk to four and the parishes had been largely con-
solidated. This paper attempts to reconstruct the earlier territories and uses the evidence to suggest a topography and
chronology of settlement in Wallingford from the Middle
Saxon period into the later Middle Ages.

Keywords

Anglo-Saxon; medieval; Berkshire; Wallingford; origins;
development; parish boundaries.

Introduction

The aim of this paper, in conjunction with those of Dr Roffe
and Dr Keats-Rohan, is to encourage new discussion on the
early origins of the town. It will consider topography and
boundaries in the light of current documentary and archaeological evidence. There are still many questions to be
answered but it is hoped that it will engender a stimulus to
further work.

The remarkable survival of Wallingford's Saxon earthen
fortifications and wet ditch with the River Thames marking
the eastern edge and the later castle earthworks defining the
north-eastern section, gave the town a visibly defined physical boundary well into the 19th century. It was not until
1972 that the water flowing into the town ditch from the
Millbrook was piped underground, with just a small stream
of water still flowing into the Thames in the south-eastern
section past St Leonard's churchyard. In times of flood,
water can often still be seen in the ditch north of the
Bullcroft and in some of the castle ditches. Yet these boundaries are deceptive; the town's influence and political
control extended far wider than their narrow confines and a
study of their hinterland is essential to an understanding of
its origins.

Until the 19th century the town of Wallingford remained
largely confined within its defences, apart from a notable
suburban area to the south which today appears to merge
seamlessly into Winterbrook in the neighbouring parish of
Cholsey. The boundary, however, is clearly delineated by
Bradford's Brook, which is bridged by Reading Road just
beyond the present hospital. A version of the name of this
stream, *Badfordes Brook*, was already in use by 1634
(Mortimer, 1995, 165). Most of the modern development of

Wallingford to date has been westwards of the town
defences in an area that was still largely fields until well into
the 20th century.

On the eastern bank of the Thames, opposite
Wallingford, lies Crowmarsh and the neighbouring former
parishes of Newnham Murren and Mongewell. The latter
are long and narrow, rising eastwards to the steep slopes of
the Chiltern Hills. This once-wooded range of hills forms
an upland area bordering the river valley which narrows to
the Goring Gap a few miles south of Wallingford. There the
ancient track of the Icknield Way comes off the westerly
Cholsey Downs to cross the river and then the Chilterns.
The Chilterns are a stark contrast to the arable lands surrounding the other sides of Wallingford.

Wallingford Bridge spans the river and the flood plain
on the Crowmarsh side, with the town boundary marked at
its eastern end and flanking either side of the bridge in a
roughly triangular shape, with ditches originally marking
its course. South of the bridge the boundary returns to the
centre of the river opposite Castle Priory, running south
until it meets the outfall of Bradford's Brook; north of the
bridge it returns across the river to the Wallingford bank
close to the outer limits of the castle earthworks.

Immediately to the north of the town the river begins to
curve slightly east before making a large sweep to the west
to a point some 400m above Shillingford Bridge, notably to
a point which is marked on the southerly bank by a detached
piece of Brightwell parish. On the eastern bank of the
Thames between Wallingford and Shillingford lies Benson,
(formerly Bensington) and beyond, north-westwards, the
old Roman town of Dorchester. The Rocque map of 1761
designates the substantial area of land enclosed by the
sweeping bend of the river as part of 'Wallingford Parish';
it was in fact a major part of All Saints parish and the area
was commonly known as Clapcot from at least the 11th
century (GDB, 61v; *DB Berks,* 33,3;4; see also Keats-
Rohan below, p. 61). This land, which includes the
medieval manor of Rush Court, has always been closely
associated with Wallingford Castle. It was of obvious defensive importance in controlling the Shillingford river crossing and the northern approach to the town. Bounding
Clapcot to the west are Sotwell and Slade End, linked to the
ancient settlements of Brightwell and Mackney.

Of further interest in this northern area is the recognition
of two enigmatic parallel banks some 140m apart which
appear to be in alignment with the two main roads through
Wallingford. Their purpose is not yet understood but their
presence is indisputable and will be further investigated (see
Edgeworth below, pp. 83–4 for a fuller discussion).

The importance of water is striking in the delineation of
Wallingford's boundaries – the River Thames and its flood

plain, local streams and water-filled defensive or boundary ditches – and there is good evidence that man has played an important role in engineering this use of water over the centuries. Bronze Age metalwork recovered from the Thames and the excavation of an eyot near the bypass bridge to the south of the town has demonstrated that the river played an important role in that period (Booth above, p. 6). The farming potential of the Thames gravels and a good source of water ensured some continuity of exploitation into the Iron Age. Activity from this period has been revealed most recently by trial trenches in a field lying immediately behind the Wallingford Medical Practice but on the southern bank of Bradford's Brook. These confirmed the presence of an extensive early to middle Iron Age settlement, for which the obvious water supply is the adjacent brook (Wessex Archaeology 2009). Since the geological stratification is such that this part of Bradford's Brook must be a man-made cut, it seems that this feature dates to at least the Iron Age. This dating is earlier than that suggested by Grayson in his article on the water systems associated with the town's development (Grayson, 2004). He clearly demonstrated that Bradford's Brook and the Millbrook are part of a system of streams flowing from west of the town which have been linked to ensure a good supply of water to the town and subsequently the castle, but the sequence in which this work was achieved is debatable.

An Old English description of the Cholsey bounds attached to a late ninth-century Latin charter of a land exchange between King Alfred and Denewulf Bishop of Winchester, dated sometime between 878 and 899, lends weight to the view that the Bradford's Brook boundary predates the Saxon town of Wallingford. The designated course of the Saxon boundary ends with a description of the route through marshy ground along the edge of Mackney, 'thence on the ancient ditch east to the Thames at Wallingford (*þonon on þone ealdan dic est to temaese aet welingaford*)' (Gelling 1976, 757; S.354). It seems highly likely that the ditch referred to is the line of Bradford's Brook, which appears as the boundary on the earliest surviving map (Cholsey 1695) and still delineates the Cholsey/Wallingford boundary today.

When the *burh* defences were constructed in Alfred's reign, there was a need to divert a flow of water to supply the new town defences (Edgeworth below, p. 80). This is the most likely time for the cutting of the Millbrook, which would have taken much of the water to the town ditch and away from the Bradford's Brook stream, potentially turning it into a winter overflow – *Winterdich* or *Winterbroc*, the name which is in use by *c.* 1153 when it is mentioned as bordering land south of the town in a proposed grant by Henry of Anjou and his mother the Empress Matilda (*Regesta*, iii, no 88). Sometime after the Norman Conquest further cuts were made to the west to divert more water to the town from the streams of the Moretons. The name Millbrook is likely to have evolved from the known mill at the south gate of the town which was fed by water from the town ditch.

The exact site of the ford which gave Wallingford its name is still an open question and one which is yet to be fully addressed. Not even the derivation of the name is clear: 'ford of the Welsh', 'strangers' ford', and 'Wealh's ford' have all been suggested – the last most recently (Gelling and Cole 2000, 75). 'Slotisford Hundred' surrounds Wallingford at the time of Domesday Book (*DB Berks*, Maps) but the location of the 'ford with the bar or bars' (Gelling 1974, 507), which gives the Hundred its name, is unknown. Two other 'ford' names lie within a five mile stretch of the river: Shillingford upstream and Moulsford downstream. It seems likely that the river may have been at least occasionally fordable at several points in the vicinity of Wallingford. Early maps and photographs show eyots and heavily reeded shallows. The stretch of river below the bridge was still so inconveniently shallow in the early 19th century that a weir and lock was built at Chalmore in 1838 to raise the water level below the bridge by 18 inches to enable barges to reach the Town Wharf above the bridge. The lock was removed in 1883 after better dredging and controls had finally deepened the navigation channel.(Thacker 1968, ii, 197–201)

The first secure reference to a bridge at Wallingford comes in the 12th century where an anonymous chronicler describes 'the bridge that ran up to the entrance to the town, and was the master-key not only of the town but of the castle on that side' (*Gesta Stephani*, 227). However, the eleventh-century account by William of Poitiers of William's crossing of the Thames 'by ford and by bridge' may possibly be an earlier reference to a bridge at Wallingford (*Gesta Willelmi*, 147). Although firm evidence is lacking, it certainly seems likely that the river was bridged here in some way when the Alfredian *burh* was created. The discovery of middle Saxon bridgework at Oxford has confirmed the local capabilities for the building of such a crossing (Dodd 2003, 75, 79–81). Could it be that the bridge was built in close proximity to the ford, as appears to be the case in Oxford? If so, it might be expected that early roads would lead to this crossing point. In 1975 Kirsty Rodwell drew attention to the fact that the main Roman road from Silchester to Dorchester bypassed Wallingford to the west on a route leading through Cholsey and Mackney, crossing the river near Shillingford. There is, nevertheless, a strong possibility that another early medieval, if not Roman, road forded the river close to the site of Wallingford Bridge. A stretch of road, known in medieval references and still in the 19th century as the Portway, approaches Crowmarsh from the south east on an alignment with Watery Lane. It has been diverted to the end of the bridge but its original course would have taken it north west across the river to a point where it could have linked the existing road north of Wallingford towards Shillingford (Edgeworth below, p. 82).

Early Saxon influence in the vicinity of Wallingford is very clearly delineated in other surviving place-names denoting natural features. Gelling and Cole (2000, xix, 41) have argued that some topographical names, particularly those relating to major concerns of settlers such as water supply and terrain, are likely to date from the settlement period of the 5th century. The link of Wallin*ford*, Shillin*ford*, Mouls*ford* and Slotis*ford* to river shallows and crossing points has already been discussed. To these can be added two islands (OE *eg, ieg)* in marshland, Chols*ey* and

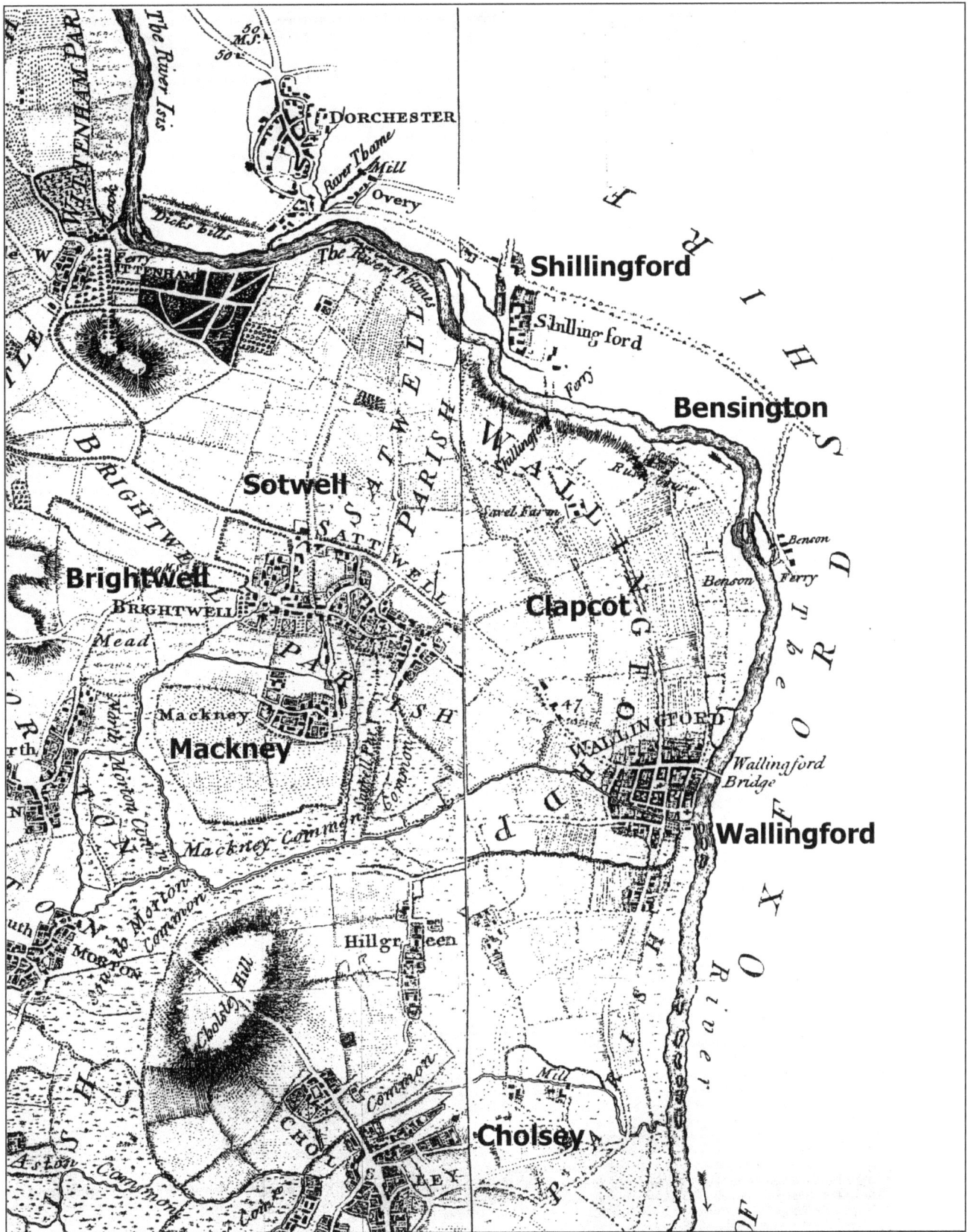

Figure 4.1 Saxon place-names in Wallingford's hinterland (base map: John Rocque, 1761).

Mackn*ey*, the marshland of Crow*marsh* and the fresh water supplies of Sot*well*, Bright*well* and Monge*well*. It is significant that the lands of these parishes, together with the River Thames, completely encircle Wallingford's boundaries (Figure 4.1).

Such evidence makes it likely that the hinterland of Wallingford was well settled in the early Saxon period. Furthermore, on the Oxfordshire side of the river, Dorchester has long been noted for its early Germanic burials at Dyke Hills, whilst burials of late Roman style at

Queenford Farm continued well into the 5th century. Recent work near the abbey (Keevil 2003) uncovered further evidence of early Saxon settlement within the town and it is likely that more will emerge during the current Discover Dorchester Project. Similarly, sunken featured buildings of the 6th century excavated at Benson reveal early Saxon settlement at a place later noted as a royal estate centre (Booth *et al.* 2007, 96; Booth above, p. 10).

Evidence of similar settlement in Wallingford itself is tantalisingly sparse at present, apart from the large cemetery in St John's Road. Helena Hamerow's article in this volume (above, p. 16) reveals the fifth-century dating of the earliest cremations here and the high status nature of some of the finds. The cemetery lies just to the south west of the town ramparts and ditch. It obviously served a local population but no clear archaeological evidence of the location of the early Saxon settlement has yet been discovered by the limited archaeology within the boundaries of modern Wallingford; just a few shards of early Saxon pottery were excavated within the late Saxon ramparts (Brooks 1965a). It is to be hoped that the Garden Archaeology programme of the present *Burh* to Borough Project may shed light on this question in due course, though the depth of such settlement layers within the later town may well be beneath the 1.2m maximum depth of the test pits.

However obscure the location of the original Saxon settlement in Wallingford may currently be, the presence of the St John's Road cemetery makes it clear that it existed somewhere in the vicinity. It is, however, the later parish boundaries that may provide the decisive evidence for the earliest phases of known settlement. These need to be considered in context with archaeological and documentary sources for the town's churches, including their links with the Saxon hinterland surrounding the town which has already been identified.

It is likely that the re-introduction of Christianity into the area by St Birinus in the mid 7th century, and the establishment of a minster at Dorchester, had an effect on the Wallingford community. However, there was a period of only about 30 years (*c.* 635 – *c.* 665 AD) before the seat of the new West Saxon bishopric was removed to Winchester. It is impossible to assess how much of the work of Birinus and his successors was eclipsed by the Mercian takeover that followed in the late 7th century but Dorchester survived as a religious centre, since it eventually re-emerged as a bishopric (Blair 1994, 58). The political disruption of the Mercians in this part of the Thames Valley did not preclude the foundation of further religious centres: there are indications that the Mercian King Wulfhere (AD 658/9–675) founded minsters at Thame, Aylesbury and Bicester. Indeed John Blair suggests that: 'The decades after 660, were the golden age of the rich cosmopolitan life of early Christian England. Never again, probably, was so much land and money devoted within such a short space of time to the expansion of the English Church' (Blair 1994, 61).

Yet apart from Dorchester, the only other known early minster in the Wallingford area is Abingdon, 15 miles (24km) away. In view of the scale of early local settlements it seems at least likely that other religious centres are yet to be identified. So what indications might there be? Such a

church was likely to be founded by the patronage of king, bishop or wealthy layman and would be free of the usual taxation. It would be an ecclesiastical settlement probably headed by an abbot, abbess or priest and supporting a group of monks, nuns, priests, or laity. Such a community might be involved in pastoral care, receive dues and exert parochial authority (Blair 2005, 3). Such sites are often associated with rivers, their water-fronts giving potential for trade and profit. 'The locations emphasize their centrality in the economic systems which were growing around them in the 7th and 8th centuries, and which ensured the re-birth of many of them as small towns between the 10th and 12th.' (Blair 1994, 67).

One possible candidate for such a religious centre in Wallingford is the church of St Leonard which stands on an east-west axis in the south-east corner of the town. The ramparts and ditch of the *burh* make a deviation south-eastwards to encompass the precincts of the church. The most likely explanation for this is that the church was already there when the rampart was built. Although the present St Leonard is the oldest church structure surviving in the town it is unlikely that it is the original building. Like so many other churches, it has been altered at various stages: it suffered considerable damage in the Civil War, the Victorians gave it a 'facelift' and a tower, but there is still clear late Saxon or early Norman herring-bone stonework surviving on the outer north face of the nave, and Saxon features on the outer south face of the chancel. There is also some interesting twelfth-century stone carving on the chancel arches inside the church.

The dedication to St Leonard is also likely to belong to the 12th century, but a papal confirmation of Honorius II (1124–30) gives a clear indication that this was actually a new name for the church (*CMF*, i, 13). It refers to a gift of 1122, recorded in the cartulary of St Frideswide, Oxford, by which King Henry I gave St Leonard, together with St Lucian, the chapel of Sotwell and 51 acres of land, to St Frideswide (*CMF*, i, 11). The papal confirmation of the gift, exact in all other detail, names the first church not as St Leonard but as Holy Trinity the Lesser. The most likely explanation is that the church had been recently re-dedicated (possibly following the rebuilding of an older structure) to avoid confusion with the more prestigious church of Holy Trinity in the northern part of the town, which had been regularized after the conquest as a priory under the powerful influence of the abbey of St Albans (Roffe below, pp. 36–7). The older dedication to Holy Trinity is often associated with an early Saxon church. Many such stone churches were simple structures, with a nave and small chancel. The south face of the present chancel has several interesting features which have not been fully analysed. A careful study of the fabric might shed more light on its origins; it is even conceivable that it incorporates elements of the earliest church.

The site on which the church stands shares several key features with early minsters: it is close to the river, standing prominently above it, and may have been bordered by a stream sourced from a spring which apparently rises under the later mill site to the west (pers. comm. Mr Boughton, last owner of the mill in the 1970s). Such a spring could

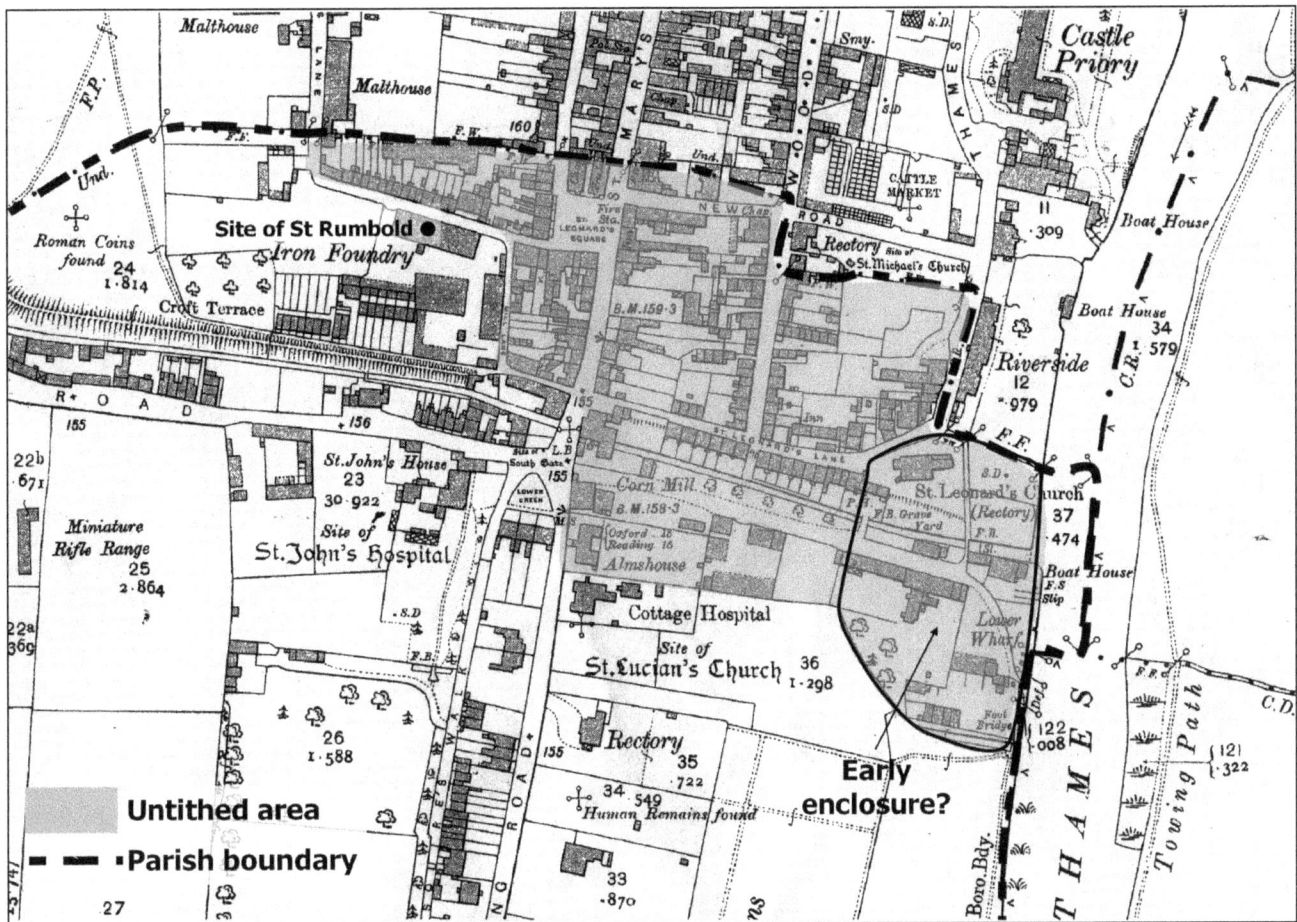

Figure 4.2 Part of St Leonard's parish, showing the untithed area and the conjectured early church and wharf boundary.

have provided a fresh water stream to a settlement area around St Leonard and have been incorporated later by the builders of the *burh* defences. The church also stands close to a neighbouring water front with a long history as the lower wharf of the town. A possible former enclosure with the river as its eastern edge is reflected in the curving southern boundary of Lower Wharf (the modern St Lucian's House) and the road pattern marking the outer boundary of St Leonard's churchyard on the northern side (Figure 4.2). This pattern has potential parallels with other minster sites such as Bisley or Bampton (Blair 2005, 197–8).

The tithe map for St Leonard reveals that a significant part of the parish is excluded from tithe. The reason is not yet fully understood, although the phenomenon is most likely to relate to the management of impropriate tithes (tithes that had passed from religious houses to lay landholders) after the Dissolution. It does seems likely, however, that the area so defined is the original parish of St Leonard. It includes the wharf, part of the southern bank of the Millbrook almost to the modern Wallingford Road, and the whole of the northern urban area of the modern parish east of the present Mill Lane. What is more, the areas immediately bordering the tithe-free part of the parish to the south and west are the likely sites of the lost churches of St Lucian and St Rumbold. St Leonard has clear links with these neighbouring churches, both of which it had incorporated by the 14th century. Significantly, St Lucian also included the chapel of Sotwell in its parish, making it potentially

even larger than St Leonards, and it too is a therefore a possible candidate for an important early foundation. A pre-conquest grant (S.517) mentions property belonging to Sotwell in the area immediately south of the *burh* and links it with three churches, for which the only known candidates are St Leonard, St Lucian and St Rumbold which suggests that all three are 10th century or earlier. (Roffe below, p. 37–8)

The histories of St Lucian and St Rumbold are more obscure than those of St Leonard. There is only sparse documentary evidence for St Lucian. Its dedication is rare and potentially early: St Lucian of Antioch was martyred in AD 312. Its early association with Sotwell is certainly notable. Of its location, Skermer, writing *c.* 1712, describes it specifically as '5 Poles southward of the Alms House. The ground extends as far as the Knowl in the footpath to Winterbrook'. He adds that 'The Minister of Wallingford paid for the ground', in other words, it was glebe land. There are nineteenth-century references to skulls being found in this area and all this accords well with medieval sources which place it to the east of the present Reading Road. Northwards the parish appears to include land 'towards the Milldam' (the town ditch) (Riley 1876, no 231). It probably bordered St Leonard's parish here, a little south of the ditch. Unlike St Leonard's, however, St Lucian's did not survive the downturn in the borough's economy in the later Middle Ages. By 1299 there was only one priest presented by St Frideswide to serve both St Leonard and St Lucian and by 1320 it was

21

requested that the churches be united as the revenues had 'become so slight that they were scarcely sufficient to maintain one chaplain' (*RRM*, 55,156).

St Rumbold or Ruald was a colourful seventh-century saint, grandson of Penda of Mercia, who lived for only three days. He was born, demanded Christian baptism, preached a sermon to his parents and died on the third day having given clear instructions about his place of burial. It is perhaps worth noting that the choice of this particular dedication for a potentially early Wallingford church could be an indication that it was founded in the time of Mercian influence discussed above. In 1982 excavations revealed between 40 and 60 east-west orientated burials on the site of the old Wilder's iron foundry south of Goldsmiths' Lane and west of Mill Lane. Some of the most easterly burials had been cut through by twelfth or thirteenth-century pits, suggesting that they were of an earlier date. Pottery from other associated pits was preliminarily dated from the mid 11th to the 13th century, suggesting a contraction of activity on the site by the 14th century.

It has been presumed that this was the burial ground of St Rumbold and it is possible that a square end of stone walling with an internal dimension of 16 feet (5m), recorded in service trenches under the old iron foundry, was a part of the foundations of the church. However, this could not be confirmed (Halpin 1983). A shadow of doubt is cast by a document of 1198 which places the *atrium* (hall or porch) of the church to the south of a tenement lying outside the south gate (*CMF*, ii, 367). If this is a reference to the church itself, it is certainly puzzling, for at present there is no other known medieval church to which the cemetery in Goldsmith's Lane can relate. It seems more likely that the reference is to an associated property rather than to the church itself, but the doubt should not be ignored (for an alternative explanation, see Roffe below, p. 38).

It is certainly clear from several references amongst the 13th and early 14th century deeds that some properties in St Rumbold parish lie south of the town. The parish appears, like St Leonard's, to span the defences. *Bruttestrete* is mentioned in several of these sources and, from the context, is clearly the name of the road leading into the town from the south. Ascertaining whether the street name continued north of the south gate, and whether its alignment was that of the later St Mary's Street (formerly Fish St) or of St Martin's Street could help place the site of the church of St Rumbold more certainly. There is much scope for further documentary research into property and boundary locations and until more evidence presents itself the exact position of the church of St Rumbold must remain an open question.

It is certain, however, that Henry I gave the church to the new abbey of Reading in 1121 (together with Cholsey) and the last recorded presentation by the abbot was in 1353. By the late 14th century St Rumbold had been joined with St Leonard and this documented decline of the use of the church of St Rumbold accords well with the evidence from the excavated churchyard.

In summary, the case is made for the existence of three churches in the southern area of the town and its environs well before the Conquest. Two of these, St Leonard (formerly Holy Trinity the less) and St Rumbold, had parishes which span the ramparts of the town, perhaps an indication of origins predating the 9th century *burh*. St Rumbold lies to the west of *Bruttestrete*; St Lucian lies to the east between *Bruttestrete* and the river, south of St Leonard. The road pattern outside the south gate reflects that of the main routes through the town, converging at the southern end close to the ancient Bradford's Brook boundary, which was probably also the southern extent of the St Rumbold and St Lucian parishes, though it should be remembered that St Lucian also held the chapel of Sotwell.

Consideration of the later usage of land in this southern area suggests further pointers that the *burh* fortifications may have been imposed on an earlier southern settlement. Apart from the existence of the wharf, which has been mentioned above, there are two other known connections with trade: a mill and a market. A mill near the south gate is documented in the 12th century when it was said to have 'been made' by Brien fitzCount (*Regesta*, iii, no 88). Mill sites, however, change so little that it is quite conceivable that this mill was on the site of a predecessor. In a similar way, references can be found to the selling of corn and possibly of bread in the area: in 1271 there is mention of a corn market in the parish of St Lucian (Riley, no 590) and it is possible that the name of the adjacent *Bruttestrete* may be a corruption of 'bred streat', a name recorded by Leland as still existing in 1542 but which has never been identified (*Leland*, i, 118).

It could be supposed that both the mill and the market were post-Conquest features, associated with a newly created extended medieval market area. This, however, does not accord well with the archaeological picture from within the fortified town which suggests that Wallingford's economy, far from expanding, was beginning to shrink in the 13th century, at a time when other local towns, such as Oxford, Abingdon and Reading were expanding. A good recent example was found in the *Burh* to Borough 2008 excavation on the Kinecroft where pottery evidence suggests that the buildings discovered had a life span from *c*. 11th-12th century, then went out of use. The only known medieval development to the south in Wallingford was the foundation of the hospital of St John, probably originating in some form as the result of the proposed grant of land *c*. 1153 by Henry of Anjou and the Empress Matilda and later through endowments by townspeople (Orme, 75; Roffe below, p. 40), although a post-Conquest French borough is also a possibility (Roffe below, p. 38). It is equally tenable that the extra-mural market is a survival from the Saxon period, an indication of trading in a pre-*burh* community based around a wharf, with a market area, churches and links to a neighbourhood of other centres to the west and north, including Sotwell, Brightwell, Mackney and, perhaps, the Clapcot area.

The extra-mural southern area has had little archaeological investigation so far but the wealth of surviving medieval documents paints a striking picture of the town's arable fields and grazing lands lying within this southern hinterland. Portmanfield, Portmanmoor and Chalmore, all lie south and west of the Saxon town fortifications and within the confines of Bradford's Brook and Millbrook – the bounds of St Leonard's parish – formerly the three

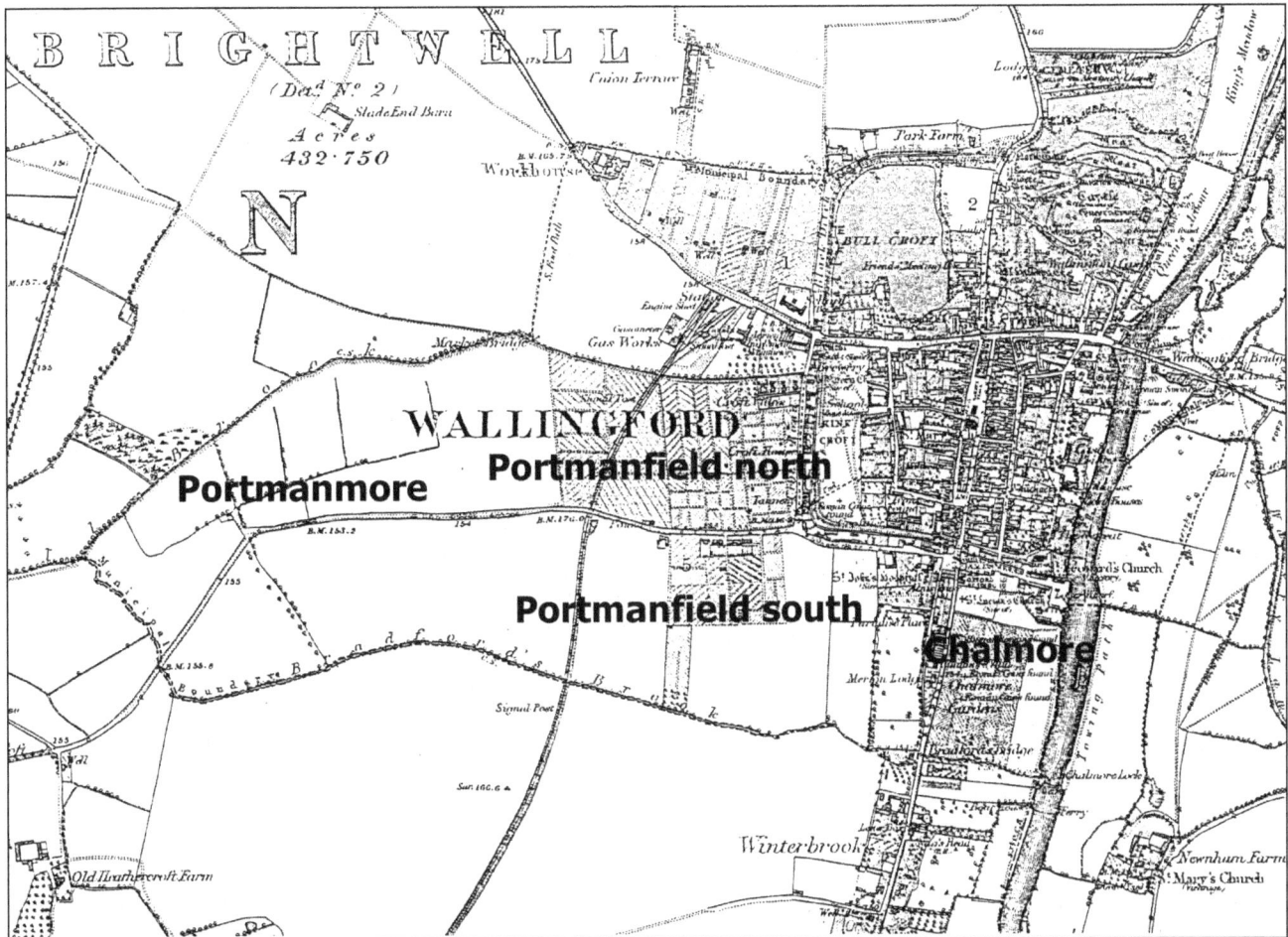

4.3 Town fields in St Leonard's parish.

parishes of St Leonard, St Lucian and St Rumbold (Figure 4.3). They reflect a system of farming which may have supported a pre-*burh* Saxon settlement and survived its creation.

The arrangement was long-lasting. Some of these lands were later given to the hospital of St John and became known as St John's Field. The hospital was dissolved in the 16th century and the tithes were divided. This is made clear in the Glebe Terriers of 1634 which reflect the continued importance of these fields. The tithes were shared between St Leonard and St Peter, as were the tithes in Chalmore. It is also striking that Sotwell was still included in the Wallingford Terriers and almost all its tithes were still due to St Leonard which had also taken over some which were formerly paid to the priory of Holy Trinity. The Sotwell terrier is unusually detailed and appears to be based on an earlier document pre-dating the sixteenth-century dissolution of the priory (Mortimer 1995, 164–183).

To place these later arrangements in context, consideration must be given to the impact of the building of the *burh* and the Norman Conquest on the parishes of Wallingford. Eleven medieval parish churches are recorded in Wallingford, one of which also served as the church of the priory of Holy Trinity (Figure 4.4). In addition there was a gate chapel of St Mary Grace at the bridge, a church of St Peter in the West (most probably a similar gate chapel), the free chapel of the hospital of St John the Baptist outside the

south gate, and the royal free chapel of St Nicholas which served the extra-parochial castle.

Of these, only St Mary le More, St Leonard and St Peter still survive, together with the churchyard of All Saints (commonly known as All Hallows by 1606), the church having been demolished in 1643 during the Civil War. These four parishes had absorbed the other seven by the end of the 14th century. St Peter (today redundant) was destroyed in the Civil War but rebuilt in the late 18th century. St Leonard also sustained severe damage and was out of use for 50 years after the war but parts of the older building survived; the Victorians gave it a new tower, rebuilt some of the interior and made changes to windows and doors. They also completely rebuilt St Mary le More, apart from its seventeenth-century tower. St Mary le More and St Leonard is now the single Wallingford parish.

Documentary records and archaeology have enabled some assessment of the lost medieval churches and their parish boundaries. Figure 4.5 shows the boundaries as they were in 1837. From at least the late 11th century until 1525 the parish of St Mary le More belonged to Holy Trinity Priory, an influential monastic institution under the authority of St Albans Abbey, which stood north of the High Street in the southern area of what is now the Bullcroft. Holy Trinity served as a parish church and the priory also presented priests for the churches of St Martin and St John on the Water. The parochial status of Holy Trinity and the ear-

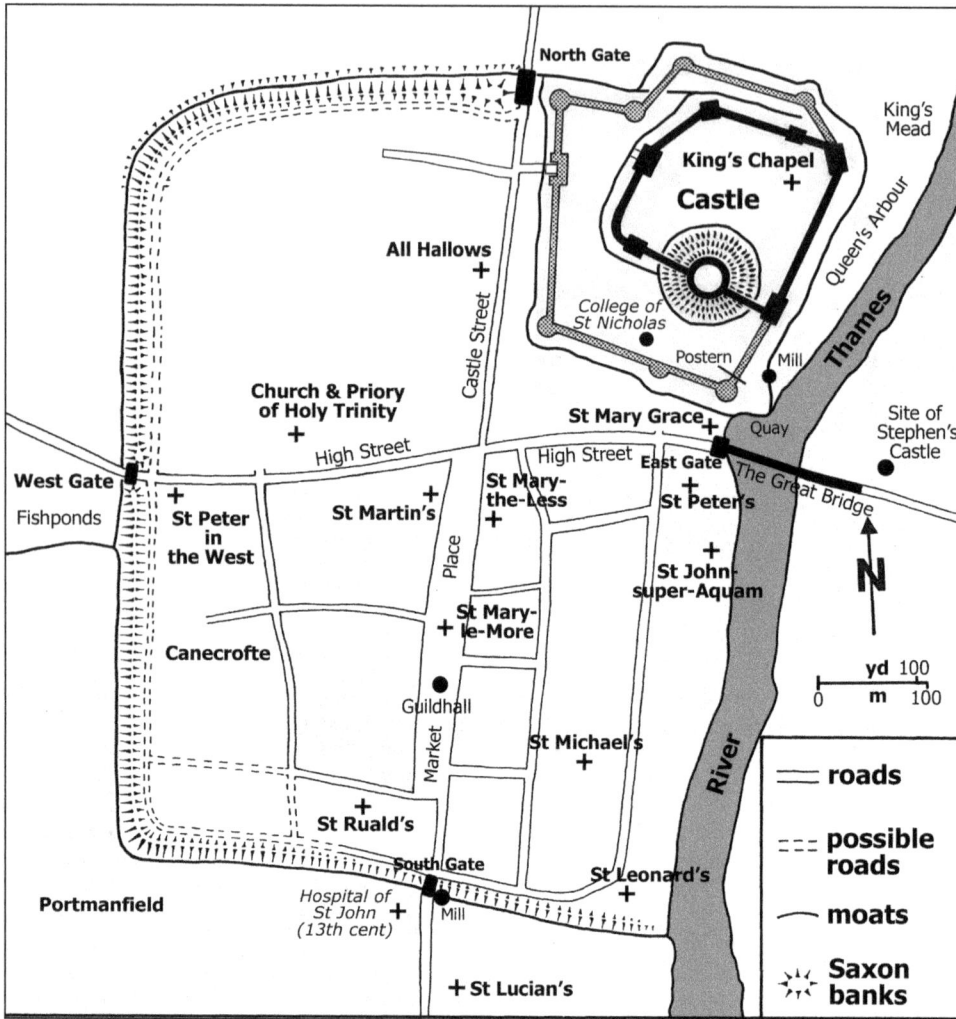

Figure 4.4 Wallingford in the 12th century.

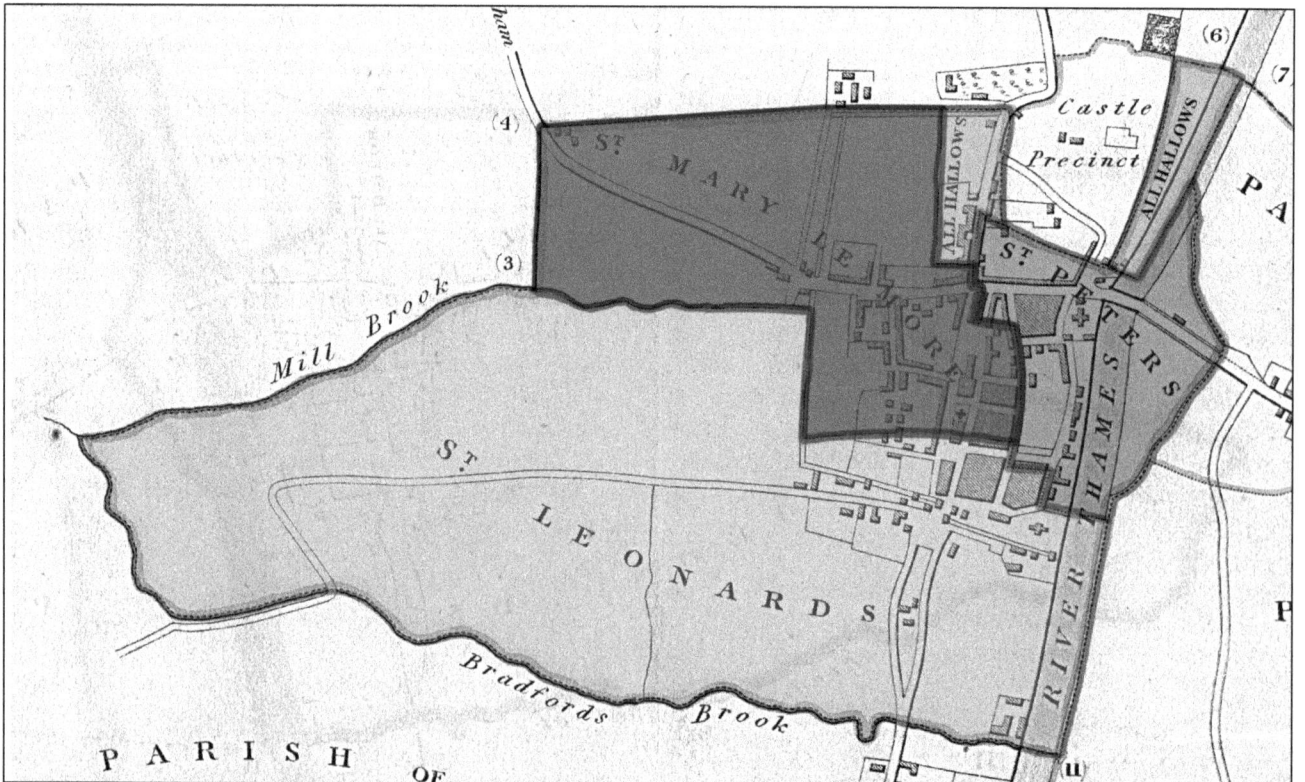

4.5 Wallingford parishes in 1837.

liest references to the church point to the possibility of its existence before the Norman Conquest and the founding of the later priory as an important episcopal foundation; the evidence for this is presented by David Roffe (below, p. 36–7).

Excavations in 2004 by Northampton Archaeology on the site of the new Waitrose supermarket on the corner of High Street and St Martin's Street uncovered the medieval churchyard of St Martin. The earliest of the 210 articulated burials discovered dated to the 10th or 11th century and the latest to the 15th century. Some of the early burials had stones, and in one case skulls, placed either side of the heads to keep them upright – so called 'ear-muff' burials. One such, with flint 'ear muffs', had a pierced scallop shell suspended round its neck (a real one, not a metal badge). This has been interpreted as an indication that the owner had made a pilgrimage to Santiago de Compostella which first became a popular destination in the 10th century. Other finds from the Saxon period included a lead crucifix with a surviving mother-of-pearl nail, two decorated hooked tags and the base of a Saxon mortar mixer which was probably used during the building of the church (Booth *et al.*2007, 267–8; Iain Soden, pers. comm.).

These discoveries point clearly to St Martin being a church of the Saxon *burh*, in existence well before the Norman Conquest. There appeared to be a significant decline in burial numbers on the site by the 15th century and it is recorded that in 1412, a licence was given to the proctors of St Mary's church 'to use the timber and stones of St Martin's church, Wallingford, which collapsed long ago and is ruined, without a rector and almost entirely without parishioners'. The churchyard was to be enclosed and future responsibility for it was placed with the parishioners of St Mary's church (*RRH,* 150).

There is no easy way of defining the individual parish boundaries of Holy Trinity, St Martin and St Mary le More since the latter appears also to have absorbed the parish of Holy Trinity after the dissolution of the Priory in 1525. Properties 'sometymes parcell of the Priorye of late purchased' are noted in the useful 1606 survey of the town (N.A. E3151369. 101–123) and Holy Trinity is known to have encompassed land outside the west gate. Otherwise, the churches are purely urban, all the rights of the extended parish of St Mary's lying within the town walls; there is no mention of holdings in the town fields which, in the Glebe Terriers of 1634, are divided entirely between St Leonard and St Peter (Mortimer, 163–193).

The origins of St Mary le More itself are obscure but its urban status and its association with Holy Trinity suggest that, like St Martin, it might be a *burh* church (Roffe below, p. 37). The church certainly had a prominent role in the medieval town; presumably its central position and the failure of St Martin gave it status which was further enhanced by the demise of the priory in 1525.

St Peter's parish incorporated three other medieval churches: St Mary-the-Less (or St Mary of the Stalls), St Michael and St John-super-Aquam. With the exception of St John, these churches all belonged to the royal free chapel of St Nicholas in the castle whose Dean presented their priests. It is particularly notable that St Peter's parish

boundary crosses the river to include land on either side of the bridge – a feature which suggests that something in its origins may derive from the foundation of the Alfredian *burh* which centred on the river crossing. Within the town area of the parish the boundaries follow roads and properties, the southern dog-leg seeming to cut into part of St Leonard's parish south of New Road to encompass the known site of St Michael's churchyard. This was excavated in 1974 by the Wallingford Historical and Archaeological Society revealing 35 medieval burials, none apparently later than the 14th century, and a thirteenth/fourteenth-century bell-pit; the church itself almost certainly lies beneath the present Cattle Market car-park (Weare 1977). The straight urban boundary lines apparently cutting into the lands of an established parish give St Michael every appearance of being a small post-Conquest urban estate church. It had gone by 1374, its parish being absorbed by St Peter.

St Mary-the-Less has similar features, probably accounting for the northern dog-leg of St Peter's parish where the boundary divides properties facing west on to St Martin's Street from those facing east on to St Mary's Street. It was probably another post-Conquest foundation which, like St Michael, failed by the late 14th century and was linked to St Peter.

St John-super-Aquam is something of an enigma: David Roffe (below, p. 37) has noted from a confirmation of endowments to St Albans Abbey by the bishop of Salisbury that it belonged to the priory of Holy Trinity from the 12th century but nothing is known of its priests or the extent of its parish before it was absorbed by St Peter's. Its name survived as an orchard in the detailed 1548 town survey (Bodleian Library, MS Top Berks b41).

North of the High Street lay All Saints, notably a dedication often associated with early Christian foundations. The 1606 survey records the church as standing on the east side of Castle Street adjoining its churchyard. However, since the line of Castle Street is known to have been shifted westwards in the 13th century (Brooks 1965a) it would presumably have been located originally on the west side of the main north road out of the town. There are further references in the 1606 survey to a parsonage house and parsonage barns on the west side of Castle Street. The parish of All Saints has some notably unusual features. It includes the large and very significant area to the north of the town, known as Clapcot, bordering Sotwell and the Slade End part of Brightwell on the west and the river on the east, taking in the land bounded by the long bend in the river. Within the town boundaries its area is small and irregular with little regard for the street pattern and it has also been split in two by the implantation of the castle or what preceded it. The castle itself is extra-parochial. Such features strongly suggest that, like St Leonard and St Lucian, All Saints is the survivor of an older ecclesiastical arrangement that possibly pre-dates both the town and castle. It deserves more attention.

Within the castle area stood the royal free chapel of St Nicholas. Until now Wallingford and Windsor have been the only chapels of this type which could not be shown to be pre-Conquest foundations. However, the work of David Roffe and Katharine Keats-Rohan now shows convincingly that the castle site was an important pre-Conquest royal base, and that the chapel is also likely to have origins predating the Norman stronghold (Roffe, p. 36; Keats-Rohan, p. 60).

In summary, a progressive pattern of development can be detected within the boundaries and parishes of Wallingford. They are surrounded by early Anglo-Saxon settlement sites, detectable from their names and the surviving water systems which were later adapted to serve the fortified *burh*. The fifth- to sixth-century pagan burial ground may have served more than those settled in the immediate vicinity of the ford; it is possible to envisage a wider population to the west in the Sotwell, Brightwell and Mackney area, and even a further community to the north of the later town in the enclosed bend of the River Thames (Roffe below, p. 42). Perhaps some of these settlements may even have incorporated survivors of a sub-Roman culture as has been observed in Dorchester (Booth above, p. 10).

From perhaps the mid 7th century there are indications that an important church, either Holy Trinity (later St Leonard) or possibly St Lucian, was established on the river side. Two others followed, including St Rumbold and an economic community was developed close by with a wharf for river trade, a market area and arable and moor land in what later became the town fields. The settlement was protected to the south by the ancient boundary of Bradford's Brook. This community had strong links with Sotwell to the west, and also Brightwell which was possibly the estate centre (Roffe below, p. 38). To the north of the ford the church of All Saints may have been the focus of Clapcot.

By the late 9th century royal activity is apparent in the Wallingford area (Keats-Rohan below, p. 53). The king acquired Cholsey to the south and chose Wallingford as the site of a defended royal *burh*. The ramparts which were constructed ignored the earlier settlement boundaries, but encompassed the churches of St Leonard, and (probably) St Rumbold within the walls on the south. St Lucian and the town fields lay outside the defences but remained within the southern boundary of the town which survived as the *Winterdich* (later Bradford's Brook). In the north, All Saints church lay inside the walls, but its lands were similarly left outside. There the boundary was the river with its crossing point near Shillingford.

The town defences focused on the ford, and quite probably a bridge was built, with the eastern boundary established at the far end of the crossing (later the bounds of St Peter's parish). The Millbrook was cut to supply a defensive moat round the ramparts. As the Saxon town developed, new town churches were established, linking the southern and northern communities (St Martin and Holy Trinity and possibly St Mary le More), while the north-eastern section of the town was developed as a stronghold with a royal palace, a royal free chapel (later St Nicholas) and possibly accommodation for the king's housecarls as guards.

By 1066 Wallingford was a royal centre in the charge of Wigod, a stronghold of note to William of Normandy who chose to bring his army there to cross the Thames, perhaps to be sure of securing it.

Of course much of this scenario lacks firm evidence, but nothing here is without some supporting material. What is certainly clear is that the town's origins are far more complex than has been previously recognized. It is to be hoped that the *Burh* to Borough Project will open the way to more detailed archaeology and research. Many debatable questions can only be resolved by holes in the ground; the present garden archaeology programme and more extensive planned excavations may help provide some answers.

There is also scope for more work on early properties. Many property holdings within the town have already been traced in detail to the 17th century, and some to the 15th century (D. Pedgley, unpublished notes, Wallingford Museum). Further research into the wealth of surviving medieval records may make it possible to link at least some of those to the 13th century or earlier.

It is greatly to be hoped that the excellent, and still all too rare, example of archaeologists and documentary historians working closely together within the *Burh* to Borough Project will finally ensure that Wallingford comes out of the footnotes and makes the headlines.

5

WALLINGFORD IN DOMESDAY BOOK AND BEYOND

David Roffe

Abstract

The Domesday account of Wallingford is a key document for an understanding of the early history of Wallingford and yet hitherto its potential has gone largely untapped. A new edition and translation is provided here and its forms and content are analysed for the fist time in the light of recent research in the representation of boroughs in Domesday Book. The data of the account are then used, in conjunction with both earlier and later documentation, to reconstruct the topography, society, and military role of Wallingford in the 11th century and beyond and to explore its origins.

Keywords

Anglo-Saxon; Anglo-Norman; Berkshire; Wallingford; Domesday Book; society, origins.

Introduction

Domesday Book is a uniquely important source for the early history of England and yet one that is often difficult to interpret. Its origins and production are complex. William the Conqueror ordered the Domesday survey at the Christmas court in 1085 at a time of crisis. King Cnut of Denmark was threatening to invade and it would seem that William wished to raise money to pay for mercenaries that he had hired for the defence of his realm and, equally importantly, to review the services owed to him by his men. All the records were brought to William at Salisbury in August 1086 and 'all those who held land in England' agreed on an extension of taxation and a redefinition of knight service. Most of those records no longer survive and the details of the meeting have to be reconstructed from the subsequent digest and re-organization of the survey that is Domesday Book. Although it contains only a fraction of the evidence collected in 1086, Domesday remains a basic source for the early history of England. It contains the first reference to the vast majority of English settlements and in most instances affords the most detailed survey before the modern period (Roffe 2007).

So it is that the Domesday account of Wallingford is central to the early history of the borough. There are a handful of pre-Conquest references to the town, but it is unparalleled in its scope and detail until the Wallingford survey of 1548 (Bodleian Library, MS Top Berks b41). It is the most important source for the history of medieval Wallingford. Hitherto it has been extensively mined by historians of Wallingford and beyond, largely for the detail that it affords of family history. Yet, surprisingly, it has never been analysed as a survey of a community, largely because its complexities have defied interpretation (Hooper 1988, 23–4). In consequence, there has been no concerted attempt

to understand the early history of the borough. This paper provides a new edition and translation of the text (Appendix) and examines the structure and sources of the account for the first time. It then uses its data to reconstruct the topography, social structure, and political role of Wallingford in the late 11th century and beyond.

The Domesday text

The Domesday account of Wallingford is entered on the dorse and verse of folio 56 of volume 1, Great Domesday Book (GDB), in the Berkshire section of the record (Figures 5.1 and 5.2). Apart from following the list of the county's tenants-in-chief (here, in fact, probably postscriptal), the account of the borough of Wallingford broadly conforms to a typical borough entry. As such, it is in apposition to the bulk of the text. Domesday Book is above all a survey of lordship. County by county it is arranged by chapters relating to the lands of each tenant-in-chief. In consequence, where a village was divided between a number of lords, it is necessary to look in the chapter of each to reconstruct a full account. The Domesday account of rural England is arranged by estates rather than settlements. Boroughs, by contrast, were enrolled as communities, that is, all the land is described together regardless of who held it. Here and there the account of a manor may refer to a property held in town. But, by and large, the bulk of the account is to be found at the head of the county folios, 'above the line' in Maitland's phrase (1897, 218), in a single entry.

This form has long been held to reflect the special nature of boroughs as communities and, in consequence, the special procedure that the Domesday commissioners applied to them (Martin 1985, 143–63; Reynolds 1986, 295–310). However, recent research has shown that it owes more to the programme of the GDB scribe than the peculiarities of urban life and the conduct of the Domesday inquest (Roffe 2007, 109–43). Detailed examination of the accounts of all the Domesday boroughs has shown that they are far from homogeneous. They draw upon numerous sources – an initial survey of the king's lands, an *inquisitio geldi*, local records, seigneurial surveys – which were originally all presented separately. They came together, and then imperfectly, only with the compilation of Domesday Book some years after the events of 1086. Here the agenda was different. Whereas the inquest had been concerned with a new agreement between king and subjects on geld and service, the GDB scribe produced the book as an administrative aid in the record of the king's dues in each county. The account of the boroughs, coupled with other dues – those sections usually called 'the county customs' – for which the sheriff was responsible to the king, were brought together to supplement the seigneurial data.

The account of the borough of Wallingford typifies the

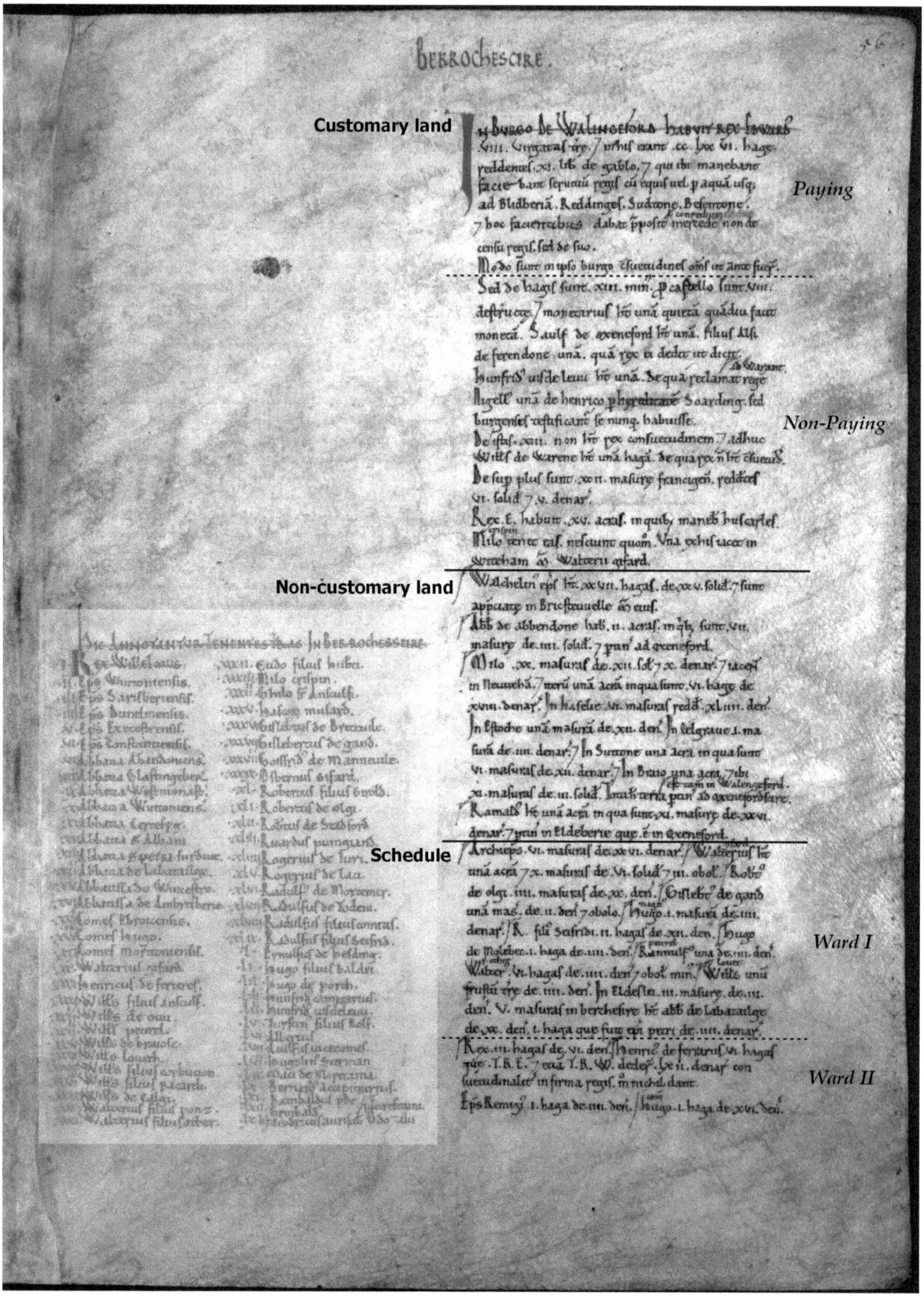
Customary land
Paying
Non-Paying
Non-customary land
Schedule
Ward I
Ward II

Figure 5.1 GDB, 56 dorse, the account of Wallingford, sections 1, II, and IIIa and IIIb (base image Alecto Historical Editions).

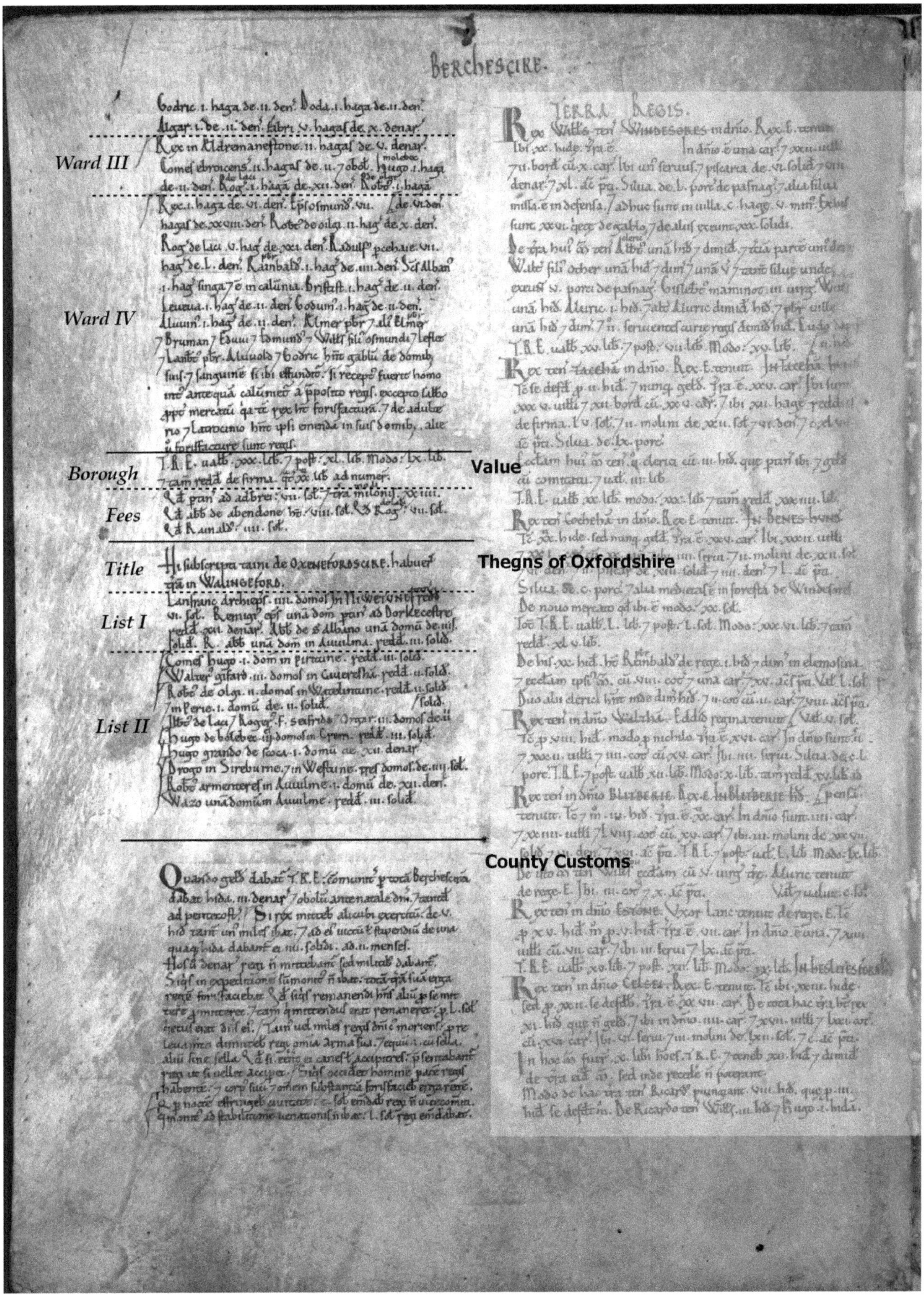

Ward III

Ward IV

Borough

Fees

Title

List I

List II

Value

Thegns of Oxfordshire

County Customs

Figure 5.2 GDB, 56 verso, the account of Wallingford, sections III c and d, IV, V, and VI (base image Alecto Historical Editions).

29

process. It was written in its entirety by the main scribe of GDB (Thorn and Thorn 2001, 37–72). Nevertheless, it is far from a coherent and integrated whole. Lines 1–68 were written first and, after a two-line space, lines 71–3. There is no title as such, but the first line of the account, 'IN THE BOROUGH OF WALLINGFORD KING EDWARD HAD…' starts with a large red drop capital and the rest of the line is written in rustic capitals and lined through in red ink to draw the eye. In general, the account is neatly drafted. Occasional interlineated glosses appear throughout, most often supplying a distinguishing surname or epithet to a holder of land but on occasion also adding or correcting material. As far as can be seen, these additions were current, that is they were added by the scribe in the course of drafting his work. However, there are signs that the scribe was writing in haste. There are two passages that are incomprehensible as they stand. A reference to Nigel [d'Aubigny] and Henry [de Ferrers] cannot be understood without extensive emendation (lines 14–15) and the *haga singa* belonging to St Albans Abbey has defied interpretation (line 59 and note for possibilities). More widely, the scribe's Latinity uncharacteristically lapses on a number of occasions. In nine instances a nominative is used where the sense demands an accusative and one vice versa (lines 32, 33, 41, 49, 50, 53, 55, 59).

The account originally ended half way down the second column at line 73. Nevertheless, the scribe seems to have anticipated that there was more information to come, for he subsequently added a valuation clause to the two blank lines 69 and 70 which he had presumably left for the purpose. All of this was executed before the rubrication of the section – highlighting important matter by shading and underlining in red ink – and probably the rest of the Berkshire text. Subsequently, a further passage was added, after a one-line space, in a hand that is slightly more cramped than that of the body of the text. Occupying lines 75–90, it is entitled 'The following thegns of Oxfordshire had land in Wallingford' and exhibits its own vocabulary. Throughout *domus*, 'house', widely used in the account of Oxford, is preferred to the *haga*, 'close', *masura*, 'messuage', or the occasional *acra*, 'acre', of the rest of the text. As far as can be seen, the passage was immediately followed after a two-line space by the enrolment of the last entry in the column, lines 94–109, the county customs; it, too, is unrubricated.

The stratigraphy of the text, then, immediately suggests that the valuation clauses, were in some way distinct from the body of the account and that the list of Oxfordshire thegns and the county customs were derived from entirely different sources. Scribal conventions, expression, and content confirm the impression. The forms of the text define a further three sections and indicate the sources of each (Figures 5.1 and 5.2).

Lines 1–22: customary lands

The account opens with the statement that King Edward had eight virgates of land in 1066 in which there were 276 closes paying £11 in rent (*gablum*) and various services to the king. There were as many tenements in 1086 which paid 'all customary dues', less 13. Eight had been destroyed in the construction of the castle and a further five had been

exempt in one way or another. William de Warenne had a further close 'from which the king does not have customary dues' and there were in addition 22 messuages of Frenchmen who were, it seems, similarly quit. The section ends with an account of 15 acres in which Edward the Confessor's housecarls had lived. These acres were held by Miles Crispin at the time of the inquest, but under what terms the jurors did not know, although one was said to belong to Walter Giffard's manor of Long Wittenham (GDB, 60; *DB Berks*, 20,3).

The status of this land was defined by its relationship to the crown. Although King Edward the Confessor is said to have held it in 1066, he was less a 'landlord' than the recipient of dues owed by the burgesses who dwelt there. These dues were the *consuetudines*, 'customs', that are referred to in the text. Of what they consisted is rarely explicit. Only rent, escort, and cartage are noticed here in the Wallingford account. It is clear from other Domesday boroughs that a tenement might also render to the king and the earl geld, heriot, tolls, landgable, mint tax, baking dues, and soke, even military service and some light labour dues (Tait 1936, 96–108). These were the types of due that the burgesses of Wallingford would have paid.

For those properties that still paid the customs in 1086 little detail is given: a single figure is the norm throughout Domesday Book and the individuals who held them are rarely recorded. The exempt tenements are more expansively described in justification of their exemption. They were of differing status. Moneyers, who had the rank of a thegn (Roffe 2007, 121–2), were regularly quit, although it is rarely made explicit, as it is in Wallingford, that the privilege was directly related to the activity of minting rather than to the property associated with it. Frenchmen also regularly held under special terms; they were usually quit of custom and in Nottingham, Norwich, and Northampton they even had their own boroughs (Darby 1977, 298–9; Reynolds 1977, 43). The plantation of foreigners seems to have been actively encouraged after the Conquest. Other tenements had been exempt on an ad hoc basis or their lords had unilaterally withdrawn the customs. The overriding point, however, was that they were properties which were or had been in a special relationship with the king.

The customary lands constituted the borough proper and their holders were the 'king's burgesses'. Indeed, in some instances, as in the accounts of Leicester and Derby (GDB, 230, 280; *DB Leics*, C3; *DB Derby,* B2), the value of the borough is recorded immediately thereafter. The customary tenements were the main focus of royal interest in the Domesday inquest and summary totals provided an adequate account of the king's dues for the purposes of Domesday Book. However, it cannot be doubted that behind the extant figures there lie more detailed records. Uniquely in the Little Domesday Book (LDB) account of Colchester (Essex) every burgess is named (LDB, 104–107; *DB Essex*, B3) and it is clear that the source of the data was an extensive inquest record (Taylor 2000, 13–14). It was almost certainly a product of the audit of regalian rights which constituted the first stage of the Domesday inquest (Roffe 2000, 128–40). Similar sources must have existed for all boroughs where the population is recorded. That the source of the account of the customary tenements in Wallingford was different from the rest of the Berkshire text is hinted at by the language in which it is expressed. Normally, the GDB scribe used the formula *x tenuit*, 'x held', to indicate who held land in 1066, but here he uses *habuit*, 'had', in the opening paragraph, a usage that is associated with records from the earlier stages of the Domesday inquest. Section three of the Domesday account of Wallingford (lines 36–68) probably preserves a fragment of the source that the scribe used (see below).

Lines 23–35: non-customary lands

A second section is signalled by the introduction of the *paragraphos*, a paragraph or gallows sign, to mark entries (Roffe 2007, 39, 77, 113, 115). There are four entries in all and each describes tenements that were attached to manors in the surrounding countryside. Bishop Walkelin of Winchester's closes belonged to Brightwell (GDB, 58; *DB Berks*, 2,3); the abbot of Abingdon's to unspecified estates in Oxford[shire], Miles Crispin's to Newnham Murren, Haseley, North Stoke, Chalgrove, Sutton Courtenay, and Bray (GDB, 57, 57v, 159–159v; *DB Berks*, 1,22,37; *DB Oxon*, 35, 2,6,10,11), all said to lie in Oxfordshire; and Rainald's in Albury (GDB, 161; *DB Oxon*, 59,22), also in Oxfordshire.

Again, the type is widely evidenced in the accounts of Domesday boroughs. Tenements that were attached to a manor paid their customs to its lord rather than the king and they were not considered to be 'of the borough', but to be an integral part of the rural estate. The account of the manor of Brightwell underlines the distinction. Bishop Walkelin's tenements in Wallingford were unequivocally urban. Medieval inquest records and the Wallingford surveys of 1548 and 1606 indicate that some, at least, were situated on the north side of High Street between Castle Street and the east gate (*CI* 14, nos 326, 332; Bodleian Library, MS Top Berks b41; NA, E315/369, pp 101–23). And yet it is recorded that 25s came 'from the pleas of the land which belongs to this manor in Wallingford' (GDB, 58; *DB Berks*, 2,3). Suit of court was paid to Brightwell. The land was a separate fee within, but not part of, the borough. Historiographically, the manors to which this type of tenement belonged have been known as 'contributory manors', that is, they looked to the borough (Ballard 1904, 11–36). In 1086 the reality was the exact opposite: the urban properties were contributory tenements in that their dues went to the rural estate.

As such it is clear that the source of the information was the survey of the lands of tenants-in-chief which followed the *inquisitio geldi*, the second stage of the Domesday inquest (Roffe 2000, 140–6). Thus, a further seven non-customary fees in Wallingford are described only in the account of their parent manors. A close in Wallingford is recorded in the account of the king's manor of Sutton Courtenay; three closes in the bishop of Winchester's manor of Harwell; a church held by Roger the priest in the bishop of Salisbury's manor of Sonning; eight closes in the manor of Sotwell of St Peter's Abbey, Winchester; five closes in the abbot of Battle Abbey's manor of Brightwalton; eight closes in Walter Giffard's manor of Long Wittenham; and

five closes in William fitzCorbucion's manor of North Moreton (GDB, 57v, 58, 59v, 60, 61; *DB Berks*, 1,37.2,3.3,1.10,2.15,1.20,3.27,2). Closes recorded in the accounts of the manors of Faringdon and Thatcham are unlocated but may also have been situated in Wallingford, although they have not been identified in later sources (GDB, 56v, 57v, 62v; *DB Berks*, 1,2,34;50,1; Hooper 1988, 25). These entries were presumably overlooked by the GDB scribe when he came to compile the account of Wallingford. A further 14 (lines 74–89) in Oxfordshire were picked up only at a late stage in the production of the Wallingford Domesday (see below). Elsewhere the scribe did not bother to collect together such entries at all. What account there is of Winchester, for example, is to be found only in the description of manors that held property in the city (Roffe 2007, 118–9).

Lines 36–68: schedule

The *paragraphos* marks the exceptional status of the non-customary land. In the following section it merely indicates divisions of a schedule, that is a systematic listing of lands. There are four divisions in all. Each consists of a continuously written list of holders of land (although small in-line *paragraphoi* mark individual entries in sections 1 and 2), the number of tenements they held – sometimes expressed as *hagae*, sometimes *masurae* – and a small sum of money. The only deviation from this pattern is a list of ten especially privileged people appended to the last entry which is again written continuously. Most of the individuals named in the body of the schedule were tenants-in-chief who held land in the surrounding area, but just under a quarter – eight out of 34 – were more minor figures. 'The smiths (*fabri*)', who held five closes at 10d, must be entirely local; the remainder are difficult to identify but, by the same token, were clearly of modest means. Again, the ten individuals in the appendix appear to be predominantly local.

It is the status of these latter that suggests the identity of the schedule. Almær the priest, another Almær the priest, Brunmann, Eadwig, Edmund, William son of Osmund, Leofflæd, Lambert the priest, Alweald, and Godric are said to 'have rent from their houses and [the fines due for] bloodshed, if it is shed therein [and] the perpetrator has been arrested there before he is claimed by the king's reeve, except on Saturday, on account of the market, because then the king has the fine; and they have the fines for adultery and theft in their houses; other fines, however, are the king's' (lines 61–8). These liberties are akin to what would elsewhere have been known as 'sake and soke' (Roffe 2007, 120–4). The tenements in which they were enjoyed were constituted as urban fees, that is, they were estates within the borough but not of it as an institution. Nothing more is known about them. Typically, such liberties manifest themselves in the 13th century as small urban courts with the assize of bread and ale. No such courts have, as yet, come to light in medieval Wallingford. In Stamford and Lincoln similarly enfranchised townsmen were lawmen (GDB, 336, 336v; *DB Lincs*, C2–3.S5) and, despite the presence of Leofflæd, a woman, it is possible that the ten were constituted as a comparable panel of doomsmen. It is perhaps more likely, though, that they represent individual, specifically urban, interests. The three priests in particular suggest that the liberties were associated with churches (although it should be noted that three priests were lawmen in Lincoln).

The juxtaposition of those who 'have rent from their houses' with the main list suggests that rent was paid by the others to the king. Indeed, it is explicitly said of Henry de Ferrers' five closes that they 'TRE and also TRW gave 62d. customarily in the king's farm; now they give nothing' (lines 46–8). Some of the tenements evidently belonged to rural manors. Three closes were attached to Ilsley, probably Bishop Osmund's manor; one of the king's closes was appurtenant to Aldermaston; and Battle Abbey's five can almost certainly be identified with those that are recorded in the account of its manor of Brightwalton (GDB, 58, 59v; *DB Berks*, 1,44.3,1.15,2). They may have all been non-customary, although they were not necessarily so (tenements might render rent to the king and yet might still belong to a rural manor). Nevertheless, by and large, custom defines the list: it describes rents due to the king.

Identical in form, all four of its divisions would appear to have come from the same source. That source was evidently not a tenurially arranged one, for the lands of some individuals occur in more than one section. The holdings of the king and Robert d'Oilly are each described in three of the divisions of the schedule, Hugh de Bolbec's in two, and so on (Figure 5.3). Rather the pattern suggests a geographical circuit, albeit with a description of the king's lands entered first. Elsewhere the initial survey of boroughs often seems to have proceeded from one ward of the borough to another. In Cambridge the fact is explicit – there is an entry for each ward – and in Huntingdon and York the ferdings and shires of the borough and city had a major influence on the form of the text (GDB, 189, 203, 298, 298v; *DB Cambs*, B1–9; *DB Hunts*, B; *DB Yorks*, C). The Wallingford schedule is suggestive of a similar procedure. In the early 13th century, as subsequently, there were four wards in the town (Rotulus de Redditibus, BRO F/T 1) and their association with the four gates of the borough suggests that it had always been so. The schedule was probably organized by wards.

As a source it has affinities with the list of burgesses 'who render all custom' in Colchester; there are also parallels with the Domesday account of Oxford to which a schedule is likewise appended (GDB, 154; *DB Oxon*, B). But its closest parallel is the survey of Winchester *c.* 1110 (Barlow 1976). There too there was a circuit (albeit from street to street) and customary land is juxtaposed with the occasional notice of other types of land. Above all, rents due to the king are given. The Wallingford schedule looks like a preliminary survey of the king's dues of a similar kind emanating from the earliest stages of the Domesday inquest in Wallingford. As such, it seems likely that it was the source behind the bland statement of the number of customary tenements given in the first section of the account of the borough. If so, then it would appear that its figures duplicate those of the earlier total but incompletely so: in total it lists only 95 properties out of the 262 said to have been there in 1086.

Lines 69–73: value

After finishing the schedule, the scribe left a space of two lines and then wrote down the value of the lands of *Albrei* (an unidentified person or place), Miles Molay, the abbot of Abingdon, Roger de Lacy, and Rainald. It might seem, then, that the figures refer to the lands in the schedule which the scribe had just written. In reality, however, only Roger de Lacy's lands appear there. Rather non-customary land seems to be the referent for the others. Nevertheless, the information did not come from exactly the same source as that part of the text. Although it has been argued that Miles Molay is possibly a different person from Miles Crispin (COEL), it seems more likely that they two are identical: the value of his land at 24s correlates reasonably well with the 23s 4d in value recorded in the non-customary lands. The other figures, by contrast, are much higher than those given earlier (Figure 5.4). To what they refer and why these five fees alone are valued is unknown. Comparable values are rare in other boroughs, but are found in identical terms in the account of the king's manors of Nakedthorn (possibly in Compton), Shrivenham, and Faringdon in the body of the Berkshire text (GDB, 57v; *DB Berks*, 1,24,33,34).

Figure 5.3 The order of entries in the schedule.

I	II	III	IVa	IVb
Archbishop	*King*	*King*	*King*	Almær the priest
Walter Giffard	Henry de Ferrers	Count of Evreux	*Bishop Osmund*	Almær the priest
Robert d'Oilly	Bishop Remigius	*Hugh of Bolbec*	*Robert d'Oilly*	Brunmann
Gilbert de Ghent	Earl Hugh	*Roger de Lacy*	*Roger de Lacy*	Eadwig
Hugh the Great	Godric	*Robert d'Oilly*	Ralph Piercehedge	Edmund
R. fitzSeifrid	Dodda		Regenbald the priest	Will. s Osmund
Hugh de Bolbec	Algar		St Albans	Leofflæd
Ranulph Peverel	The Smiths		Beorhtric	Lambert the priest
Walter fitzOther			Leofgifu	Alweald
William Lovet			Godwine	Godric
Ilsley (?Bp Osmund)			Alwine	
Battle Abbey				
Bishop Peter				

Italicized names appear in more than one group

Figure 5.4 Values.

Lord	Valuation clause	Non-customary lands	Tenements
Albrei	7s		
Miles Molay	24s	23s 4d	51
Abbot of Abingdon	8s	4s	7
Roger de Lacy	7s	2s 9d	6
Rainald	4s	2s 2d	11

The postscriptal addition to the valuation clause merely states 'TRE it was worth £30; and afterwards £40; now £60, and yet it renders at farm £80 by tale.'. There can be no doubt, however, that the value in question was that of Wallingford to the king, for the value of all borough is couched in very similar terms (Roffe, 2007, 138–41). As the round totals suggest, the figures must in some sense be conventional sums. System is apparent: a unit of £30 is found throughout the country. In Northampton the sum is said to represent a farm of three nights, that is the supply of three day's worth of food to the king's court (GDB, 219; *DB Northants*, B36). It might be suspected that the value of Wallingford was similarly related to the farm. And yet the king received a premium from whoever 'farmed' the borough. Whether that was the sheriff, the reeve, or the burgesses is unrecorded (Tait 1936, 148).

Lines 75–90: the thegns of Oxfordshire

This list, headed 'The following thegns of Oxfordshire had land in Wallingford', was entered into the record in a single stint sometime after rubrication of the text. However, layout defines two distinct sections. The Wallingford houses of the clerics are described continuously in a single paragraph. By contrast, those of the laymen are accorded a separate entry, each of which, with one exception, is signalled by a *paragraphos*. In the use of the past tense, *habuerunt*, 'they had', and the English *taini*, thegns', the title would suggest that the individuals held in 1066. In fact, as far as can be determined, they all held at the time of the Domesday inquest. All but two entries name the manor – Newington, Dorchester, Ewelme, Pyrton, Caversham, Watlington, Waterperry, Crowmarsh, Shirburn, South Weston (GDB, 155, 157, 157v, 158, 158v, 159v; *DB Oxon*, 2,1.6,1.15,1,2.20,1,3.28,1,9,22.38,2) – to which the houses belonged and a sum of money. The clerics and the first three of the laymen held in their capacity as tenants-in-chief, the remainder as tenants of other lords.

Despite the difference in layout and status of individuals, there seems to be no marked difference in tenure. Belonging to rural manors, the tenements would seem to be non-customary lands, the money the rent they paid. None is mentioned in the account of the parent manors to which they belonged and it seems likely that the houses came to light only when the GDB scribe came to write up Oxfordshire, one of the last shires to be engrossed (Roffe 2007, 98–104). However, although the order of entries follows the sequence of chapters in the Oxfordshire folios, it is possible that he did not simply cull the information from seigneurial returns, that is the details of his estates that each lord provided at the time of the Domesday inquest. The reference to 'thegns' in the title may suggest that the scribe also consulted and updated an older, if not necessarily pre-Conquest, English schedule. Similar sources are well-attested elsewhere in Domesday Book (Harvey 1971, 753–73). In Nottinghamshire, for example, a pre-Conquest list of holders of sake and soke was modified to include two Normans (GDB, 280v; *DB Notts*, S5).

Lines 94–109: county customs

Apart from the three-line space that separates it from the 'thegns of Oxfordshire', the distinctiveness of the customs section is signalled only by an enlarged capital Q for the first word *Quando...*, 'When...'. The passage consists of a disparate collection of what can only loosely be called 'customs'. It is written continuously, but paragraphoi distinguish six entries (Figure 5.5).

Figure 5.5 The county customs.

Entries	Subject matter
a ll.94–6	Collection of the geld twice yearly
b ll.96–103	Military service
c ll.103–6	Heriots
d ll.106–7	Penalty for killing a man under the king's peace
e l.108	Penalty for breaking into the city
f l.109	Penalty for not game-beating

This, and similar sections in other boroughs, have usually been treated as in some way related to the main account, here Wallingford (Roffe 2007, 127–32). In fact, with the possible exception of the fifth entry (itself generic rather than specific), none of the customs relates specifically to the borough. The section, while of great interest, is evidently not part of the Domesday account of Wallingford. It was entered by the GDB scribe as part of his programme of transforming the inquest records into a useful source of information for the administration of the county. Its sources are debateable, but clearly diverse. The disparate nature of the entries suggests that the Domesday scribe picked up whatever material he could find. All the matters impinged in one way or another on the main business of the inquest, but it is not inconceivable that he drew it from routine administrative sources dating from any time up to the compilation of Domesday Book.

Wallingford in 1086

The composition and sources of the Domesday account of Wallingford are summarized in Figure 5.6. The account is

Figure 5.6 The composition and sources of the Domesday account of Wallingford.

Section	Content	Source
I	Customary land	Audit of regalia, 1st stage of inquest, summary
II	Non-customary lands	Survey of seigneurial land, 3rd stage of inquest
II	Schedule	Audit of regalia, 1st stage of inquest, initial survey
IV	Value	Geld survey?, 2nd stage of inquest
V	Oxfordshire thegns	OE schedule, survey of seigneurial lands

clearly a compilation and, moreover, it is evident that it was the GDB scribe who assembled the material. Had there been an earlier draft, then it might have been expected that the account would have been more integrated and coherent. The Oxfordshire thegns would surely have been incorporated into the non-customary section of the account; the schedule would, perhaps, have been omitted as irrelevant; and the valuation clause would have been tidied up and positioned where it made more sense. Instead, there is evident haste and confusion. Like the county customs that follow it, the Domesday account of Wallingford is clearly a mish-mash of what the GDB scribe had to hand when he came to write GDB.

Its forms and content were chosen, within the limits of what was available, to suit his programme. What represented the business of the inquest for the king in 1086, by contrast, was probably confined to the more limited and summary sections I, II, and IV, customary lands, non-customary lands, and value. It was these items that told William the Conqueror what income he had from Wallingford in land and geld and what was the value of the land of his tenants-in-chief there, the main objectives of the three stages of the Domesday inquest. The Wallingford account is more or less as comprehensive as was required in 1086. That is not to say that it was an exhaustive survey. If the resources of the king, geld, and service were the three major subjects of the inquest, then data were collected to illustrate these its concerns (Roffe 2007, 306–19). Where people and resources were not assessed to such burdens, they were not of interest to the Domesday commissioners and thus go unrecorded. On its own, then, the Domesday account of Wallingford is partial and incomplete. However, taken together with contemporary and later evidence, it provides the framework for a fairly detailed picture of Wallingford in 1086.

Tenements, population, and extent

Calculating the size of Wallingford presents a number of problems and ultimately it can only be assessed comparatively by relating it to others boroughs in 1086 and to itself at later periods. Three terms – *hagae*, *masurae*, and *domus* – are employed in different parts of the account, along with seven instances of acres and 'a piece of land (*frustrum*)' (Figure 5.7). Usage seems largely to depend on source and it is likely that these terms are roughly equivalent (Roffe 2007, 137–8). The number of customary *hagae* is unambiguous: there were 276 less 8 that were destroyed in the construction of the castle. The exempt tenements are explicitly included in this total and context would suggest that the 22 *masurae* of the Frenchmen were too. Likewise, the 95

predominately customary tenements listed in the schedule are probably duplicates. That leaves 122 non-customary tenements to add to the customary, giving a total of 390 in all.

Figure 5.7 Population.

Section	1066	1086
Customary paying	276	268h = 268
Customary exempt		14h+22m = 36
Non-customary		33h+63m = 96
Schedule		65h+30m = 95
Oxfordshire thegns		26d = 26

h=*haga* m=*masura* d=*domus*

This total is evidently a minimum. There is no way of knowing how accurate were the figures for the customary lands, but the non-customary tenements are clearly underrecorded. The tenements of the nine townsmen and one woman in section three who did not pay custom are omitted. Later evidence suggests that there may have been others. In the mid 12th century Robert son of Fulcred, lord of Padworth, had the advowson of a portion of the church of St Lucian in Wallingford, which was described as an appurtenance of the church of Padworth (*Salisbury Acta*, nos 85–6). The relationship looks like one between non-customary land and a rural manor. And yet there is no indication of it either in the Domesday account of Wallingford or of Stephen son of Erhard's manor of Padworth (GDB, 63v; *DB Berks*, 64,1). It was probably simply overlooked in the Domesday inquest. There were further suggestive relationships between the manors of Aston Rowant, Basildon, Clapcot, and possibly Hungerford, all in Berkshire, and the borough in the 13th century (*Oseney Cartulary*, iv, 436–7; Riley 1876, no. 238; *Rot. Orig*, 300; *Boarstall Cartulary*, nos 678, 738).

There were, then, probably 400 or more properties in Wallingford in 1086. What that figure means in terms of population is impossible to say. Elsewhere in Domesday Book burgesses were counted rather than tenements and so it has been usual to suppose that each unit of survey – whether *burgensis*, *haga*, *masure*, or *domus* – represents a family. With an assumption of five persons per household, the population of Wallingford has been calculated in excess of 2500 (Hooper 1988, 23). Such reasoning, however, is largely meaningless. The units of the survey are all legal entities that owed dues to the king: *masura* and its cognate variant *mansio* were interchangeable with *manerium*, 'manor', in the early stages of the Domesday inquest, indicating a measure of *service* (Roffe 2007, 137–8). How these units relate to real houses, and thus to families, is simply unquantifiable. By the same token, there are difficulties in comparing Wallingford with other Domesday boroughs. The number of tenements recorded will largely depend on how pronounced were the interests of the king in each. A better measure of comparative size is the farm that was paid to the king (Roffe 2007, 138–41). In these terms, it is evident that Wallingford at £80 was in the first division of English boroughs rather than the premiership of the likes of Lincoln, Norwich, and York.

The evidence for the physical extent and organization of Wallingford in 1086 is somewhat more robust. The 390 tenements of Domesday can be compared with the 107 recorded in the 1548 survey of the borough (Bodleian Library, MS Top Berks b41). Wallingford was evidently larger in the 11th century than it was in the mid 16th. Indeed, it is clear from mapping those properties that can be more or less confidently located that its physical extent in 1086 was much as it was before late nineteenth-century expansion (Figure 5.8). The customary tenements were apparently scattered throughout the borough. They cannot be located from the Domesday evidence alone but are represented by the 160 or so individuals who paid landgable in a series of thirteenth-century rent rolls (Rotulus de Redditibus; BRO, FT, 1–9). They are more or less evenly distributed between the four wards of the town.

The customary lands belonging to rural manors exhibit a similar distribution. It has already been noted that three of the bishop of Winchester's tenements that belonged to his manor of Brightwell were located on the north side of High Street (lines 23–4). A series of medieval sources and the Wallingford surveys of 1548 and 1606 indicate that they are represented today by St Michael's House, no 89, and the George Hotel (*CI* 14, nos 326, 332; Bodleian Library, MS Top Berks b41; NA, E315/369, pp 101–23). Similar sources identify the bishop of Lincoln's property that belonged to

Figure 5.8 Domesday topography (base map reproduced by permission of Oxford Archaeological Unit).

Dorchester as 7 Market Place, now represented by Boots the Chemist (line 78; Bodleian Library, MS Top Berks b41). Hugh de Bolbec's tenements belonging to the manor of Crowmarsh were close by at and around no 14 St Mary's Street (Bodleian Library, Charters Oxon D.1; *CI*, 17, 312; Bodleian Library, Charters Oxon D.1). Others can, as yet, be assigned no more precisely than to a parish. The property belonging to William fitzCorbucion's manor of North Moreton was probably in Holy Trinity parish (*Mon Ang*, iii, 80b). Nigel d'Aubigny's manor of West Henred or Willington held land in St Mary le More's (*Mon Ang*, iii, 279–80; *VCH Berks*, ii, 539–46) and the monks of Winchester's manor of Sotwell in St Lucian's outside the south gate (see below).

In the absence of detailed archaeological data (Creighton *et al.* below, p. 72), it is impossible to gauge the density of settlement with any precision, but there must have remained many open spaces in Wallingford in 1086. The west end of High Street, for example, seems to have been under-developed, for on the foundation of Holy Trinity Priory in the north-west quadrant of the borough after the Domesday inquest 'land' (*terra*) was granted rather than tenements (*messuagia* or whatever) for the construction of its conventual buildings (*BF*, 111). Throughout the Middle Ages the Bullcroft and Kinecroft were probably largely pasture despite tentative expansion in the 11th or 12th century in one area of the latter (*ibid.* below, p. 72). Nevertheless, there was clearly widespread development within the defences and outside the south gate in 1086.

This spread of settlement was paralleled by a precocious institutional infrastructure. If its four wards were already in existence, as section 3 of the Domesday account suggests, so too in large measure was the parochial structure of medieval Wallingford. Only one church is recorded in the Domesday text. Roger the priest held it although, according to the Domesday account, it rightly belonged to the bishop of Salisbury as of his manor of Sonning in the account of which it is duly recorded (GDB, 58; *DB Berks*, 3,1). However, five further priests are noted (lines 45, 58, 61, 63), two of whom, Bishop Peter and Regenbald, were notable royal clerics (Keynes 1987, 185–222). The record of priests implies the existence of the churches which they served. None of these clerics can be assigned to any particular foundation, but a further seven churches can be identified in 1086 (Figure 5.8).

The chapel of St Nicholas and the church of All Saints

The chapel of St Nicholas in the castle was, according to the Oseney Cartulary, founded by Miles Crispin (*Oseney Cartulary*, iv, 415). The initial foundation consisted of probably three prebends, the churches of North Stoke, Chalgrove, and All Saints in Wallingford with a mill outside the south gate, and land in Newnham Murren and Haseley (*Rot Chart*, i, 75b, 81a, 118b, 200a; *CRR*, i, 415). In 1278 the chapel was re-founded by Edmund, earl of Cornwall, as a college consisting of a dean and five priests, six clerics, and four choristers (*VCH Berks*, ii, 103–6). Throughout its recorded history, St Nicholas was a royal free chapel, that is, it was a peculiar that was, at least as regards the chapel itself and All Saints church, exempt from ordinary jurisdiction

(Denton 1970, 124–6, 131–6; *Rotuli Parliamentorum*, i, 344b).

There is no reason to doubt that Miles Crispin had a role in the history of the foundation. Its endowment was closely related to his Wallingford lands in 1086 (lines.27–33); he must have had a significant benefactor. If the Domesday account is taken literally, then it must have been founded after 1086. However, it is not clear that St Nicholas was an entirely new institution. The dedication is post-Conquest but in some sources St Nicholas is linked with St Mary which may represent an earlier patron saint (*CChR 1257–1300*, 209). Moreover, royal free chapels are regularly associated with pre-Conquest foundations of some antiquity (Denton 1970, 134–6). St Nicholas in Wallingford has been held to be post-Conquest on the ground that it was situated within a castle. However, earlier antecedents cannot be dismissed. Elsewhere, as in Dover and Leicester (Blair 2005, 365–6), pre-Conquest churches were not infrequently incorporated into post-Conquest fortresses.

The origins of St Nicholas' church itself must await archaeological investigation, but there is some evidence that its prebends had a pre-Conquest identity. Most of the TRE holders of the lands – Queen Edith, Thorkil, Edwin, Alwine son of Cypping, Tovi (GDB, 63v, 159, 159v; *DB Oxon*, 35,2,6,10; *DB Berks*, 1,22,37.65,6) – are unexceptional or unidentifiable. The only one that is remarkable is the Engelric who held Newnham Murren before the Conquest or shortly after (GDB, 159v; *DB Oxon*, 35,11). The name is a rare one. Elsewhere in Domesday Book it refers to a single individual, the priest who founded or re-founded the royal free chapel of St Martin le Grand in London (Davis 1972, 9–26; Taylor 2000, 16). No positive identification can be made here, but the coincidence is striking. More clearly All Saints church must have been in existence at the time of the Domesday inquest. Its parish was extensive, encompassing the north-eastern quadrant of the borough, apart from the evidently intrusive area of the extra-parochial castle, and the territory of Clapcot to the north (see Dewey above, p. 25). The estate that the parish represents, and the nucleus that the church marks, were clearly primary features of Wallingford.

Holy Trinity

Holy Trinity Priory, in the Bullcroft in the north-west quadrant of the borough (Figure 5.8), was a cell of St Albans Abbey in Hertfordshire. It was endowed with the churches of St Mary le More, St Martin, and St John-super-Aquam and extensive lands in and around Wallingford (*VCH Berks*, ii, 77–9). According to an inquest in the Book of Fees, dating from 1212, the founder of the priory was Geoffrey the chamberlain (*BF*, 111). Geoffrey was the chamberlain of the king's daughter (Green 1997, 397) and in 1086 he held one house in Winchester of the king's manor of Basingstoke and the manor of Hatch Warren in Hampshire in chief (Barlow 1976, nos 246, 270, 272; GDB, 49; *DB Hants*, 67,1). There is no record in Domesday Book of him holding in Wallingford. However, the land he held, or was to hold, can be identified. Holy Trinity subsequently held the demesne tithes of Geoffrey the chamberlain in North Moreton and it is thus clear that, in part at least (Geoffrey also held land of the king in Moulsford in Cholsey), it is represented by the five closes that belonged to William fitzCorbucion's manor in Moreton in 1086 (GDB, 61; *DB Berks*, 27,2; Bodleian Library, Wallingford Charters, no 1). A Geoffrey held of William in Charlton and Mappleborough in Warwickshire, but North Moreton was in the possession of a certain Ralph (GDB, 61, 243; *DB Berks*, 27,3; *DB Warks*, 28,11). It would therefore seem that Geoffrey founded the priory after the Domesday inquest. According to St Albans tradition (*Mon. Ang.*, iii, 279a), it dates from the time of Abbot Paul (1077–93) and Archbishop Lanfranc (1070–89) advised on its foundation, so a date range of 1086–9 can be suggested (but see Haggar 2008, 391–2).

It was not, however, a foundation entirely *de novo*: the priory was established within a pre-existing church dedicated to the Holy Trinity. Its existence is recorded in a catalogue of benefactors of St Albans. Nigel d'Aubigny, the brother of Abbot Richard, (1097–1119), is said to have granted West Hendred to the abbey, along with 'the church of Christ in Wallingford, half of another church consecrated in honour of St Mary, and Easole (*Estwellam*)' in Kent (*Mon. Ang.*, iii, 279a-b). Christchurch here stands in for Holy Trinity, a common early medieval equation (Morris 1986, 82–3). The grant of Hendred is recorded in Domesday Book without any reference to property in Wallingford (GDB, 59v; *DB Berks*, 12,1). Holy Trinity and St Mary le More may be silently included in this entry or in the account of the close or house that St Albans held in the borough in 1086 (lines 58, 79). But it is unclear whether the grant of the churches was integral or separate, contemporary or later. There is another possible tenurial context for the churches. In 1086 Nigel held one close in the borough of Henry [de Ferrers] along with the manor of Willington in Didcot (line 14; GDB, 60v; *DB Berks*, 21,8). He is said to have held it 'of the inheritance of Swærting' who may be identical with the Svertingr who minted coins in Wallingford between 1068 and 1083–6 (*Sylloge, sn* Wallingford). Both churches, then, could have been appurtenant to this fee. Alternatively, they could have been entirely separate properties.

The origins of the priory in an earlier borough church are evident in the parochial functions attached to it throughout the Middle Ages: it remained a parish church (*VCH Berks*, iii, 539–46; *TE, sn* Wallingford). In the 11th century that foundation was probably of somewhat higher status than a simple parish church. Writing in the 13th century but using the roll of Adam the cellarer of the mid 12th century (Haggar 2008, 374), Matthew Paris hints at a context in which such a relation can be understood. He records that after the church of Holy Trinity in Wallingford was given to St Albans, Abbot Paul 'sent monks there, constructed buildings, and with the advice of Archbishop Lanfranc determined (*constituit*) that the rule of the church of St Albans be observed there inviolate' (*Mon. Ang.*, iii, 279a). The emphasis on the rule and its observance suggests that Matthew's understanding of the foundation of the priory was in terms of a regularization of an existing community of priests. Holy Trinity was probably a college of secular canons.

The priory's later endowment of the churches of St Mary le More, St Martin, and St John-super-Aquam may, then, represent something of the extent of its *parochia*. If it is not absolutely clear that the moiety of St Mary le More granted to St Albans by Nigel d'Aubigny was already appurtenant to Holy Trinity, then it was evidently in the same tenurial context. There is no record of the holder of the other half. St Martin, or just possibly St John-super-Aquam, was probably the church held by Roger the priest and claimed by the bishop of Salisbury in 1086: the patronage of all the other borough churches are otherwise accounted for by other patrons (GDB, 58; *DB Berks*, 3,1; *VCH Berks*, i, 335). Ownership, vested as it was in the individual priests of the foundation, was fragmented in the late 11th century as in many a similar collegiate foundation (Blair 2005, 345–8, 361–7). In origin, however, the college may have been an episcopal church. As late as the mid 12th century the bishops of Salisbury would seem to have claimed proprietary rights in it, for Bishop Joscelin (1142–1184) issued a charter confirming to St Albans all the lands of the priory of Holy Trinity (*Mon. Ang.*, iii, 279a-b). The transaction was effectively a quitclaim. Thereafter, only a vestige of Salisbury's former jurisdiction survived: despite holding no land there, the bishopric retained right to tithes of the manor of North Moreton, to which much of the priory's lands had belonged in 1086, throughout the Middle Ages (*VCH Berks*, iii, 492–8).

The churches of St Rumbold, St Lucian, and St Leonard

The church of St Rumbold or Ruald is dimly perceived in the medieval records. A reference to an orchard on Goldsmith's Lane 'that was formerly a cemetery' in the survey of Wallingford of 1548 and the discovery of a burial ground at the south end of the same has been held to fix the site of the church (Bodleian Library, Top Oxon b41; *VCH Berks*, iii, 539–46) Medieval evidence, by contrast, tends to suggest that St Rumbold was extra-mural. In 1198 there is a notice of the hall (*atrium*) of the church which lay to the south of a tenement outside the south gate. In 1300 there was a grant of arable between the churchyard and *Bruttestrete*, which ran through Chalmore, and in 1306 the parish is said to lie outside the south gate (*CMF*, ii, 367; Riley 1876, no. 592; BRO, RTb 45, 68). The church was given by Henry I to Reading Abbey along with the church of Cholsey (*Reading Cartularies*, 159, 161–2); some late presentations are known, but it seems to have been united with St Leonard in the 14th century (*VCH Berks*, iii, 539–46). However, it appears that it had always had an association with St Lucian and St Leonard.

The church of St Lucian also no longer exists, but its site is well-documented: it stood on the east side of the Cornmarket outside the south gate (Riley 1876, nos. 85, 590). St Leonard still stands in the south-east corner of the borough and displays vestiges of eleventh- and twelfth-century fabric (Dewey above, p. 20). The two churches were given to the monastery of St Frideswide, Oxford, on its foundation by Henry I in a single grant (*CMF*, i, 11). The dedication of both is decidedly post-Conquest, but a confirmation of Pope Honorius II of 1124–30 suggests that St Leonard at least was a re-dedication (*CMF*, i, 13). It seems that it was formerly known as the church of the Holy Trinity the Lesser (in contra-distinction to Holy Trinity Priory). The two churches had been united by 1291 and St Leonard became the main and then only parish church (*VCH Berks*, iii, 439–46).

The later medieval and early modern parish of St Leonard was extensive (Dewey above, pp. 20–1), encompassing part of the southern quarter of the borough within the defences, the area to the Cholsey boundary to the south, Chalmore and Portmanfield to the south west, and the vill of Sotwell to the west (Slade End would seem to have looked to Brightwell). The boundaries of St Rumbold's parish cannot now be determined. Nor is that of St Lucian known for certain (Dewey above, pp. 21–2). However, it is clear that the chapel of Sotwell belonged to this latter church rather than to St Leonard in the 12th century, for between 1155 and 1165 the bishop of Salisbury confirmed to Monk Sherborne Priory its church of Padworth with St Lucian and its chapel of Sotwell (*Salisbury Acta*, nos 85–6; *CMF*, i, 29; ii, 364–5). Since St Frideswide still retained an interest in St Lucian at this date, the reference must be to a part of the church. Indeed, in 1291 Sherborne was taxed on only a portion of the combined rectory of St Lucian and St Leonard (*Salisbury Acta*, no 86; *TE, sn* Wallingford). The priory came into possession through its patron, the de Port family. Hugh de Port held Sotwell of the abbot of St Peter's, Winchester, in 1086 (GDB, 59v; *DB Berks*, 10,2) and so it is likely that the eight closes in Wallingford belonging to the same manor were, in part or whole, in the vicinity of St Lucian's church.

The relationship seems to have been of some antiquity and so facilitates the identification of the three churches in an earlier document. A Latin charter of supposedly 945 purports to record the grant by King Eadred of Wessex (946–55) to his minister Æthelgeard of 30 hides, of which 10 were in Brightwell, 15 in Sotwell, and 5 in Mackney (S.517). It is a twelfth-century forgery, but attached, 'in good Old English' (Gelling 1979, 37–8), is a boundary clause that describes the parishes of Brightwell with Mackney and Sotwell. There then follows a memorandum, again in English, that there were 36 acres and a mill north of the borough of Wallingford, 'property inside the *port* from the east gate to the brook, on the north side of the street, and seven houses (*heorthas*) and three churches outside it' (for a copy, see S.523). The tenements on the north side of the street near the east gate were clearly the closes that belonged to the bishop of Winchester's manor of Brightwell on High Street (see above). The seven houses outside can be identified with the 8 closes that belonged to Sotwell in 1086. There seems no doubt, then, that the churches were St Leonard, St Lucian, and the neighbouring St Rumbold (being outside the borough *qua* institution if not physically). All three were evidently pre-Conquest in origin.

Their status and origins can be only a matter of conjecture. Royal they were evidently not. How Henry I came into possession is unclear, but it is probable that the crown had only recently acquired a right to them. Had they belonged to the king in 1086, it is likely that they would have been recorded in Domesday Book since the initial survey of royal regalia had included an article on churches (Roffe 2007, 76–7). Local foundations like Cholsey are seemingly fully recorded (GDB, 57; *DB Berks*, 1,7). A context within the bishop of Winchester's manor of Brightwell is clearly more appropriate. It is possible that one of the three churches was a minster of some kind and the other two daughter churches. (With its dependent chapelry, St Lucian looks the most important despite the fact that only St Leonard survives). The speculation would go some way to explaining another early twelfth-century royal initiative in the area. In 1153 Henry of Anjou and his mother the Empress Matilda granted to Master Benedict land outside the south gate as far as the Winterbrook to build a college of priests (*Regesta*, iii, no 88). This seemingly abortive foundation could well have proposed a regularization of an existing collegiate institution in the area. On the other hand, it may ultimately have resulted in the foundation of the Hospital of St John outside the south gate which, by the 16th century, was held to have been founded by the townsmen of Wallingford (*VCH Berks*, ii, 99–101).

However, there are features of St Rumbold, St Lucian, and St Leonard that are not consistent with such an analysis. The three churches seem to have discrete identities whereas the constituent elements of a minster are rarely noticed in early sources. Furthermore, it might be expected that Brightwell was part of the complex, if not the primary foundation: there is no sign of an ecclesiastical link between that church and the other three. On balance, then, it is perhaps more likely that St Rumbold, St Lucian, and St Leonard were simple estate churches. Rural manors frequently had churches on the lands they held in town: tithe was a seigneurial appurtenance before the Conquest. Superficially, the connection between Sotwell and its eight closes in Wallingford appears to be like that of any other rural manor with land in the central borough. However, the inclusion of the manor within the parish of an urban church suggests a closer, more structural, link. St Lucian, and presumably the related St Leonard and St Rumbold, were probably integral elements of the estate: the Sotwell/Brightwell complex extended into the borough and the churches mark nuclei within it.

Social structure and administration

Occupying the north-east quadrant of the borough, the castle dominated the community in 1086 as it was to do so throughout the Middle Ages and beyond. It was a potent symbol of a very real royal power (Keats-Rohan below, pp. 56–7). It had been built on the orders of William the Conqueror between 1067 and 1071 by Robert d'Oilly who became its first constable. Miles Crispin was his successor in 1086. He came into his lands through marriage to Matilda, the daughter of Robert and Ealdgytha, the daughter of Wigod of Wallingford (COEL). Miles' interests in Wallingford were considerable (lines 27–33), but, like Robert before him, he was not its lord: Wallingford remained a royal borough. Miles was a *minister*, a royal servant. He was typical of many another landholder in Wallingford. Ralph fitzSeifrid's status is unclear, but his brother Roger who held Brightwell Baldwin in Oxfordshire is explicitly described as a *minister regis* (GDB, 160c; *DB*

38

Oxon, 58,7, *Terra Ricardi et aliorum ministrorum regis*). Henry de Ferrers (lines 14, 46–8) probably held in Wallingford as the successor to Godric the sheriff: he derived much of his Berkshire land from him and may have succeeded to his office. Ælfsige of Faringdon (line 11) and Alwine son of Cypping (line 61) were closely identified with royal power: both survived the Conquest and were granted lands by William the Conqueror. The service they rendered is unknown, although it may be significant that an Alfsi was the predecessor of Geoffrey the chamberlain of the king's daughter in Hatch Warren in Hampshire (GDB, 49; *DB Hants*, 67,1). Alweald (line 63), described as a thegn, was a chamberlain, probably to the queen since he held in succession to Edith in Carswell (GDB, 63v; *DB Berks*, 65,15). Leofflæd (line 62), who held in Sutton Courtenay (GDB, 57; *DB Berks*, 1.13), may have similarly been in the service of the queen. Geoffrey the chamberlain served the king's daughter (GDB, 49; *DB Hants*, 67,1). In the vicinity of Wallingford there were numerous sergeancies that owed various other services.

Much of the land that these *ministri* held was appurtenant to their office. Although it appears to be held in chief in 1086, seemingly with full title, in the course of time it

was lost to their families or became subject to the overlordship of neighbours. The land of the housecarls tended to come into the honour of Wallingford, even though in 1086 Miles Crispin apparently held only the land in the borough on which they had lived. Geoffrey the chamberlain lost his land in Moulsford and it was given to another *minister*, Henry the larderer, before it was granted to Holy Trinity Priory by Henry I (Bodleian Library, Wallingford Charters, no 1). Even the honour of Wallingford may have been precariously held (Keats-Rohan below, pp. 62–3). The crown maintained a tight control of its agents and their land in Wallingford and the surrounding area.

Provided they rendered the customs, the burgesses had a somewhat greater right in their tenements. Nevertheless, they still had obligations to the king. Wallingford was assessed at 8 virgates, that is 2 hides (line 2), notionally 240 acres. The figure is perhaps consonant with the limited extent of the borough's fields, but it can hardly be a measure of its full obligation to the king in terms of geld and service. Domesday notes that 'they who dwelt there did service for the king with horses or by water as far as Blewbury, Reading, Sutton Courtenay, [and] Benson' (lines 3–7), The burgesses, it would seem, were liable to escort duty and

Figure 5.9 Rural manors with tenements in Wallingford.

Ref	Manor	Lord in 1086	Lord in 1066	County	Tenements
1.22	Long Wittenham	Miles Crispin	Queen Edith	Berks	1a
1.23	Brightwell	Bishop Walkelin	Bishop [sic] Stigand	Berks	27
1.25	Oxford	Abbot of Abingdon		Oxon	7
1.27–8	Newnham Murren	Miles Crispin	Engelric	Oxon	20
1.29	Haseley	Miles Crispin	Queen Edith	Oxon	6
1.30	North Stoke	Miles Crispin	Edwin	Oxon	1
1.30–1	Chalgrove	Miles Crispin	Thorkil	Oxon	1
1.31–2	Sutton ?Courtenay	Miles Crispin		Berks	6
1.32–3	Bray	Miles Crispin	Alwine son of Cypping	Berks	11
1.35	Albury	Rainald		Oxon	11
1.43	East Ilsley	[?Bp of Salisbury]		Berks	3
1.44–5; 59v	Brightwalton	Battle Abbey	Earl Harold	Berks	5
1.52	Aldermaston	King	Earl Harold	Berks	2
1.77–8	Newington	Archbp Lanfranc	Archb. of Canterbury	Oxon	4
1.78–9	Dorchester	Bishop Remigius		Oxon	1
1.80	Ewelme	Abbot R		Oxon	1
1.81	Pyrton	Earl Hugh	Archbishop Stigand	Oxon	1
1.82	Caversham	Walter Giffard	Swein	Oxon	3
1.83	Watlington	Robert d'Oilly		Oxon	2
1.84	Waterperry	Robert d'Oilly		Oxon	1
1.86	Crowmarsh Gifford	Hugh de Bolbec		Oxon	3
1.88	Shirburn	Drogo		Oxon	3
1.88	South Weston	Drogo		Oxon	
1.89	Ewelme	Robert d'Armentieres	Ulf	Oxon	1
1.90	Ewelme	Wazo		Oxon	1
57v:1,37	Sutton Courtenay	King		Berks	1
58:2,2	Harwell	Bishop of Wnchester	Bishop [sic] Stigand	Berks	3
58:3,1	Sonning	Bishop of Salisbury		Berks	ch
59v:10,2	Sotwell	St Peter's, Winchester	Monks	Berks	8
60:20,3	Long Wittenham	Walter Giffard	Queen Edith	Berks	8
61:27,2	North Moreton	William fitzCorbucion	A free man	Berks	5

a=acre ch=church

cartage under the supervision of the reeve (Roffe 2007, 120, 267). Military service must also have been part of the equation. Most boroughs were constituted as separate hundreds with military and peace-keeping responsibilities (Roffe 2007, 124). No such obligations are noted in relation to Wallingford but the existence of wards is suggestive in this context. There is no evidence as to how they operated in the borough, either in Domesday or later, but if they were typical of those found in other boroughs and cities, then they would have functioned as something like rural vills – subdivisions of hundreds – in coordinating watch and ward (Creighton and Higham 2005, 184–92). What is clear is that the borough had its own court from an early period. In common with most boroughs in Wessex, it did not meet within the defences, but outside the borough: the moothall and gallows were in Clapcot until perhaps the thirteenth century (*Boarstall Cartulary,* 708; Hedges 1881, ii, 344).

In the reign of Henry II the burgesses were granted a charter of liberties (*CChR 1257–1300*, 68), but already in 1086 they may have farmed the borough, that is, assumed its financial administration (*pace* Tait 1936, 148). Wallingford was leased at £80 rather than at its £40 value, so they would have had to pay as much again as the normal issues of the borough (lines 70). If it is impossible to determine whether the ten privileged townsmen and woman of the schedule were constituted as a formal body like the lawmen of the northern and eastern England, it cannot be doubted that they formed some sort of patriciate: they were the sorts of people who made up the movers and shakers of the later borough.

Whether they were joined at this period by the lords of the rural manors that held land in Wallingford is again unclear. In total 20 lords are recorded in the text, holding some 31 manors (Figure 5.9). Most are tenants-in-chief with seemingly full title to their lands, but three or four are represented by local clients. This may well have been the reality for most of them in 1086. It is unlikely, however, that many, either lords or men, were permanently resident; their presence was probably required, if at all, only for court sessions. By the 13th century their successors had largely withdrawn from the borough, the relationship between the tenements and rural manor amounting to little more than the payment of a quitrent. Of the townsmen who actually occupied their tenements in 1086 there is no information. Elsewhere they differed little in status from the burgesses despite rendering customs to their lord (Roffe 2000, 123–4), and it must be suspected that those in Wallingford were no different: no distinction in the status of burgesses has been detected in the later Middle Ages.

Wallingford before 1086

The Domesday inquest was about taxation and service in 1086, but in assessing those matters the commissioners concerned themselves with changes in resources in the previous twenty years. Thus it was that information was collected not only for the state of affairs in 1086, but also for when the estate was acquired by its current lord and *Tempore Regis Edwardi*, 'in the time of King Edward', that is in 1066 or before. History is part of the fabric of Domesday. Unfortunately, that history is somewhat attenuated in the case of Wallingford. It is recorded that Edward the Confessor was the lord of the borough and the number of customary tenements in 1066 is noted, along with the value of the borough in 1066 and 'after'. Otherwise there are no details of earlier landholders in the borough. The deficit can, however, be made good in the case of the non-customary lands, for a pre-Conquest lord is usually recorded in the accounts of the manors to which they belonged (Figure 5.9).

The borough in 1066

The construction of the castle had seen the destruction of eight customary tenements (line 9); it is likely that other, non-customary, properties were also destroyed but there is no record of the fact. At some point prior to 1086 22 Frenchmen had also been settled in the town (line 18–19). No evidence has come to light to indicate where, but there is a distinct possibility that they had their own borough. The Cornmarket in the parish of St Lucian, outside the south gate, first mentioned in 1212 (*BF*, 113), is a likely location, for, although properties there were subject to the borough court in the 13th century, there are indications that the area was in some contexts extra-burghal (*NI*, 7b). It is directly comparable in both status and situation to the sites of the well-documented French boroughs in Northampton, Norwich and Nottingham (Foard 1995; *CA* 170, 64–71; Roffe 1997; Roffe 2007, 133). The plantation of the Frenchmen there might account for the resumption of the advowsons of the churches of St Rumbold, St Lucian, and St Leonard by the king. Apart from these changes, Wallingford appears otherwise to have been as extensive in 1066 as it was in 1086. At least seven of the eight churches of 1086 were in existence. The eighth, the chapel of St Nicholas, may have been newly founded when the castle was built; equally it could have had pre-Conquest antecedents. Wallingford's growth was not a Norman phenomenon.

Nor was its royal character. Domesday indicates that the borough was a significant royal centre in 1066: as in 1086, *ministri regis* figure large. The priests are most visible. Bishop Peter, Regenbald, and Engelric (if he was the priest of that name) were all royal chaplains. There were also the counterparts of the post-Conquest household officers, most notably the housecarls whose land Miles Crispin held in 1086 (lines 20–2). None of these housecarls is named, but Tovi the Wend, 'a housecarl of King Edward', may have been of their number, for his land in Gloucestershire passed to Ælfsige of Faringdon whose son held a close in Wallingford in 1086 (GDB, 164; *DB Gloucs*, 1,66). The Tovi who held Bray was probably the same person (GDB, 57, 63v; *DB Berks*, 1,22.65,6). By 1086 his manor had passed to Alwine son of Cypping who also held a close in Wallingford, probably of Miles Crispin (line 61). There must have been other housecarls among Miles' various predecessors in Berkshire and Oxfordshire, but for only two is there any sort of evidence. In 1066 Ludric and Beorhtweard, held the manors of Fulscot and Purley (GDB, 62v, 63; *DB Berks*, 49,2–3). At the time of the Domesday inquest their manors were in the tenure of Roger fitzSeifrid along with Brightwell Baldwin in Oxfordshire to which Roger or Ralph fitzSeifrid's land in Wallingford was probably attached (line 40; GDB, 160c; *DB Oxon*, 58,7). In the

12th century, however, all three were held by the Huscarle family of the honour of Wallingford (*VCH Berks*, iii, 417–22; for two further Huscarle estates, neither of which had close links to Wallingford itself, see Keats-Rohan below, p. 56). The implication must be that a housecarl survived the Conquest with his lands. Katharine Keats-Rohan has tentatively suggested (pers. comm.) that Roger and Ralph's father Seifrid may have been identical with the free man Seaxfrith who held a manor in Clapcot in 1066 (GDB, 61v: *DB Berks*, 33,4). Alternatively, the Huscarles held under a Norman, or the Norman tenant took on the name, perhaps through marriage. The 15 acres on which the housecarls lived in Wallingford has not been identified.

Wigod of Wallingford can be added to this list of *ministri* (Keats-Rohan, below pp. 56–7). He is said in a late source to be a kinsman of Edward the Confessor. He was certainly an officer of the royal household and a substantial lord in his own right in southern England: as a king's thegn he held manors in probably as many as 12 counties from Sussex to Gloucestershire. He came to terms with William the Conqueror shortly after the Battle of Hastings and continued to hold his lands until his death sometimes before the Domesday inquest. His toponymic 'of Wallingford' appears to indicate that he was lord of the borough, but Domesday Book indicates otherwise. Wigod is not mentioned in the account of Wallingford; that is not surprising since no predecessors are mentioned in the text. However, it is clear that King Edward was in receipt of the issues of the borough in 1066 (line 1) and William the Conqueror continued to hold them in 1086. Wigod can have been no more than a custodian, probably in the capacity of a staller, that is a kind of military governor.

The profile of the lords who held rural manors with tenements in Wallingford was much the same as it was in 1086, that is, it was largely the greater lords of the shire who had property in the borough. Only one stands out as exceptional: the un-named free man who was the predecessor of William fitzCorbucion in North Moreton may have been a tenant. As in 1086, there is no evidence that their urban tenements had any special function beyond that of the standard burgage. It is likely that they were little more than detached manorial appurtenances, recorded as much for their income as function.

The earlier borough

Beyond 1066, Domesday Book is silent: in the absence of systematic archaeological investigation, the earlier history of Wallingford is largely a matter of speculative inference from the later evidence. With that proviso, a number of suggestions can be made as to the origins and development of the borough. What characterizes Wallingford above all else in both 1086 and 1066 is the royal presence. It had probably always been closely associated with royal authority. The existence of the borough of Wallingford is first noted in the late ninth- or early tenth-century document known as the Burghal Hidage, a list of Wessex boroughs and the number of hides attached to each for their defence (Hill and Rumble 1996; Haslam 2005). A network of boroughs had been set up by King Alfred to counter the Danish attacks on southern England in the 870s. The Burghal Hidage indicates that

Wallingford was a key site in the system: assigned 2400 hides, it was paralleled in importance only by Winchester which was assessed at a similar sum. Commanding the middle Thames valley it evidently retained its strategic importance into the 11th century. The reference to the land of the housecarls in Domesday Book suggests that a royal garrison was maintained there for its defence as late as the reign of Edward the Confessor (Hooper 1984, 171; Hooper 1988, 23). It is likely, then, that there was a royal hall, probably even a palace, in Wallingford from an early period. The castle is the most likely site. It is adjacent to the apparently early church of All Saints and the fact that only eight customary closes were destroyed in its construction (lines 9–10) in an area central to the borough must suggest that the area was of high status rather than under-developed in 1066 and before.

If All Saints and possibly St Nicholas mark the early centre of royal power within the borough, then Holy Trinity was probably its ecclesiastical counterpart. Its date of foundation can only be determined, if at all, by archaeological investigation. However, it is unlikely that it pre-dates the borough. Its parish, and the putative *parochia,* were modest in extent and almost entirely intra-mural: Holy Trinity extended outside the west gate, but the bulk of its parish was within the defences (Riley 1876, no. 590); St Martin, St Mary, and St John-super-Aquam had no share at all in the fields of the borough (Dewey above, p. 23). If Holy Trinity with its satellites was truly an episcopal foundation, as Salisbury's claims would suggest, then it is probably no earlier than the reign of Edward the Elder (899–924). The see of Wilton, subsequently moved to Ramsbury and then after the Conquest to Salisbury, was created out of the diocese of Winchester in 909 (Barlow 1979, 220–1). Excavation has shown that it is from about this period that the earliest burials associated with the church of St Martin date (Booth *et al.* 2007, 267–8). Holy Trinity may prove to have been founded at a formative stage of the development of the borough of Wallingford.

The borough proper, that is the zone assigned to the burgesses and the lords of the surrounding area, was laid out to the south and east around the market place. What provision was made for the early burgesses is unknown. By contrast, there is some indication that lords were originally assigned large blocks of land. The 15 acres on which the housecarls dwelt is unique as a reference to a garrison. It is also unusual, in an intramural urban context, in the units that it uses: acres tend to be a measure of agricultural land rather than houses. In Wallingford, however, there are a further six references to urban properties so defined in Domesday Book. The abbot of Abingdon had 2 acres on which there were seven messuages; Miles Crispin 3 separate acres in which there were six hagas, and six and 11 messuages respectively; Rainald 1 acre with 11 messuages; and Walter Giffard had 1 presumably with 10 (lines 25, 28, 31, 32, 34, 37). The acre was apparently a measure of a group of tenements. None has, as yet, been identified, but it is likely that these acres were comparable to the early sokes found in other English towns such as London and Huntingdon (Tait 1936, 43).

The defences were constructed to encircle the whole complex. Whether the present circuit represents the original one is unclear. It has usually been assumed that the existing bank and ditch date in their entirety from the foundation of the borough. The fact seems to be more or less explicit in the Burghal Hidage. Attached to one of the versions of the document is the following formula:

> For the establishment of a wall (weal-stilling) of one acre's breadth, and for its defence (*waru*) sixteen hides are required. If each hide is represented by one man, then each pole (*gyrd*) can be furnished with four men (Rumble 1996, 30, 34).

This formula translates as follows: each perch (16½ feet, about 5 metres) of borough wall was to be defended by four men and each hide was to provide one man. Assessed at 2400 hides, Wallingford should from the beginning have had a wall of 3300 yards. In reality no more than 2800 yards are apparent on the ground. Various adjustments to the defences have been suggested to make up the shortfall. Some analyses have proposed lengthening the defences by including a hypothetical wall to the east by the Thames or the so-called bridgehead across the river (Robertson 1956, 496). More radically, others have asserted that the Mercian pole of 15½ feet was employed (Fernie 1991, 3; Huggins 1991, 22–3).

All of this probably takes the formula too seriously. It is true that it seems to predict the length of the defences of Winchester and Wareham, but in most of the remaining Burghal Hidage boroughs it misses the mark completely or can be made to fit only with special pleading (Hill 1996, 74–86). The fact points to a different reality. Neat formulas are ubiquitous in Anglo-Saxon and medieval sources, but they express ideals rather than reality. The whole taxation system, for example, was founded in the fiction that the hide was a more or less standard measure of land. In fact it was a fiscal unit, in effect a basis for negotiation on tax liability (Roffe 2007, 190–7). The Burghal Hidage formula, then, does not have to be seen as prescriptive. It is inherently unlikely that the extent of defences was determined by some quill-pusher in Winchester: soldiers knew that such matters depend on circumstances and locality. Rather the formula was probably intended to guide on the basis of rule of thumb and then only in a general way.

There is no necessity, then, to believe that the present circuit represents the original defences of Wallingford. In fact, the existing earthworks may well be multi-period. As has already been seen, the first reference to St Leonard, situated as it is snugly in the south-east corner of the defences, asserts that it was outside the borough, although this may mean nothing more than that it was not part of the institution rather than physically without the defences. A late date for the southern line of the defences might also explain the apparent contradiction between the archaeological and the historical evidence for the site of St Rumbold's Church.

In the absence of targeted archaeological research, the extent and location of the earliest defences remain unclear. What is apparent, however, is that the borough was not a primary feature of the tenurial landscape. In the documented period its fields were always modest in extent compared to those of the surrounding settlements; its low assessment to the geld in 1086 suggests that there had never been a great amount of arable land attached to the borough. The bishop of Winchester's manor of Brightwell and its appurtenant land and churches in Wallingford probably represent an older, pre-burghal, order. It has already been argued that the best reading of the evidence suggests that the south gate area of Wallingford was an integral element of the episcopal estate. Manors of this type, either within the defences or adjacent to them, are a common feature of pre-Conquest boroughs (Roffe 2007, 125–7). Many are specifically related to burghal functions. Commonly, the earl had a substantial hall and curia which mirrored that of the king and the bishop often also had an estate close at hand. As leading figures in the shire and the borough court, both needed substantial establishments in town. Others, by contrast, have proved to be primary settlement nuclei, that is, they are elements that were independent of the borough or preceded it. Brightwell was clearly of this type. While there is no evidence that any of the land or churches belonged to Brightwell before the mid 10th century (S.517, 536), the estate itself is perceptively earlier than the Alfredian borough. Brightwell, assessed at 30 hides like the later Brightwell, Mackney, and Sotwell, first appears in a substantially authentic Winchester charter of 858 (S307, S517; Kelly 2007, 300).

The estate was probably part of a larger complex that included North Moreton, South Moreton, and Cholsey. All four were situated on high ground around an area of moorland which they seem to have shared as a common resource. As late as 1066 there are signs of tenurial connections between them – the pre-Conquest fees display a similar structure, suggesting a common origin (Roffe 2007, 291–304) – and at an earlier period they may all have been royal (S.307, 354, 496). No concrete evidence has come to light to indicate how Clapcot and All Saints fitted into this tenurial structure before the borough was constructed, although topography would suggest that it was an integral element of the complex. Wallingford itself, by contrast, was inserted into this older landscape. It was evidently a new town of the late 9th century. Whether its site was determined by an existing crossing of the Thames or it superseded an earlier one is again unknown. The original Wallingford, that is the crossing of the Thames from which the borough took its name, may have been further to the south. If taken literally, the boundary clause of a supposedly ninth-century Cholsey charter suggests that it was close to the outfall of the modern-day Bradford's Brook (S354, Gelling 1974, 535–6). Alternatively, there may have always been a number of crossings (Dewey above, p. 18). Whatever the case, the construction of the borough saw a shift of tenurial and settlement focus from the high ground to the west to the present town and the bridge over the Thames.

The borough and the shire

In 1086 Wallingford was the principal town of Berkshire, for it alone is entered at the head of the county folios. It is not known whether the shire court met in the borough before the Conquest. At least on one occasion in the late 10th century it was held at Scutchamer Knob on the Ridgeway in East Hendred, while in the 12th century it

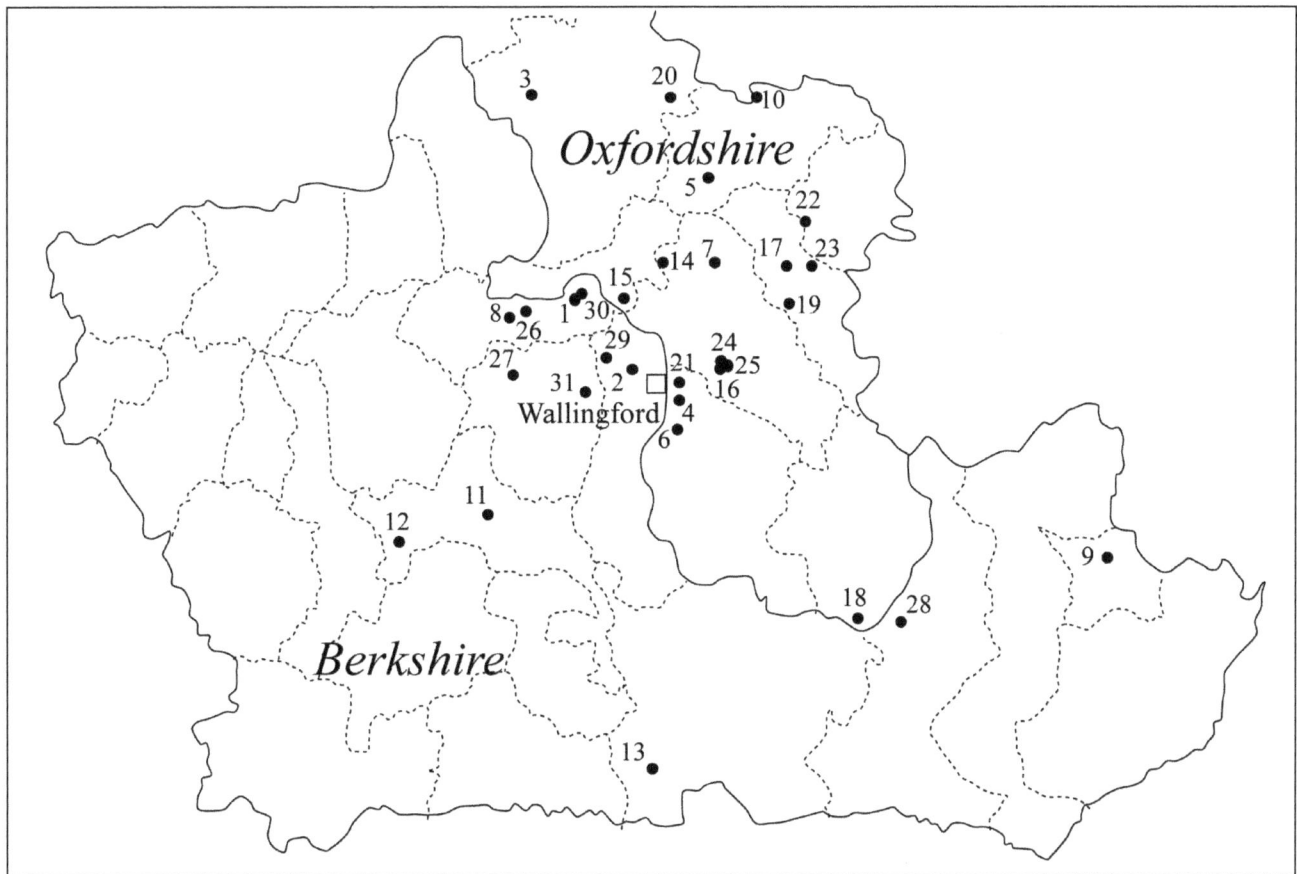

Figure 5.10 distribution of manors with properties in Wallingford.
Key: 1. Long Wittenham, 2. Brightwell, 3. Oxford, 4. Newnham Murren, 5. Haseley, 6. North Stoke, 7. Chalgrove,
8. Sutton ?Courtenay, 9. Bray, 10. Albury, 11. East Ilsley, 12. Brightwalton, 13. Aldermaston. 14. Newington, 15. Dorchester,
16. Ewelme, 17. Pyrton, 18. Caversham, 19. Watlington, 20. Waterperry, 21. Crowmarsh Gifford, 22. Shirburn, 23. South Weston,
24. Ewelme, 25. Ewelme, 226. Sutton Courtenay, 27. Harwell, 28. Sonning, 29. Sotwell, 30. Long Wittenham, 31. North Moreton.

usually met at the southern end of Oxford bridge in Hinksey (S.1454; see also *ASC*, 88 which suggests that Scutchamer was the traditional site of the shiremoot). However, although there is no record of the fact, it seems likely that the sheriff was based in the town. As has been seen, his land must be represented by the six closes held by Henry de Ferrers who succeeded to the lands of Godric the pre-Conquest sheriff (lines 46–8).

The extent of the shire he administered was substantially that of the historic Berkshire until its dismemberment in 1974. The whole county was assessed at 2495 hides in 1066 (Palmer 2007). That total is very close to the Burghal Hidage assessment of 2400 hides (Rumble 1996) and, indeed, the Domesday hidation must substantially date from about the time that document was written. The ancient assessment founded in the land of the family had been displaced by an assessment based on the plough by 900 (Hart 1992, 289–305). The pre-Conquest assessments of Berkshire are based on the original five-hide unit and Anglo-Saxon charters indicate no great change until the post-Conquest period when a degree of beneficial hidation is apparent in Domesday Book (*pace* Hooper 1988, 5–6). Nevertheless, the 2496 hides of 1066 cannot encompass the same area as the 2400 of the Burghal Hidage, for there was a second borough in Berkshire with a separate assessment. Shaftsey, or what is now known as Sashes, an island in the

Thames next to Cookham, was assessed at 1000 hides (Brooks 1964, 79–81; Rumble 1996).

The Berkshire of Domesday cannot be the territory assigned to Wallingford in the late 9th or early 10th century. The contributory tenements of the borough of Wallingford may provide a clue to its earlier extent. It has already been noted that there were properties in the borough that belonged to 31 rural manors, only to dismiss them as simple manorial appurtenance in both 1066 and 1086. They were of little moment to their lords in the mid 11th century. At an earlier date, however, they were probably related to their lord's obligation to fortify and defend the borough (Maitland 1897, 213–63). In that context it is clearly significant that over a half (18 out of 31) of those in Wallingford belonged to manors in south-east Oxfordshire, all but two of which were situated to the east of the River Thame (Figures 5.10). Topographically, this area of the county appears to be an appendage, a subsequent addition to a formerly smaller entity. It is probably not coincidental, then, that the assessment of Oxford in the Burghal Hidage was less than its Domesday total of 2434 hides (Palmer 2007). Either 1300 or 1500 hides were assigned to the borough at the earlier date – the two main recensions of the Burghal Hidage disagree at this point (Rumble 1996).

There is no comparable evidence for Sashes. The borough was apparently short-lived – it does not even appear in Domesday Book – and there is no reference to contributory manors (if they ever existed) unless the land in Boveney in Buckinghamshire that belonged to the church of Cookham is a vestige of one such (GDB, 146; *DB Bucks*, 11,1; for an enigmatic reference to service due from Hedsor to Sashes, see Berk 2008). But, like Wallingford, Sashes is situated across the Thames from another seemingly anomalous area: southern Buckinghamshire south-east of the Thame again looks as if it has been tacked onto the county and again the Burghal Hidage assessment attached to Buckingham was less than its Domesday counterpart, 1600 hides as against 2130 in 1086.

It can be suggested, then, that the territories of both Wallingford and Sashes extended across the Thames into what is now Oxfordshire and Buckinghamshire respectively. The definition of boundaries in terms of hides is problematic. With the present evidence it is not possible to reconcile the Domesday assessments with those of the Burghal Hidage (*pace* Bailey 1992, 88–9). The three counties of Berkshire, Buckinghamshire and Oxfordshire had a combined assessment of 7060 hides in 1066 (Palmer 2007) where there were 6300 or 6500 (the combined assessments of Wallingford, Sashes, Oxford, and Buckingham) at the earlier period. The discrepancy may be due to the transfer of hundreds from other counties, piecemeal re-assessment, exemption, or simple error. These are imponderables.

However, the figures may make sense in terms of hundreds. The hundred was notionally a hundred hides, but in reality it was rarely assessed at that amount. It had its own court to which the free men of the area paid suit and it was the basic unit of military organization. After the Conquest, when its operations are first evidenced in detail, it seems to have been subordinate to the shire court. In origin, however, the hundred was an independent institution, and somewhat earlier, often representing ancient folk moots (Richardson and Sayles 1963, 25 n3). Like many another feature of the social landscape, its area was not immutable. Hundreds might divide, amalgamate, or otherwise change. But in some areas there was considerable continuity of numbers

and assessments. Worcester, for example, in a later addition to the Burghal Hidage, was assessed at 1200 hides as was Worcestershire in the early eleventh-century County Hidage, while there were 12 hundreds in the shire in 1086 assessed at 1189 hides (Maitland 1897, 525, 579). It may be significant, then, that Berkshire, Oxfordshire, and Buckingham in total encompassed 63 hundreds in 1086 where the Burghal Hidage would suggest 63 or 65 (Thorn 1988a; Thorn 1988b; Thorn 1990). A reconstruction of the territories of the four boroughs can be attempted more meaningfully in these terms (Figure 5.11).

The assessment of Sashes at 1000 hides implies that 10 hundreds were assigned to it. There are six hundreds in the southern portion of Buckinghamshire – the three Chiltern Hundreds of Desborough, Burnham, and Stoke, along with Aylesbury, Risborough, and Stone – with a combined assessment of 748 hides. Corresponding with the this block of land, there are a further four hundreds – Charlton, Beynhurst, Ripplesmere, and Bray – across the Thames in eastern Berkshire assessed at 292 hides. That makes 1040 hides in all. The territory of Wallingford can be similarly defined. The south-eastern portion of Oxfordshire encompassed 5½ or 6 hundreds – Binfield, Benson, Langtree, Lewknor, Pyrton, Thame – at the time of Domesday assessed at 664 hides, while the 18 remaining hundreds in Berkshire (that is, the 22 hundreds of Domesday less the 4 hundreds assigned to Sashes) were assessed at 2203. This would approximate to the 24 hundreds predicted by the Burghal Hidage, but the actual assessment is 2867 hides. With few topographical clues as a guide, how the remaining 29 or 31 hundreds might have been distributed between Oxford and Buckingham is unclear.

By its nature, this reconstruction is speculative. In itself it raises further possibilities. If the territories of Wallingford and Sashes spanned the Thames, then did that of Oxford? The Vale of White Horse may well have been attached to the borough in the early 10th century. More fundamentally, the assessments may never have been intended to inform a rigid system of administration like the shire (Brooks 1996,

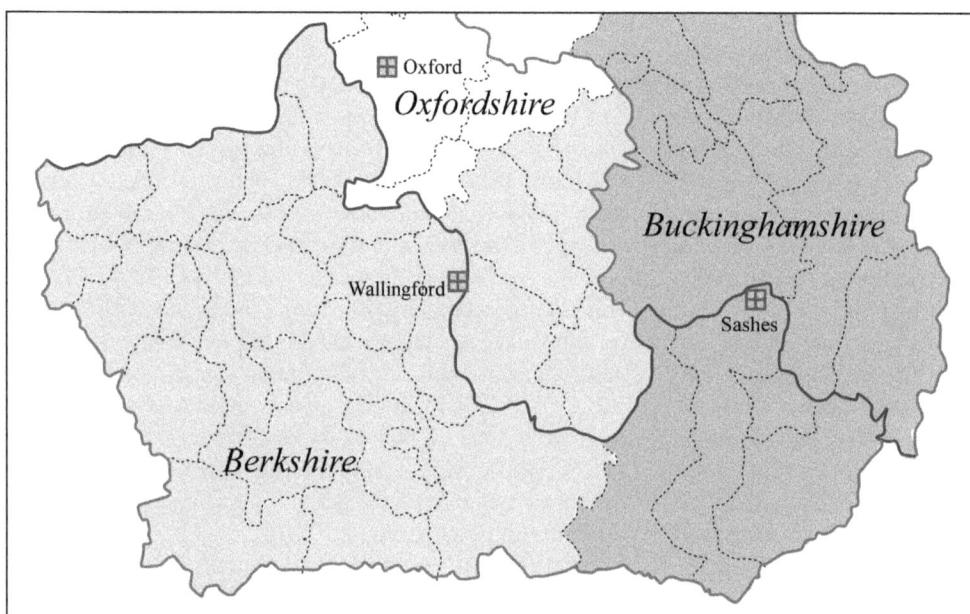

Figure 5.11
The territories of Wallingford and Sashes at the time of the Burghal Hidage.

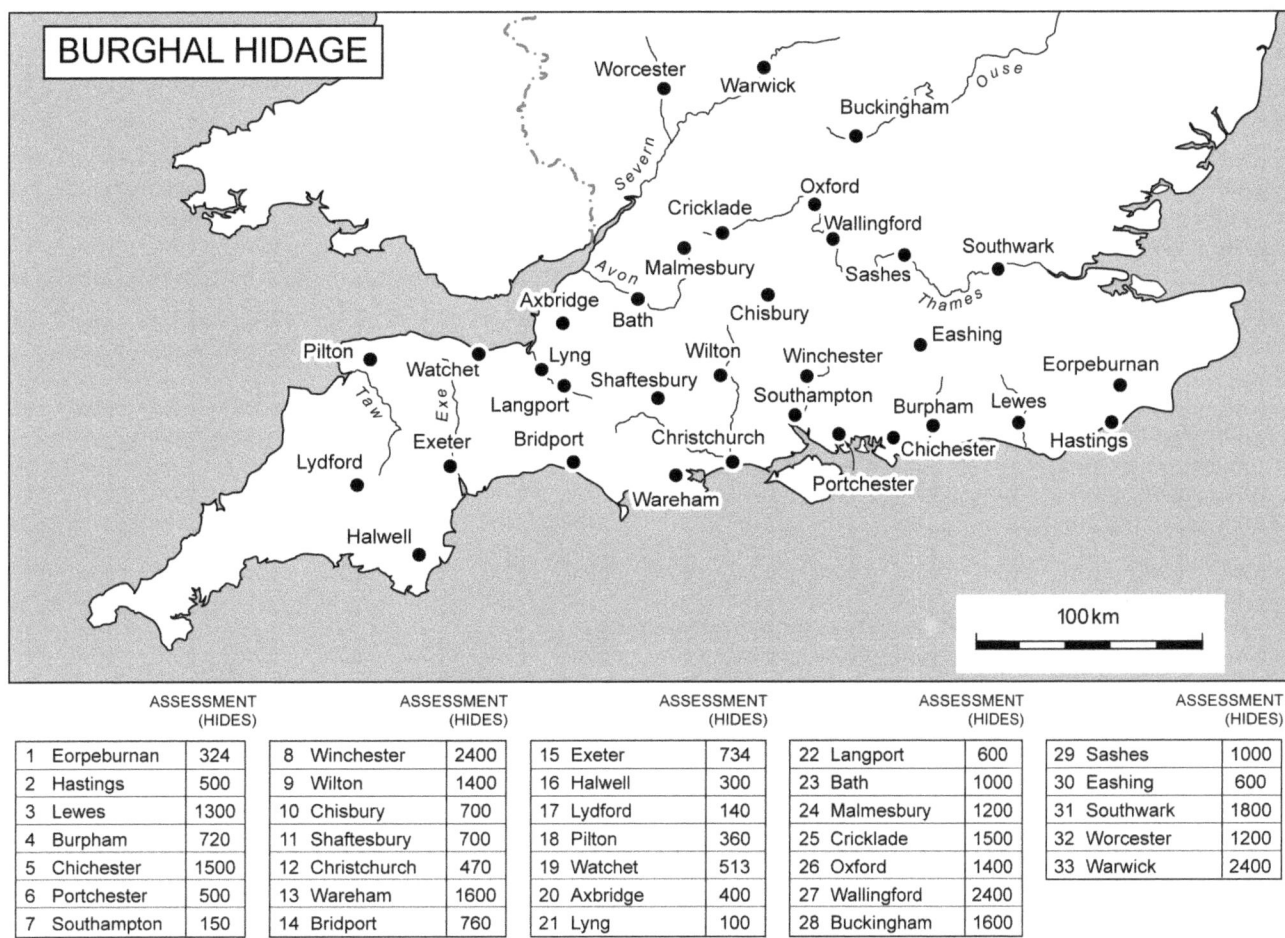

BURGHAL HIDAGE

	ASSESSMENT (HIDES)			ASSESSMENT (HIDES)			ASSESSMENT (HIDES)			ASSESSMENT (HIDES)			ASSESSMENT (HIDES)
1	Eorpeburnan	324	8	Winchester	2400	15	Exeter	734	22	Langport	600	29	Sashes	1000
2	Hastings	500	9	Wilton	1400	16	Halwell	300	23	Bath	1000	30	Eashing	600
3	Lewes	1300	10	Chisbury	700	17	Lydford	140	24	Malmesbury	1200	31	Southwark	1800
4	Burpham	720	11	Shaftesbury	700	18	Pilton	360	25	Cricklade	1500	32	Worcester	1200
5	Chichester	1500	12	Christchurch	470	19	Watchet	513	26	Oxford	1400	33	Warwick	2400
6	Portchester	500	13	Wareham	1600	20	Axbridge	400	27	Wallingford	2400			
7	Southampton	150	14	Bridport	760	21	Lyng	100	28	Buckingham	1600			

Figure 5.12 The Burghal Hidage boroughs.

134). What is striking about the Burghal Hidage is that it described a *national* system of defence (Figure 5.12). The list of boroughs starts at *Eorpeburnam,* probably on Romney Marsh in Kent, proceeds westward along the coast to Devon, and then returns along the northern boundary of Wessex to Southwark in Surrey. The boroughs were clearly intended to operate as an integrated whole. Indeed, the sources show that garrisons acted in a concerted fashion on more than one occasion (Haslam 2005). It seems very likely, then, that Oxford, Wallingford, and Sashes worked together in the defence of the middle Thames valley. Their resources in manpower and taxation may therefore have been assigned to each as the need required (cf Brooks 1996, 137–8).

Conclusion

The Domesday account of Wallingford is a difficult text. It was compiled from disparate sources at one remove from the processes that produced the evidence on which it is based and it was shaped by a programme that was other than that of the original enterprise. The Domesday scribe may have wanted the account to be as comprehensive as possible, but it could never be more than the sum of its parts: the inquest was about tax and service and data were collected to illuminate these its concerns. It is a very difficult text indeed. It cannot answer all the questions asked of it by the historian and the archaeologist. Nevertheless, it does provide a framework in which the early history of

Wallingford can be understood. This paper has attempted to tease what it can out of the account; it has also used the conclusions to ask further questions about the origins of the borough. With further documentary research more flesh will be put on the bare bones of the account presented here. However, it is archaeological investigation that will test the hypotheses that have emerged. Equally importantly, it will reveal new evidence which will enable the documents to be interrogated in different ways. The future of Wallingford's past is with the *Burh* to Borough Project.

Acknowledgements

I am grateful to Katharine Keats-Rohan and Judy Dewey for inviting me to contribute to this collection of essays on the early history of Wallingford. I remember with great pleasure the brain-storming sessions we had on the early history of the borough: I have benefited from their encyclopaedic knowledge of the history of the town at almost every point in the argument. Thanks are also due to David Pedgley. I have made great use of his transcripts of medieval documents deposited in Wallingford Museum and he was kind enough to identify the modern counterparts of various tenements noted in the 1548 and 1606 surveys. All errors of fact and interpretation remain my own responsibility. Figures 5.1 and 5.2 are published with the permission of Alecto Historical Editions and Alecto Historical Editions and the Oxford Archaeologic Unit gave permission to use Figure 5.8).

Appendix: text and translation of the Domesday account of Wallingford

The text of the Domesday account of Wallingford GDB, 56–56v) has been transcribed line by line in a continuous sequence from the Alecto facsimile of the manuscript. The County Customs section has been appended. Although long considered an integral element, it is not part of the account but it has been included here since it illustrates the programme of the GDB scribe and his working methods. Interlineated material is indicated by vertical |lines| at the beginning and end of the addition or gloss. Unless ambiguous, all contractions have been expanded. Paragraphoi are represented by paragraph marks (¶), but otherwise all punctuation has been modernized. No attempt has been made to reproduce the rubrication scheme which, it must be suspected, is largely mechanical.

As far as possible, the translation follows the line-numbering of the text. Interpolated material is enclosed in square brackets where the text is deficient or ambiguous. Otherwise, words that were intended to be understood have been silently incorporated. The orthography of the personal names follows that of the Alecto edition of Domesday Book.

> IN BURGO DE WALINGEFORD HABUIT REX EDWARDUS
> viii virgatas terrae et in his erant cclxxvi hagae
> reddentes xi libras de gablo et qui ibi manebant
> faciebant servitium regis cum equis vel per aquam usque
> 5 ad Blidberiam, Reddinges, Sudtone, Besentone
> et hoc facientibus dabat praepositus mercedem |vel conredium| non de
> censu regis sed de suo.
> Modo sunt in ipso burgo consuetudines omnes ut ante fuerunt,
> sed de hagis sunt xiii minus: pro castello sunt viii
> 10 destructae et monetarius habet unam quietam quamdiu facit
> monetam; Saulf de oxeneford habet unam; filius Alfsi
> de Ferendone unam quam rex ei dedit ut dicit;
> Hunfridus vis de leuu habet unam de qua reclamat regem |ad warantum|;
> Nigellus unam de Henrico per haereditatem Soarding, sed
> 15 burgenses testificantur se numquam habuisse.[1]
> De istis xiii non habet rex consuetudinem et adhuc
> Willelmus de Warene habet unam hagam de qua rex non habet consuetudinem
> De super plus sunt xxii masurae francigenarum reddentes
> vi solidos et v denarios.
> 20 Rex Edwardus habuit xv acras in quibus manebant huscarles.
> Milo |crispin| tenet eas, nesciunt[2] quomodo. Una ex his jacet in
> Witeham manerio Walterii gifard.
> ¶ Walchelinus episcopus habet xxvii hagas de xxv solidis et sunt
> appreciatae in Bricsteuuelle manerio eius.
> 25 ¶ Abbas de abbendone habuit[3] ii acras in quibus sunt vii
> masurae de iiii solidis et pertinent ad oxeneford.
> ¶ Milo xx masuras de xii solidis et x denariis et iacent
> in Neuueham et iterum unam acram in qua sunt vi hagae de
> xviii denariis; in Haselie vi masuras reddentes xliiii denarios;
> 30 in Estoche unam masuram de xii denariis; in Celgraue i ma-
> suram de iiii denariis. Et in[4] Suttone una acra in qua sunt
> vi masuras[5] de xii denariis. Et in Braio una acra et ibi
> xi masuras[6] de iii solidis. Tota hac terra pertinet ad oxenefordscire |est tamen in Walengeford|.
> ¶ Rainaldus habet unam acram in qua sunt xi masurae de xxvi
> 35 denariis et pertine[n]t[7] in Elderberie quae est in oxeneford
> ¶ Archiepiscopus vi masuras de xxvi denariis. Walterius |gifard| habet
> unam acram et x masuras de vi solidis et iii obolis. Robertus
> de olgi iiii masuras de xx denariis. Gislebertus de gand
> unam masuram de ii denariis et obolo. Hugo |magnus| i masuram de iiii
> 40 denariis. R.[8] filius Seifridi ii hagas de xii denariis. Hugo

---

[1] **Nigellus…habuisse**: this passage is obscure. The testimony of the burgesses could suggest that there is a dispute here. Alecto understands the passage as indicating that Nigel was making a claim against Henry. However, in that context the burgesses' evidence does not make obvious sense: the *se* must refer back to the burgesses. Why should they say that they never had it? It would make slightly better sense to emend *se* to *eum* or even *ipsos*; then the reference would be to Nigel, Henry, or Swærting. But the passage may be best understood in the broader context of the account of custom withdrawn. Nigel d'Aubigny was the man of Henry de Ferrers in Willington (in Didcot) and it is likely that he was also his tenant in Wallingford. The issue was probably whether either of them had a legitimate right to royal dues. Were the burgesses saying that Swærting never had the *consuetudines* and that therefore Nigel should not have them? The passage can be emended thus: *Nigellus unam de Henrico per haereditatem Soarding, sed burgenses testificantur ipsos numquam habuisse consuetudinem*.

[2] **nesciunt**: the 'they' in question refers to the jurors of Wallingford, cited above as 'the burgesses'.

IN THE BOROUGH OF WALLINGFORD KING EDWARD HAD
8 virgates of land, and in these were 276 closes
rendering £11 in rent, and they who dwelt there
did the king's service with horses or by water as far as

5 Blewbury, Reading, Sutton Courtenay, [and] Benson,
and to those who did this the reeve gave cash or kind not from
the income of the king but from his own.
Now all the customary dues in this borough are as they were before;
but of the closes there are 13 less: 8 were destroyed for the castle,

10 and a moneyer has 1 quit so long as he does
the coining; Sæwulf of Oxford has 1; the son of Ælfsige
of Faringdon 1, which, he says, the king gave him;
Humphrey Visdeloup has 1, for which he claims the king's warranty;
Nigel 1 of Henry through inheritance from Swærting, but

15 the burgesses testify that they never had [the customary due].
From these 13 the king does not have customary due[s]; and in addition
William de Warenne has 1 close from which the king does not have any customary due.
Over and above these are 22 messuages of Frenchmen rendering
6s. 5d.

20 King Edward had 15 acres on which housecarls dwelt;
Miles Crispin holds them, they do not know how. One of them belongs to
Long Wittenham, a manor of Walter Giffard.
¶ Bishop Walkelin has 27 closes rendering 25s., and they are
appraised in his manor of Brightwell.

25 ¶ The Abbot of Abingdon had 2 acres on which are 7
messuages rendering 4s., and they belong to Oxford.
¶ Miles [has] 20 messuages rendering 12s. 10d., and they belong
to Newnham Murren; and also 1 acre on which are 6 closes rendering
18d; in Haseley 6 messuages rendering 44d;

30 in North Stoke 1 messuage rendering 12d; in Chalgrove 1
messuage rendering 4d. In Sutton Courtenay there is 1 acre on which are
6 messuages rendering 12d. In Bray there is 1 acre, and there
are 11 messuages there rendering 3s. All this land belongs to Oxfordshire, and yet it is in Wallingford.
¶ Rainald has 1 acre on which are 11 messuages rendering 26d.,

35 and they belong to Albury which is in Oxford[shire].
¶ The archbishop has 6 messuages rendering 26d. Walter Giffard has
1 acre and 10 messuages rendering 6s. 1½d. Robert
d'Oilly 4 messuages rendering 20d. Gilbert de Ghent
1 messuage rendering 2½d. Hugh the Great 1 messuage rendering

40 4d. R. fitzSeifrid 2 closes rendering 12d. Hugh

---

³ **habuit**: the scribe wrote *hab* with a suspension mark through the ascender of the final letter. The natural reading is *habuit*, 'had' but the context suggests *habet*, 'has', was intended.

⁴ **Et in**: the change from a rustic initial I to a square one, along with a change to the nominative, signals a separate entry and, perhaps, distinguishes the land described.

⁵ **una acra in qua sunt vi masuras**: *recte* unam acram in qua sunt vi masurae

⁶ **in Braio una acra et ibi xi masuras**: *recte* in Braio unam acram et ibi xi masurae.

⁷ **pertin'**: the subject could be *unam acram* or *xi masurae*.

⁸ R. could be either Ralph (so Phillimore) or his brother Roger who both held in chief of the king, anomalously sharing a single chapter (GDB, 62v, 63: *DB Berks*, 49).

de Molebec[9] i haga[10] de iiii denariis. Rannulfus |peurel| una[11] de iiii denariis.
Walterus |filius other| vi hagas de iiii denariis et obolo minus. Willelmus |louet| unum
frustrum[12] terrae de iiii denariis. In[13] Eldeslei iii masurae de iii
denariis. v masuras in berchesire habet abbas de labatailge
45 de xx denariis. i haga quae fuit episcopi Petri de iiii denariis.
¶ Rex iii hagas de vi denariis. Henricus de ferrariis vi hagas
quae TRE et etiam TRW dederunt lxii denarios con-
suetudinaliter in firma regis, modo nihil dant.
Episcopus[14] Remigius i haga[15] de iiii denariis. Hugo |comes| i haga[16] de xvi denariis
50 Godric i haga[17] de ii denariis. Doda i haga[18] de ii denariis.
Algar i de ii denariis. Fabri v hagas de x denariis.
¶ Rex in Ældremanestone ii hagas de v denariis.
Comes ebroicensis ii hagas de ii[19] et obolo. Hugo |molebec|[20] i haga[21]
de ii denariis. Rogerus |de laci| i hagam de xii denariis. Robertus |de olgi| i hagam de vi denariis.
55 ¶ Rex i haga[22] de vi denariis. Episcopus osmundus vii
hagas de xxviii denariis. Robertus de oilgi ii hagas de x denariis.
Rogerus de laci v hagas de xxi denariis. Radulfus percehaie vii
hagas de l denariis. Rainbaldus |presbyter| i hagam de iiii denariis. Sanctus Albanus
i haga singa[23] et est in calumnia. Bristist i hagam de ii denariis.
60 Leueua i hagam de ii denariis. Goduinus i hagam de ii denariis.
Aluuinus i hagam de ii denariis. Ælmer presbyter et alius Elmer |presbyter|
et Bruman et Eduui et Edmundus et Willelmus filius osmundi et Leflet
et Lanbertus presbyter, Aluuold et Godric habent gablum de domibus
suis et sanguinem, si ibi effunditur, si receptus fuerit homo
65 inter antequam calumnietur a praeposito regis excepto sabbato
propter mercatum quia tunc rex habet forisfacturam et de adulte-
rio et latrocinio habent ipsi emendam in suis domibus. Alie
vero forisfacturae sunt regis.
TRE valebat xxx libras et post xl libras, modo lx libras
70 et tamen reddit de firma quatuor xx libras ad numerum.
Quod pertinet ad adbrei[24] vii solidos et terra milonis |moli| xxiiii.
Quod abbas de abendone habet viii solidos. Quod Rogerus |de laci| vii solidos.
Quod Rainaldus iiii solidos.

75 Hi subscripti taini de OXENEFORDSCIRE habuerunt
terram in WALINGEFORD.
Lanfranc Archiepiscopus iiii domos in NIWETVNE |pertinentes| reddentes
vi solidos. Remigius episcopus unam domum pertinentem ad Dorkecestre
reddentem xii denarios. Abbas de Sancto Albano unam domum de iiii
80 solidis. R abbas[25] unam domum in Auuilma reddentem iii solidos.
¶ Comes Hugo i domum in Piritune reddentem iii solidos.
¶ Walterus gifard iii domos in Caueresham reddentes ii solidos.
¶ Robertus de olgi ii domos in Watelintune reddentes ii solidos
et in Perie i domum de ii solidis.
85 Ilbertus de laci et Rogerus filius Seifride et Orgar iii domos de ii|ii| solidis.
¶ Hugo de bolebec iii|es| domos in Crem reddentes iii solidos.
¶ Hugo grando de scoca[26] i domum de xii denariis.
¶ Drogo in Sireburne et in Westune tres domos de iiii solidis.

[9] **Molebec**: *recte* Bolebec.

[10] **Haga**: *recte* hagam

[11] **una**: *recte* unam; hagam is to be understood.

[12] **frustrum**: a rare word in Domesday, otherwise only found in three Isle of Wight entries (GDB, 39v, 56: *DB Hants*, 1W6; IoW, 7,16.IoW 8,2), where it is linked with the render of *vomeres*, 'ploughshares', an equally rare word in Domesday Book.

[13] **In**: the initial I is enlarged, rusticated, and rubricated, apparently to distinguish this entry.

[14] There is a somewhat greater space between this entry and the previous one, but it seems to be incidental. There is no indication that the entry is postscriptal and the extra spacing was probably occasioned by the size of the initial 'E' of *Episcopus* at the beginning of the line.

[15] **haga**: *recte* hagam

[16] **haga**: *recte* hagam

[17] **haga**: *recte* hagam

[18] **haga**: *recte* hagam

[19] **omission**: denariis omitted

[20] **Molebec**: *recte* Bolebec.

de Bolbec 1 close rendering 4d. Ranulph Peverel 1 rendering 4d.
Walter fitzOther 6 closes rendering 4d. less a halfpenny. William Lovet 1
plot of land rendering 4d. In Ilsley 3 messuages rendering
3d. The Abbot of Battle has 5 messuages in Berkshire rendering
45 20d. There is 1 close, which belonged to Bishop Peter, rendering 4d.
¶ The king [has] 3 closes rendering 6d. Henry de Ferrers 6 closes
which TRE and also TRW gave 62d. customarily
in the king's farm; now they give nothing.
Bishop Remigius [has] 1 close rendering 4d. Earl Hugh 1 close rendering 16d.
50 Godric 1 close rendering 2d. Dodda 1 close rendering 2d.
Algar 1 [close] rendering 2d. Smiths [have] 5 closes rendering 10d.
¶ The king [has] in Aldermaston 2 closes rendering 5d.
The Count of Evreux 2 closes rendering 2½[d]. Hugh de Bolbec 1 close
rendering 2d. Roger de Lacy 1 close rendering 12d. Robert d'Oilly 1 close rendering 6d.
55 ¶ The king [has] 1 close rendering 6d. Bishop Osmund 7
closes rendering 28d. Robert d'Oilly 2 closes rendering 10d.
Roger de Lacy 5 closes rendering 21d. Ralph Piercehedge 7
closes rendering 50d. Regenbald the priest 1 close rendering 4d. St Alban
1 close *singa* [sic], and it is in dispute. Beorhtric 1 close rendering 2d.
60 Leofgifu 1 close rendering 2d. Godwine 1 close rendering 2d.
Alwine 1 close rendering 2d. Almær the priest and another Almær the priest
and Brunmann and Eadwig and Edmund and William son of Osmund and Leofflæd
and Lambert the priest, Alweald and Godric have rent from their houses
and [the fines due for] bloodshed, if it is shed therein [and] the perpetrator has been arrested
65 there before he is claimed by the king's reeve, except on Saturday,
on account of the market, because then the king has the fine; and they have the fines for adultery
and theft in their houses; other
fines, however, are the king's.
TRE it was worth £30; and afterwards £40; now £60,
70 and yet it renders at farm £80 by tale.
What belongs to *Adbrei* [is worth] 7s.,and the land of Miles Molay 24[s].
What the Abbot of Abingdon has, 8s.; what Roger de Lacy [has], 7s..
What Rainald [has], 4s.

75 The following thegns of OXFORDSHIRE had
land in WALLINGFORD:
Archbishop Lanfranc 4 houses belonging to NEWINGTON rendering
6s. Bishop Remigius 1 house belonging to Dorchester
rendering 12d. The Abbot of St Alban's 1 house rendering
80 4s. Abbot R [...] 1 house [belonging] to Ewelme rendering 3s.
¶ Earl Hugh 1 house [belonging] to Pyrton rendering 3s.
¶ Walter Giffard 3 houses [belonging] to Caversham rendering 2s.
¶ Robert d'Oilly 2 houses [belonging] to Watlington rendering 2s.,
and 1 house to Waterperry rendering 2s.
85 Ilbert de Lacy, Roger fitzSeifrid, and Ordgar, 3 houses rendering 4s.
¶ Hugh de Bolbec 3 houses [belonging] to Crowmarsh Gifford rendering 3s.
¶ Hugh the Great of Scoca 1 house rendering 12d.
¶ Drogo, [belonging] to Shirburn, and South Weston, 3 houses rendering 4s.

---

[21] **haga**: *recte* hagam

[22] **haga**: *recte* hagam

[23] **haga singa**: *recte* hagam singam. *Singa* is obscure. *VCH* amends to *singula*, 'single', but the word would be redundant. Phillimore suggests emendation to *(con)sueta* or *diruta*, 'disused', discontinued', 'ruined, broken down'. Alecto does not attempt a translation. *Dingis* (ab. pl.), translated as 'shops', 'cellars', appears in the Domesday account of York (GDB, 298: *DB Yorks*, C3), but the term is only known from the North (Palliser 1990, 16 and n119). Katharine Keats-Rohan (pers. comm.) suggests emendation to *hagam signatam set est in calumnia*, '1 close assigned [as a prebend], but it is in dispute', citing Fauroux 1961, no 197, p.382.

[24] **Adbrei**: Phillimore suggests *adbt* for Adelbertus, OE Aeðelbeorht. There is no such landowner recorded in either the Berkshire or Oxfordshire folios. Although the context is a list of personal names, the reading *A(l)d(e)beri* for Albury in Oxfordshire is possible. The scribe may have inadvertently copied the place-name instead of the lord Rainald. The other values refer to non-customary land of a similar kind.

[25] **R. abbas**: 'Possibly Abbot Rhiannon [*recte* Rivallon] of the New Minster at Winchester [later Hyde Abbey], 1072–1088' (*DB Berks*, B9n).

[26] **Scoca**: possibly Stoke Talmage. Hugh Grand occurs in Domesday Berkshire and Wiltshire and is possibly identical with Hugh Grand of Stoke, ancestor of the Talemasche family of Stoke Talmage (COEL).

¶ Robertus armenteres in Auuilme i domum de xii denariis.

90 ¶ Wazo unam domum in Auuilme reddentem iii solidos.

Quando geldum dabatur TRE communiter per totam Bercheciram

95 dabat hida iii denarios et obolum ante natale domini et tantundem
ad Pentecostam. ¶ Si rex mittebat alicubi exercitum de v
hidis tantum unus miles ibat et ad eius victum vel stipendium de una-
quaque hida dabantur ei iiii solidi ad ii menses.
Hos vero denarios[27] regi non mittebantur sed militibus dabantur.

100 Siquis in expeditionem summonitus non ibat, totam terram suam erga
regem forisfaciebat. Quod siquis remanendi habens[28] alium pro se mit-
tere promitteret et tamen qui mittendus erat remaneret pro l solidis
quietus erat dominus eius. ¶ Tainus vel miles regis dominicus moriens pro re-
leuamento dimittebat regi omnia arma sua et equum i cum sella

105 alium sine sella. Quod si essent ei canes vel accipitres, presentabantur
regi ut si vellet acciperet. ¶ Siquis occideret hominem pacem regis
habentem et corpus suum et omnem substantiam forisfaciebat erga regem.
¶ Qui per noctem effringebat civitatem, c solidos emendabat regi non vicecomiti.
¶ Qui monitus ad stabilitionem venationis non ibat, l solidos regi emendabat.

---

[27] **Hos vero denarios:** *recte* Hi vero denarii.

[28] **siquis remanendi habens:** to make sense of this passage, something like *causam* must be interpolated to read *siquis causam remanendi habens*. Cf GDB, 172: *DB Worcs*, C5 where the provision is more comprehensible.

50

¶ Robert d'Armentieres, [belonging] to Ewelme, 1 house rendering 12d.
90 ¶ Wazo, 1 house [belonging] to Ewelme rendering 3s.

When geld was commonly paid TRE, throughout the whole of Berkshire,
95 a hide gave 3½d before [the Feast of] the Nativity of the Lord and as much
at Pentecost. ¶ If the king sent out an army anywhere
only 1 thegn went from 5 hides, and for his sustenance or pay
4s. for 2 months was given him from each hide.
This money, however, was not sent to the king but given to the thegns.
100 If anyone summoned on military service did not go he forfeited all his land to
the king. But if anyone having [good reason] to stay behind promised
to sent another in his stead, and yet he who should have been sent stayed behind,
his lord was quit for 50s. ¶ When a thegn or a knight of the king's demesne was dying
he left all his weapons to the king as heriot, and 1 horse with a saddle
105 and 1 without a saddle. But if he possessed hounds or hawks these were presented
to the king, to have if he wished. ¶ If any one slew a man who had the king's peace,
he forfeited both his person and all his possessions to the king.
¶ He who broke into the city at night paid a fine of 100s. to the king, not to the sheriff.
¶ He who was summoned to beat game in the hunt [and] did not go, paid a fine of 50s. to the king.

6

THE GENESIS OF THE HONOUR OF WALLINGFORD

K. S. B. Keats-Rohan

Abstract

From a twelfth-century perspective, the honour of Wallingford appears to be a typical Norman institution. However, a re-examination of its constituent parts indicates that through marriage it was largely derived from the lands of Wigod of Wallingford and his family. Wigod appears to have been one of Edward the Confessor's stallers and the estates that he held were what was effectively a pre-conquest 'castlery' with origins in a period before the formation of the county of Berkshire. Throughout its history the honour was to remain under the tight control of the crown, reflecting its strategic role in the defence of the middle Thames valley.

Keywords

Anglo-Saxon, Anglo-Norman, Berkshire, Wallingford, history, castlery; honour; Wigod of Wallingford.

Introduction

On 14 October 1066 an army led by William of Normandy defeated the English in battle and killed their king, Harold II son of Earl Godwine of Wessex, and thereby changed the course of English history. It was not, however, a decisive victory. There was no immediate offer of the crown to William: indeed, Edgar the Ætheling, a kinsman of Harold's predecessor Edward the Confessor, rejected as Edward's heir in January 1066 on account of youth and inexperience, now attracted a band of supporters in London who appear to have elected him king (*ASC*, 143; *Gesta Willelmi*, 146). Unable to take London directly from the south, William set fire to Southwark, at the foot of London Bridge, and then moved westwards along the left bank of the Thames, aiming to create an arc of terror culminating with a descent on London from the north. To achieve this he had first to cross the Thames. Like the Danes of 1013 (ASC, 143–4) he crossed at the key strategic ford at Wallingford where he received the submission of the controversial Archbishop Stigand of Canterbury (*Gesta Willelmi*, 146), moving on to Berkhamstead where, according to the Anglo-Saxon Chronicle, Archbishop Ealdræd of York, accompanied by Edgar, offered the surrender of the country to him (*ASC*, 144). The Chronicle does not mention the crossing at Wallingford because the final surrender took place elsewhere, but it is mentioned by the Norman chroniclers who understood that the river crossing was a key event. None of these sources mentions Wigod of Wallingford, who appears as such only in the folios of Domesday Book, written over 20 years later, when Wigod and his son Toki were dead. References to Wigod in Domesday Book, discussed below, suggest that he survived 1066 in the service of the Norman

king. It also shows a clear link between him and the manors that constituted the honour of Wallingford after 1066. These holdings form the starting point for a discussion of the honour's formation.

Let us start with a brief reminder of why Wallingford was important (Figure 6.1). Lying on the river terrace, protected by a hinterland of well-watered higher ground and surrounded by fertile agricultural land, it was an ideal settlement area, well placed for the eventual development of a town. In 1066 Wallingford was the last place upstream at which the Thames was fordable without bridge or boat. It was a significant crossing point on a major waterway which had been exploited by the Saxons during the migration period in the 5th and 6th centuries, and subsequently developed for both defensive and economic purposes. In its hinterland were the confluences of tributaries of the Thames, such as (from the south, moving north), the Kennett, the Thame, the Ock and the Cherwell. Not far from a major Roman road from Silchester to Dorchester and beyond, it lay close to much older routes such as the Icknield Way and the Ridgeway which connected East Anglia to Marlborough and the prehistoric complex at Avebury, crossing the chalk uplands known variously as the Marlborough, Lambourne or Berkshire Downs (recently re-named the North Wessex Downs). Direct access to Bath and Bristol was provided by a road from Marlborough. This road linked the spring-line settlements of the Vale of the White Horse, at the foot of the Berkshire Downs, to the market at Wallingford, and formed part of a major route from London to Gloucester. It was also close to a road going southwards, through Winchester to Southampton. The old road known as the Portway coming from the south and apparently crossing at Wallingford and continuing through Clapcot to Shillingford is likely to have been of some antiquity, perhaps even a secondary Roman road (Dewey above, p. 18, and Edgeworth below, p. 82). Wallingford was within easy reach of several major royal holdings at Sutton Courtenay, Benson and Cholsey, other *burh* and minster sites at Reading, Oxford and Abingdon, as well as the former Roman and episcopal town of Dorchester.

The importance of its riverine location is shown in the requirement, revealed in Domesday Book, that those who lived in Wallingford should do service for the king by horse or by water as far as Reading, Blewbury, Sutton Courtenay and Benson. We know of Wallingford's existence by the end of Alfred's reign (871–99) as a *burh* intended to defend a major angle in the Middle Thames against incursions by the Danes into what became English Mercia and Wessex, thanks to the late ninth- or early tenth-century Burghal Hidage (Haslam 2005; Hill and Rumble 1996). As such, it was one of an integrated system of *burhs*, a maximum of 40 miles apart, including five, at Southwark, Sashes (now an

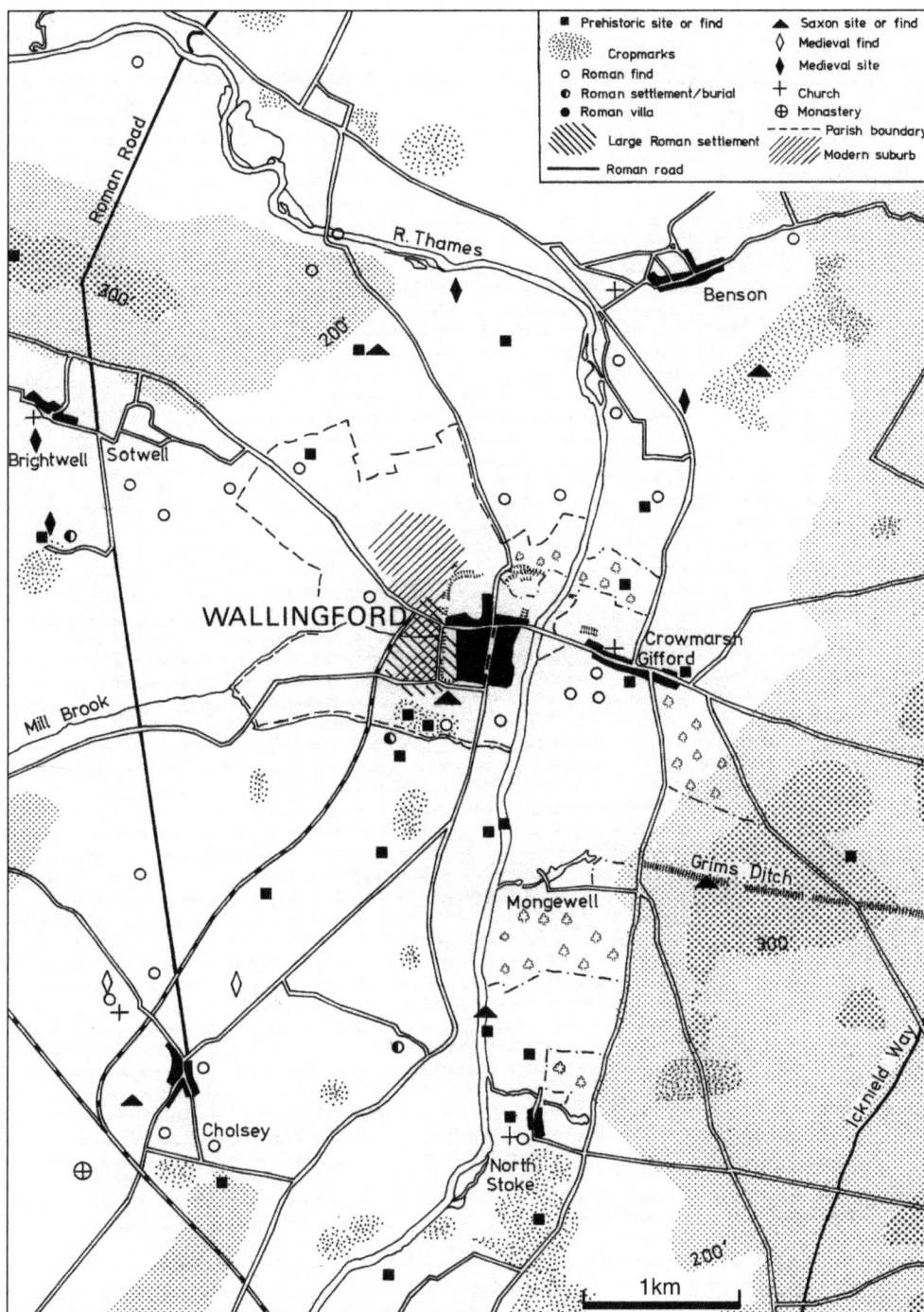

Figure 6.1 Wallingford
and its hinterland (based
on Airs *et al.* 1975,
by permission of Oxford
Archaeological Unit).

island in the Thames near Cookham), Wallingford, Oxford and Cricklade, that guarded the River Thames. Wallingford's strategic importance and its future role as a royal administrative centre can be seen from around the time of its foundation when King Alfred made a number of local land transactions. He acquired estates at Cholsey and Moulsford, East Hagbourne and Basildon from Bishop Denewulf and the church of Winchester (S.354; Gelling 1974, 757), and acquired land at Appleford in exchange for land in East Hendred from one Deormod (S.355; Gelling, 1979, no. 30). The church of Winchester – the site of the only other *burh* of comparable size to Wallingford, according to the Burghal Hidage – probably then held the estate at Brightwell, Sotwell and Mackney that was granted by King Æthelwulf in 854 but temporarily alienated in the 10th

century, before returning to Winchester's control some time before 1066 (Roffe above, pp. 38, 42). These estates protected the site of the new *burh* on the right bank of the river. With the exception of Appleford, in the hundred of the royal vill at Sutton Courtenay, all these places lay in Slottisford Hundred. Since there is reason to believe that the Alfredan *burh* either enclosed or replaced one or more existing settlements at a place where the Thames was fordable in several places (Dewey above, p. 18; Roffe above, p. 42), it is possible that the otherwise unidentified Slottisford ('ford with a bar or bars', Gelling 1979, 507) was the name of a settlement swallowed up by the new *burh*. There is no further documentary reference to the *burh* until an undated, but evidently pre-Conquest Old English memorandum attached to a forged charter from Winchester (S.517, S.523; Gelling

1979, nos. 50, 55), which shows an active town or 'port'. At this time Sutton Courtenay and Cholsey, as well as Benson on the other side of the river, were also important local royal estates. The only other pre-Conquest documentary references we have come from the Anglo-Saxon Chronicle, which relates that Wallingford twice attracted the attention of the Danes, who burnt it in 1006 (*ASC*, 88), and then passed through it *en route* to Bath in 1013 (*ASC*, 92). Only with the production of Domesday Book does Wallingford emerge from documentary obscurity to become well-evidenced as the main royal and administrative centre of the Middle Thames.

Berkshire was a peculiarly royal county during the 11th century, as probably also during the 10th. Nicholas Hooper (1988, 8–10) has calculated that in 1086 the king held one fifth of all the land in Berkshire, combining the estates held previously by King Edward, his queen Edith and Earl Harold. The abbey of Abingdon had nearly as much again, for which it rendered the service of 30 knights and castle guard at Windsor to the king. In terms of value, however, the king's holdings far exceeded those of the abbey. The situation in 1086 mirrored that of 1066 to a large extent. King Cnut had taken Berkshire for himself in 1016, though eventually part of it was granted to Earl Godwine of Wessex and later to his son (and future king) Harold (Hooper 1988, 7–9). The comital holdings, such as those at Faringdon and Aldermaston, were held by the king in 1086. King Edward had been the dominant landowner in 1066. As Domesday Book shows, a large number of thegns had held fairly small estates from him scattered throughout the county; a handful of estates belonged to earls other than Harold, and a few were held by Edward's wife, Harold's sister Edith. King William took over many of these smaller estates and effectively abolished the comital presence in Berkshire. What was left was parcelled out to some of the richest and most powerful of his Norman followers, many of whom were prominent in other regions. These included men such as Henry de Ferrers, a major landholder in Derbyshire and Nottinghamshire, who was successor to the holdings, and perhaps also the office, of Godric the sheriff in Berkshire (Green 1990, 26), and Geoffrey de Mandeville, lord of the honour of Pleshy in Essex, successor of Esger the staller and probable Norman sheriff of Essex (Green 1990, 39). An unusually high number of men, from these great landowners to humble sergeants, in the king's service held land in the county with appurtenant properties located in Wallingford. Hooper's survey of the thegnly predecessors of these ministers of the king showed that this concentration of king's ministers and sergeants in the Berkshire of 1086 reflected the position in and before 1066 (Hooper 1988, 16–17). David Roffe's new study of the Domesday borough in this volume (above, pp. 40–1) makes the point even more clearly in relation to Wallingford.

A concentration of holdings of king's barons and sergeants in a shire town is found elsewhere. These towns were already developing as the administrative hubs of their shires before 1066, when the king's business was conducted by the sheriff. Like other such places, Wallingford was a thriving town, supported by and supporting the (still mainly agricultural) trades of its hinterland, and it had a royal mint. It was also a fortified *burh* capable of defending its strategic location and the people dependent upon it. The symbiotic relationship between a successful borough as a centre for organized defence, an administrative centre and as a town with a flourishing economy is central to understanding the role of places like Wallingford before and after the Conquest.

Differences there certainly were, both between Wallingford before and after 1066 and between Wallingford and other major boroughs and honours, but also some remarkable similarities, due principally to continuing links to pre-Conquest jurisdictions. In what follows I hope to demonstrate some of these continuities and differences by examining the composition of what was known by the early 12th century as the honour of Wallingford, how it came into being, and its significance. The route will prove circuitous, taking us back before the Conquest and forward to the late 13th century.

The formation of the honour

The Norman honour was a collection of estates held by one man from the king in chief in return for a fixed military obligation based on the service of one or more knight's in the king's host, to be provided by those who held parts of the manors under the tenant-in-chief as sub or 'median' tenants. The tenant-in-chief was directly answerable to the king. The fully-developed system was later referred to as 'tenure by barony'. David Roffe's work has shown that there are close correlations between the whole or constituent parts of these honours with the pre-Conquest 'honours' previously held by individual king's thegns with sake and soke, a complex of rights and jurisdictions that alone gave full right to land and brought its holder into a special relationship with the king (Roffe 1990; Roffe 2007, 152). Before 1066 king's thegns were an important nexus of power and influence, partly due to their 'nighness to the king', characteristic also of their post-Conquest successors, the tenants-in-chief or 'barons'. The text of Domesday Book is notoriously difficult to decode, since the scribe's ideas about how to excerpt the results of the different documents emanating from the survey changed as he set about writing them up in what is now Domesday Book. Among the casualties of the process of enrolment was the gradual abandonment of the mention of the manor (*manerium*), i.e. a tributary centre, usually the lord's hall, where the dues from the tenants of the appurtenant estates were rendered to the lord (Roffe 2007, 178). The names of the holders in 1066 are also often omitted. When they are named, the reference can sometimes be to one or more dependents or clients of an unidentified king's thegn. Hence clear evidence about the holder of sake and soke in 1066 is often lacking. The land held with sake and soke by a king's thegn was known as bookland, a precious resource that was heritable, though indivisible, and theoretically derived from a king, one of whom, at some time in the past would have granted it by means of a charter or 'book'. One of the products of the Domesday inquest was the recognition that grants of the holdings of former king's thegns to the new tenants-in-chief, normally intended as for one lifetime only, had in fact often conveyed the sake and soke of these manors, and hence both the title to the land itself and the accompanying right of inheritance (Roffe 2007, 182). Rights in other forms of tenure, such as loan-land, granted for three life terms, or family land, of a thegnly predecessor did not automatically pass to the new-comer, though they were negotiable (Roffe 2007, 171–3). Roffe has identified clues in Domesday diplomatic about the manorial or sake and soke status of estates and their holders where these are not stated. A primary clue is the phrase *X tenuit* (X held), which indicates a king's thegn holding with sake and soke. He has also noted that in most if not all cases Norman baronial castles were built on the site of the hall belonging to a manor held with sake and soke (Roffe 2007, 174–5).

In 1212 the honour of Wallingford consisted of 102½ knight fees (*BF*, 120) spread over nine counties (Berkshire, Oxfordshire, Buckinghamshire, Wiltshire, Bedfordshire, Gloucestershire, Surrey, Middlesex, Hampshire). At that date the honour was a fully-fledged post-Conquest legally-constituted entity. Following the retirement of Brien fitzCount *c.* 1150 it had either been held directly by the king, or was granted to a close royal kinsman such as Richard I's brother John, afterwards King John, and then Henry III's brother Richard, earl of Cornwall, who appointed a constable. When Edward the Confessor died in 1066 a significant part of the extensive estates that became the honour of Wallingford had been held by Wigod or his son Toki, or by their men. Both Wigod and Toki are either expressly named in the Domesday text as thegns of King Edward or occur in an *X tenuit* formula. We know that Wigod's daughter married the Norman Robert d'Oilly very soon after the Conquest, and that Robert's own daughter and heiress, Matilda, married Miles Crispin around 1084 (*BF*, 116). By 1086 much of Wigod's land was held by Miles, though some remained with Robert until he and his wife Ealdgyth died, around 1092. A few other manors associated with Wigod or his son, including those held by Earl Roger of Shrewsbury in Middlesex, were attached to the honour after 1100. The composition of a significant part of the honour of Wallingford out of the lands of an undisgraced Englishman and his family, including his Norman grand-daughter, was very unusual, otherwise only being paralleled by the barony (and later earldom) of Edward of Salisbury.

Very few of the post-Conquest tenants-in-chief had been pre-Conquest landholders. Much of the Old English nobil-ity had perished on the field of Hastings; those that survived the battle automatically forfeited their lands. Some Englishmen who had not taken part in the battle were allowed to retain their lands, as tenants of the new lords, though often on terms that reduced them to penury. Domesday Book shows that Wigod himself survived the turmoil and continued to have influence among Englishmen, like the unnamed freeman who was forced to buy back his hide in Tiscott, Hertfordshire, for the extraor-dinary price of 9 ounces of gold and who turned to him for protection (GDB, 137v: *DB Herts*, 19,1). As we have seen, many of the new honours were created by giving the bulk of the estate held with 'sake and soke' (*saca et soca*) of one king's thegn, or a group of such thegns, to a single tenant-in-chief (Roffe 1990). The land of Godric the sheriff of Berkshire, who died at Hastings (or perhaps briefly sur-

vived, compare GDB, 60v: *DB Berks*, 21,13 with *Abingdon*, i, 222, and 201 n453), was given to Henry de Ferrers, for example. In a handful of cases certain key English adminis-trators prepared to work for the Normans retained their estates until the end of 1087. The few surviving examples at the end of William's reign were men strongly associated with borough and shire administration, such as Edward sheriff of Salisbury; among a handful of lesser men was Alfred *nepos* (presumably meaning 'nephew', though pos-sibly either 'cousin' or 'grandson') of Wigod, also a tenant of the honour of Wallingford (Williams 1995, 100, 102; GDB, 159v: *DB Oxon*, 35,31,43). Wigod's survival in 1066 is something of a puzzle. As a Berkshire thegn, Wigod was liable to fund a man to fight in the royal army (*fyrd*) for each five hides of land held, and to fight for his lord in person. Failure to fight for his lord (King Harold) would have entailed forfeiture and ignominy had Harold won, and fight-ing for him should have entailed forfeiture after William's victory. His continued influence with the English after 1066 indicates that the reasons for his (and his son's) absence from Hastings must have been honourable. Possibly he had fought at the battle at Stamford Bridge, three weeks before the battle at Hastings, and for some reason, perhaps injury, had left the army and returned to Wallingford – we do know from the Peterborough and Worcester versions of the Anglo-Saxon Chronicle that Harold engaged William at Hastings before the assemblage of his troops was complete (*ASC*, 143). Whilst we cannot know where Wigod or his son Toki were on 14 October 1066, it seems certain that they had not thereafter rallied to the cause of the ætheling Edgar. Indeed, it seems likely that Wigod was with Archbishop Stigand at Wallingford, and, like him, was a pragmatist who preferred surrender in the face of overwhelming odds to the pointless destruction that defiance would have entailed (cf. *ASC*, 144).

In addition to the surrender of Wallingford in 1066, Wigod is likely to have rendered a second service to the Conqueror by inducting his son-in-law into the running of Wallingford as an administrative, military and commercial centre; many of the surviving English played similar roles for the newcomers (Williams 1995, 98–125). Robert soon put a distinctively Norman seal on the change by overseeing the erection of the castle, known to have been completed by 1071, when it became the prison of the abbot of Abingdon (*Abingdon*, i, 226–7). Robert's marriage is one of a handful of examples of Normans specializing in local administra-tion who took English wives the better to embed themselves in local society (Keats-Rohan 1999, 27– 8). Ultimately, he and his family became more closely associated with Oxford, where Robert oversaw the building of another royal castle and, towards the end of his life in 1091/2, 'a massive stone causeway to carry traffic across the Thames flood-plain on the ancient southern approach to Oxford: 700 metres long, with seventeen flood-arches, it is probably the oldest post-Roman bridge built entirely of stone in western Europe' (Blair 1990, 19; *Abingdon,* ii, 34; OHER, ref. PRN 6628). Robert's organizational and military talents were at William's disposal both in England and in Normandy throughout the reign. He was at least briefly at the side of the king during the siege of Sainte-Susanne (1083–6), in the county of Maine, since Domesday Book records that 1½ hides in Ludwell, Oxfordshire, were granted to him there (GDB, 158v: *DB Oxon*, 28,24). He was in England on 31 March 1084 when he entertained at Abingdon Abbey a party comprising the king's 15–year-old son Henry, his tutor Osmund bishop of Salisbury, and Miles 'of Wallingford, surnamed Crispin' (*Abingdon*, ii, 16–19). Although Robert d'Oilly continued to maintain interests in Wallingford – he occurs among those named holding burgages in Domesday Book – Miles was certainly lord of the honour of Wallingford by 1086, when the data later excerpted in Domesday Book were gathered, having married Robert's daughter. Unlike Robert, Miles does not occur in William's *acta* until 1077, and then as witness to a confirmation given in Normandy for the abbey of Bec (*Regesta* Bates, no. 166); his only other attestation suggests that he may well have first come to England in 1080, accompanying William when he left Normandy some time after Pentecost in that year, as appears from a subsequent confirmation which was several times updated at Bec, but which essentially belongs to the period 1081 to 1087 (*Regesta* Bates, no. 167), in which his grants of tithes throughout the honour of Wallingford to the abbey occur. Since the bulk of his grants to Bec were of demesne tithes, the only reference to Bec in the Domesday account of his manors was in Swyncombe, where the monks held 2½ hides of demesne land (GDB, 159v: *DB Oxon*, 35,33). A number of his grants, for instance of tithes at Goring and Iver, must have been made after the death of Robert d'Oilly, who held them in 1086. During Miles' lordship a number of changes were made to Wallingford's ecclesiastical structures, including his own endowment of the castle chapel, probably refounding a pre-Conquest institution (discussed below). There is clearly quite a contrast between Robert and Miles as lords of Wallingford, but both were successors to the lands and office of Wigod. A closer examination of what that office was may help us better to understand the origins of the honour of Wallingford.

Housecarls and stallers

As noted above, Wallingford was dominated by officers of the king's administration to a greater extent than most other major boroughs. One of the most significant entries in the borough account is the reference to the 15 acres belonging to King Edward on which housecarls dwelt, which were then held by Miles Crispin. The exact location of the tenements of these houscarls is uncertain, but they could be linked with the land surrounding the castle on the east, or the northward extensions of the castle precinct into the extensive 'hamlet' of Clapcot (see below, p. 61). Although the collection of dues for the maintenance of housecarls is known from other Wessex boroughs mentioned in Domesday, at Wareham, Dorchester, Bridport and Shaftesbury in Dorset (GDB, 75: *DB Dorset*, B1–4), this entry is unique in identifying the only known permanent station of royal housecarls. One of these acres belonged to Long Wittenham, a manor of Walter Giffard (GDB, 56: *DB Berks*, B1). The Domesday jurors claimed not to know how Miles came to hold these acres, but as will appear, we can have no difficulty in identifying Wigod of Wallingford as

Miles's predecessor in the role. The housecarls were an innovation of the Danish king Cnut. Often described as a sort of private army, they seem to have been something like royal bodyguards, trusted royal servants close to the king's person who were given rural estates the better to serve regional royal interests (Hooper 1984). The association of royal land and the housecarls land is unparalleled elsewhere and suggests a Saxon palace site with attached garrison, perhaps, as Lawson has suggested, there to back up the authority of the king's officials in a key area dominated by royal holdings (Lawson 1993, 180). Almost all known examples of housecarls, 28 out of 32, bore Scandinavian names (Lawson 1993, 180). One of them was Toki, son of Wigod of Wallingford. He was described as *huscarle* when named as a predecessor of Earl Roger in the Middlesex manor of Ickenham (GDB, 129: *DB Middx*, 7,8).

Others can be identified. Among those named as holding burgages in Wallingford in 1086 were Roger fitzSeifrid and his brother Ralph. They also held a sergeanty of the king at Purley and Fulscot, Berkshire, while Roger held a sergeanty at Brightwell Baldwin in Oxfordshire (GDB, 160v: *DB Oxon*, 58,7). Together with Miles's Surrey manors of Beddington and Chessington – held from him by William fitzTurold and apparently later held in demesne by Miles's successor Brien fitzCount (*Boarstall Cartulary*, 322) – all these holdings were part of the honour and in the hands of a family surnamed Huscarle by 1156 (GDB, 62v: *DB Berks*, 49,2–3; *Boarstall Cartulary*, 322). The name of the family is striking and quite possibly links them to Wigod and his family. As an institution, essentially bodyguards loyal to their royal lord unto death, housecarls had effectively been eradicated by the murderous battles that occurred in short succession in late 1066. Wigod may himself have originally have been a housecarl. His association with Wallingford, a cognomen attached to him primarily in the Buckinghamshire Domesday (GDB, 150, 150v: *DB Bucks*, 23,7,12,33), was evidently significant and must have included the control of the military functions of the borough and its hinterland. Indeed, John Hudson, most recent editor and translator of the History of the Church of Abingdon has translated *oppidanorum Walingafordensium dominus* in reference to Wigod as 'lord of the garrison of Wallingford' (*Abingdon*, i, 214). By 1086 both he and his son Toki, who died saving the life of William the Conqueror at Gerberoy in 1079 (*ASC*, 159–60), were dead, and Wigod's ministry – that is, his official function – was exercised by Miles Crispin.

The career of Robert d'Oilly is perhaps more informative than Miles' as to what Wigod's ministry actually was. It has been suggested, on the basis of a writ of William I concerning the lands of the Berkshire abbey of Abingdon and its lands in Berkshire, Oxfordshire and smaller holdings in Gloucestershire and Warwickshire, that Robert was sheriff of Oxfordshire during part of the Conqueror's reign (*Regesta* Bates, no. 5). Wigod himself possibly acted in a similar capacity, to judge from the evidence of a single writ of the Confessor, discussed below. Neither Wigod nor Robert can be associated with any other shrievalty, including Berkshire, of which Wallingford was (apparently) the county town. In the Norman period a royal castle in a county town was the headquarters of the county sheriff; occasionally, as in Worcestershire and Gloucestershire, the constable of the castle was also the sheriff (Green 1997, 267–8). But too little is known about early sheriffs or the shrievalty for this to be a profitable approach to the roles of Wigod or Robert. Indeed, the fragmentary evidence we have from Domesday Book and the History of Abingdon suggests that the sheriffs of Oxfordshire and Berkshire were men of only local influence (*Abingdon*, i, 200–1, 224–5; ii, 172–3).

Robert's power and influence most likely derived from the fact that he assumed Wigod's role as lord of the garrison of Wallingford and subsequently became constable of a second royal castle at Oxford (*castelli urbis Oxenefordensis oppidanus*: *Abingdon*, ii, 10). Lords of the barony of Hook Norton, his successors retained their links with the castle and frequently occur styled constable of Oxford (*Chartulary of Oseney*, nos. 13A, 492; *Regesta*, iii, no. 475). The word is sometimes used to translate the title of staller which occurs among a small number of men who were appointed by Edward the Confessor. Like housecarls, stallers were a Danish institution introduced by Cnut (Mack 1984). These men, close personal advisors of the king and the wealthiest of his thegns, were responsible for the running of the king's military household; after 1066 they were specifically associated with royal castles. Edward's stallers were men of considerable standing who held property worth in excess of £100 per annum. They often occur in late documents of the Confessor's reign, or post-Conquest re-workings of them, as personal servants of the king, such as butlers and stewards, and also as key administrators who outranked sheriffs but occasionally also acted as sheriffs, with responsibility for the administration of the royal demesne (Clarke 1994, 126–8). An example was Esger the staller, whose post-Conquest successor, Geoffrey de Mandeville, was constable of London; it was Esger who would eventually admit the Normans into London late in 1066 (*Carmen*, 40–2). Another, who submitted to William before the battle of Hastings, was Robert fitzWimarc, a Norman who was kinsman to both Edward the Confessor and William (Keats-Rohan 2001, 977). Wigod was a king's thegn and a man of social standing and wealth. The value of the lands with which he was explicitly associated in Domesday Book exceeded £100. The sole writ of Edward the Confessor to 'his dear kinsman Wigod of Wallingford' might suggest that Wigod himself was sheriff of Oxfordshire, since he was instructed to give Islip to the king's new foundation at Westminster (S.1148; *Writs*, 104, pp.334–7; 368–9), but could equally well relate to Wigod's wider ministry in the region. The writ may have been issued at the Christmas court of 1065, shortly before Edward's death. A charter concerning Waltham Abbey written later by someone with reliable information describes Wigod as Edward's *pincerna*, that is butler (Clarke 1994, 144; Barlow 1970, 163 n1). Though there is no extant description of Wigod as a staller, this fragmentary information strongly suggests that he exercised the functions of a staller, and that his son-in-law succeeded him in that office. Indeed, though a few of Robert's appearances in the writs and charters of William I (*Regesta* Bates, nos. 189, 219, 277, 286, 301–2,

335, 338, 341) may relate to his status as baron of Hook Norton in Oxfordshire, most of them make better sense if seen in relation to his role as lord of a major strategic castlery to which an estate spread over eight counties was attached, rather than as sheriff of any one of them. This is probably the best interpretation of Wigod's role as *oppidanorum Walingafordensium dominus*; it certainly seems to indicate a more expansive role than that of a mere constable. Interestingly, both Miles Crispin and his successor Matilda, wife of Brien fitzCount, were styled 'of Wallingford', but the style of constable does not seem to have attached to Miles and indeed appears to be specific to Oxford. Brien fitzCount, as lord of Wallingford, is only styled as constable in a charter of Henry I in 1131 (*Regesta*, ii, no. 1688; discussed by the editors on p. xv) and of King Stephen in 1136 (*Regesta*, iii, no. 944). From an entry in the Pipe Roll of 31 Henry I (p.139) it appears that he paid the princely sum of £166 13s and 4d 'for the ministry [i.e. the constableship of Oxford castle] and part of the land of Nigel d'Oilly'. Nigel was the brother and successor of Robert I d'Oilly and seems to have died around 1116. His son Robert II occurs as constable after 1139.

Wigod, his family, and the honour

The bulk of what became the honour of Wallingford consisted of land that had been held by Wigod or members of his family in 1066. Much of it at the time of the Domesday survey in 1086 was held by his granddaughter's husband Miles, but some remained with his daughter and her husband Robert until their deaths, shortly after Robert's last charter attestation in 1092. Much of this remainder consisted in the fees held by members of the Basset family, thus contradicting the thirteenth-century lawyer Bracton who claimed that the Basset fees were the *maritagium* of Robert's daughter (*Bracton's Notebook*, 3:516). Further holdings, associated with Wigod's nephew Turold and his son William, were added before 1113. So what and where were these holdings, and how do they link to what we might know about Wigod and his family?

For the whole Anglo-Saxon period vastly fewer English charters survive than we would like, and many of those that do pose problems because they are often copies made in later times by scribes who either sought, usually on behalf of a monastery, to improve them, or who simply misunderstood them. These are the problems we must confront in trying to understand Wigod and the composition of his estate. As we have seen already, he occurs in a very few documents, largely unsatisfactory, of the last years of Edward the Confessor's reign, from which we glean the information that he was a kinsman of the king. The relationship, if there really was one, is likely to have been distant, but represents a plausible route to royal favour. Since he clearly had some responsibility for Wallingford, a major town, royal administrative centre and garrison, we should expect to find that some at least of his holdings were linked to the office he held. It would be reasonable to assume that by the date of the Domesday survey such holdings would be in the hands of Miles Crispin, whom the borough entry clearly shows was lord of the honour of Wallingford in 1086, but not of the borough itself.

If we plot all the locations directly associated with either Wigod or Toki, and those that formed part of the honour as it was by c. 1120 (Appendix), they will be seen to lie in a 60–mile radius of Wallingford. They form a number of clusters, in the vicinity of *burhs* or royal centres such as Wallingford itself, Oxford, Reading and Gloucester, Aylesbury, and Buckingham, as well as Marlborough and Chippenham. They include the third major strand in the composition of the honour, the holdings of the thegn Beorhtric in Buckinghamshire, to which we shall return. Another contributor to the honour was the small number of estates in Middlesex held by King William's close friend Earl Roger, whose heirs spectacularly disgraced themselves and forfeited their lands in the reigns of William's sons. These included a large manor of Colham, now in Hillingdon, formerly held by Wigod, as well as Harmondsworth, once held by Alwine, Wigod's man, and Ickenham, all about 13 miles from Westminster (GDB, 129: *DB Middx*, 7,3,5,8). Hillingdon had been held by Ulf, thegn of King Edward, probably the Ulf housecarl who had held Hanworth (GDB, 129: *DB Middlx*, 7,2,6) At Ickenham Toki was described as Edward's housecarl (GDB, 129: *DB Middlx*, 7,8); his 2 hides and 3 others, including that of Alwine, Wulfsige son of Manni's man, had been added to the land of Colham 'where it was not before 1066'; also added to Colham was Dawley, held before 1066 by Godwine Ælfgyth, Wigod's man. Ickenham lay five miles north east of Toki's Buckinghamshire manor of Iver (GDB, 149: *DB Bucks*, 19,1). Roger's estates in Surrey (GDB, 34–34v: *DB Surrey*, 18) do not seem to have come to Wallingford, though his tenant was a certain Turold, successor of Osmund (conjectured to have been his father by Williams 1995, 102). Elsewhere, at (Hampton) Meysey in Gloucestershire, Earl Roger's tenant was Turold nephew (*nepos*) of Wigod (GDB, 166v: *DB Gloucs*, 27,1). The name of this manor associates all these Turolds as the same man, whose estates eventually passed to a family surnamed de Maisy. As shown above, another of Roger's tenants was Alfred nephew of Wigod, and William fitzTurold, probably a son of Turold nephew of Wigod, occurs as a tenant of Miles Crispin at Beddington in Surrey (GDB, 36v: *DB Surrey*, 29,1). William fitzTurold's holding of Miles at Henton, Oxon (GDB, 159v: *DB Oxon*, 35,20), like that of Turold of Earl Roger at Hampton Meysey, had been held in 1066 by a man named Leofnoth. An entry for Chessington in Surrey (GDB, 36v: *DB Surrey*, 29,2), a manor of Miles Crispin, states that Wigod did not have this manor when (King) William came into the country. This might mean that Wigod was given it by William, though it could also mean that he had given it to Miles, despite its not having previously been Wigod's. Chessington, like Beddington, was held by the Huscarle successors of William fitzTurold at Beddington by 1166.

One cluster, in the region of Swindon in Wiltshire, is particularly interesting. Apart from Manton and Rodbourne (GDB, 71: *DB Wilts*, 28,9,12), held by Wigod, and Brinkworth, held by Toki (GDB, 71: *DB Wilts*, 28,8), it included the manor of Ogbourne St George, formerly held by Earl Harold and held in 1086 by Miles Crispin (GDB, 71: *DB Wilts*, 28,11). A second much larger manor of

Ogbourne St Andrew was then held by the king (GDB, 65v: *DB Wilts*, 1,22), but a contemporary geld roll for Wiltshire describes it as being 'of the land of Wigod' (Williams 1995, 100 n11). These 30 hides perhaps included Ogbourne Maizey, named from the same family to which the Domesday holdings of Turold nephew of Wigod passed. Both Ogbournes were given to the abbey of Bec by Miles's successors, Matilda of Wallingford and her husband Brien fitzCount, before 1133 (*Bec*, nos. 18, 37, 47–8).

These lands provide some clues to the origins of Wigod's family. Ogbourne occurs in the will of the Earldorman Æthelwold I who died in 946 (S.1504). His will disposes of land 'acquired from the king' and included the gift of Ogbourne to his brother Eadric. Another brother, Earldorman Æthelstan 'Half-king' of East Anglia, a benefactor of Abingdon Abbey, was willed the manor of Broadwater in Sussex. Wigod also held this in 1066, together with Bepton and a site in Chichester, right in the heart of Godwine territory (GDB, 23v, 26v, 28v: *DB Sussex*, 11,15;12,21;13,30). In the case of Broadwater at least it appears that it was lost to his heirs when William de Braose's Rape of Bramber was formed in Sussex (Fleming 1991, 199; GDB, 50v: *DB Hants*, 69,40). It is impossible to know if Wigod was a descendant of Æthelwold or his brothers, and the Sussex holdings, although said in Domesday Book to have been held of King Edward, perhaps simply indicate that Wigod's ministry continued under King Harold as it had under Edward. On the other hand, the Norman conquest was not the first such disruption to English landholding that had occurred in the 11th century. Following the Danish conquest of 1016, King Cnut had dispossessed many of the surviving English nobles in favour of his Danish followers. The Danish names of Wigod and Toki, and their association with housecarls are a likely indication that the father of Wigod was one of these Danish 'new men' who had been given royal estates formerly associated with the family of Æthelwold. A relationship to the half-king's family cannot be completely excluded, however. Although Wigod bore a Danish name, that of his daughter Ealdgyth was certainly English, suggesting that he had an English wife or mother (or both). Given that Wigod was described as 'kinsman' in Edward the Confessor's writ, a possible link can be suggested: the Confessor's paternal grandmother Ælfthryth had first been married to the half-king's son Æthelwold II, by whom she had at least one son, Leofric (Hart 1992, 589).

Although Wigod is not always mentioned as Miles' predecessor, there must be a strong presumption that a large proportion of his holdings had belonged to Wigod or to Wigod's men. Fragmentary evidence occasionally survives, such as the name of *Wigodeslande*, part of the honour's large manor of Aston Rowant (Oxon) (Cam 1963, 139). However, Wigod was not invariably Miles' predecessor (*antecessor*). The thegn Leofnoth had held before 1066 the manors of Wootton Basset, Drayton Foliat, Hazlebury, and Walcot in Wiltshire (GDB, 71: *DB Wilts*, 28,1,6,7), Meysey Hampton in Gloucestershire (held by Earl Roger in 1086) and Henton in Oxfordshire, all of which were later held by either the Foliot or Maisey families (GDB, 166v, 159v: *DB Gloucs*, 27,1; *DB Oxon*, 35,20). Chearsley (Bucks) and

Appleton and Eaton (Berks) had been held by Healfdene a thegn of Earl (king) Harold (GDB, 150, 61v: *DB Bucks*, 23,10; *DB Berks*, 33,6–7), who had himself earlier held Ogbourne and Chilton Foliat in Wiltshire (GDB, 71: *DB Wilts*, 28,2,11). Other predecessors were the king's thegn Hemming at Cherington, Gloucestershire, and Hitcham in Buckinghamshire (GDB, 169v, 149v-150: *DB Gloucs*, 64,2; *DB Bucks*, 23,3), as well as Edward's chaplain Baldwin, who held the ungelded manors of Tidmarsh in Pangbourne and Pangbourne (GDB, 61v: *DB Berks*, 33,1–2). A significant predecessor, contributing 22 manors to the honour, was the queen's thegn Beorhtric. In discussing a charter which recorded the foundation of Waltham Abbey by the queen's brother Harold in 1062 Pauline Stafford pointed out that at 'this great meeting the lay nobility were distinguished according to their intimacy with and service to the king and queen' (Stafford 1997, 108–9). Among them was Wigod the king's butler, Baldwin the king's clerk, Azur the king's steward, who later held land in Berkshire, perhaps in Ardington, under Robert d'Oilly (GDB, 62: *DB Berks*, 41,6), possibly also at Thenford (GDB, 225: *DB Northants*, 28,2) and may have been one of Miles' predecessors at Marsh Baldon (GDB, 159v: *DB Oxon*, 35,17). Among the others was a Beorhtric, described as *princeps*. Although this man cannot be identified with certainty, it is striking that it was the name of a major contributor to the honour of Wallingford.

This Beorhtric was a thegn of Queen Edith, and possibly also of the king (Stafford 1997, 319–20). He was wealthy and well-endowed with land in several counties, ranking 35th in Clarke's list of non-earlish estates (Clarke 1994, 262–4). Clarke's figures can be debated, but he assigned Beorhtric a personal annual income of £100, and Wigod one of £117 (Clarke 1994, 356–7). Much of the land which passed from Beorhtric to the honour of Wallingford lay in Buckinghamshire and had been held by him as the queen's (and in one case the king's) thegn. Most of Edith's lands in Buckinghamshire represent lands used for the dower of English queens since at least the mid 10th century. The fact that Beorhtric occurs regularly in these manors as a thegn of Queen Edith suggests that they had retained an association with the dower lands of English queens. One of the most striking things about the honour of Wallingford is that it was only held outside the royal family for two generations after the Conquest, thereafter being used as an appanage for younger sons such as Henry III's brother Richard earl of Cornwall.

Wigod and Beorhtric were certainly king's thegns who held sake and soke and therefore heritable title to land, but in some cases they may have held royal land as loanland rather than as bookland. At any rate, the occurrence of both Wigod and Toki among Robert d'Oilly's predecessors, and the subsequent addition to the honour after 1100 of those of their holdings held in 1086 by Earl Roger, shows that a notion of family inheritance was permitted for their land during the formation of the honour in the early post-Conquest period. This may also have involved Beorhtric. In Buckinghamshire Robert d'Oilly's chief holdings were the extensive manors of Iver and High Wycombe (GDB, 149: *DB Bucks*, 19,1–2). Iver had been held in 1066 by

Toki. Of three freemen there, one had belonged to Edith's man Beorhtric. The manor was said to have been of Robert's wife's holding. Wycombe (in 1212 a borough and a *villa forinsec* of the honour, *BF*, 120) was also said to have been of Robert's wife's holding, yet it was held before 1066 by Beorhtric from Queen Edith. At the ever-present risk of over-interpreting the Domesday text, can we see this as a hint of some relationship between Wigod and Beorhtric, perhaps that Wigod may have been the son-in-law of Beorhtric?

Pauline Stafford, in a study of Queen Edith and her predecessor Emma of Normandy, has suggested that the dower lands brought into the lands of the kings of Wessex by their marriages reflect their part in the process of the unification of the country by Alfred's successors that was every bit as important as conquest, and that they are key also to defence. She highlights the strong association between old English queens and fortified places, and especially with their monasteries, a 'woman, who, as both queen and wife, could legitimate the acquisition and control of key ecclesiastical estates' (Stafford, 1997, 134–5). Of special interest are the lands given in 966 by King Edgar to Ælfgifu, who has been identified with the divorced wife of King Eadwig, Edgar's brother and predecessor, which were mentioned in her will (S.1484). Ælfgifu fell into disfavour when she and her mother Æthelgifu were discovered in a compromising position with the king at his coronation banquet. Cyril Hart has shown that these women were related to the family of Æthelstan Half-King, brother of Earldorman Æthelwold, whom we met earlier (Hart 1992, 455–66, 569–604). Many of Ælfgifu's holdings lay in Buckinghamshire and occur in Domesday Book as the holdings of Queen Edith, widow of Edward the Confessor. Several were associated with Edith's thegn Beorhtric, including land at Marsworth, held in 1086 by Robert d'Oilly and thereafter by Miles Crispin (Stafford 1997, 131). Among Edith's dower lands was the manor of Newnham, later known as Newnham Murren, as seen in a charter of King Edgar of 966, which shows that Newnham then comprised the area of the modern parish of Crowmarsh Gifford (Gelling 1979, no. 277). This area was immediately opposite Wallingford and abutted the bridgehead of Wallingford land on the Oxfordshire side. In 1086 the manor of Newnham was much smaller, with Crowmarsh Gifford and North Stoke having been carved out of it; each was rated at 10 hides, as was Newnham in 966. Crowmarsh was in the hands of a major Norman tenant-in-chief, Walter Giffard, but Newnham and Stoke both belonged to Miles Crispin, as did two other Oxfordshire manors a short distance away at Chalgrove and Great Haseley (GDB, 157v, 159: *DB Oxon*, 20,3;35,2,10). Haseley had also been one of Edith's manors. Newnham had been held by Engelric, probably the royal priest who had worked for the Normans in supervising the redemption of their lands by the English. He is known as the founder of the minster of St Martin le Grand in London (Roffe above, p. 36). English queens were often associated with the royal boroughs and often patronized one of the minsters within them. The importance of Newnham can be seen in a passage in the Domesday borough account where the tenements of Miles Crispin in Newnham, Haseley, North Stoke, Chalgrove, Sutton

Courtenay and Bray are mentioned together. The first four were all substantial manors listed elsewhere in Domesday as part of the honour's lands. Miles had given tithes from all of them to Bec by 1087 or shortly after (*Regesta* Bates, no. 167). Later these holdings, apart from the last two, are associated together with the church of All Saints in Wallingford as prebends of the canons who serve the king's chapel in the castle, St Nicholas. An inquest of 1184 preserved in the Oseney Cartulary says that Miles established these prebends, which he may well have done (*Oseney Cartulary,* iv, 415). It is clear, as has been shown already for St Leonard, St Lucian and Holy Trinity, that there was a major re-organization of churches in Wallingford after 1066 (Roffe, pp. 36–8). Since the old palace site was reconfigured as the precinct of a Norman castle, the earlier Saxon royal chapel had to be replaced with a Norman one. Continuity of some sort reflected in the prebendal arrangement is not unlikely in view of the association between Newnham and Haseley with English queens. The occurrence of senior English clerics associated with ministers, such as Regenbald at Bray and Wallingford, as well as Engelric at Newnham, is unlikely to be coincidental.

All the holdings discussed so far are mapped on Figure 6.2, together with all the manors held in 1086 by either Robert d'Oilly or Miles Crispin, with no explicit reference to either Wigod or Toki in the Domesday text but which were holdings of the honour of Wallingford by about 1120, not long after Brien fitzCount's marriage to Matilda of Wallingford; many of these (with the exceptions noted below) are very likely to have been holdings of Wigod and his son. The Appendix below lists by predecessor group all the constituent parts of the honour, accompanied by Figure 6.4, which is a breakdown of the predecessors, either named or inferred by reason of succession from Robert to Miles, of 144 manors or parts thereof. Of these 21 (14.6%) had belonged to either Wigod or Toki; 61 (42%) to kinsmen or men of Wigod; 22 (15.3%) to Beorhtric; 7 manors had belonged to Earl Harold and 1 to Queen Edith (5.5%); of the remaining 32 (22%), most can be seen to be king's thegns holding with sake and soke (as indicated by the *tenuit* phrase). Only three manors do not obviously fit the pattern: it is unclear why the honour of Wallingford should have acquired d'Oilly's manors of Rissington and Lower Turkdean in Gloucestershire (GDB, 168v: *DB Gloucs,* 48,1–2), which was held in 1066 by the thegn Siward, who had no known connection with Wigod. The other was Watlington in Oxfordshire held in 1086 by Robert d'Oilly in succession to an unnnamed predecessor (GDB, 158: *DB Oxon,* 28,1). His nephew Robert II d'Oilly gave the advowson to his newly founded abbey of Oseney in 1129 (interestingly, the first prior (1138–54) then abbot of Oseney from 1154 until his death on 2 October 1158, was named Wigod). By 1166 it was a fee of the honour of Wallingford, held by the Breton Halinald de Bidun by grant of Henry II (*Boarstall Cartulary*, 322). If these really are anomalous holdings they are perhaps linked to Brien fitzCount's purchase of the office and part of the land of Nigel d'Oilly around 1129/30 (see above, p. 57).

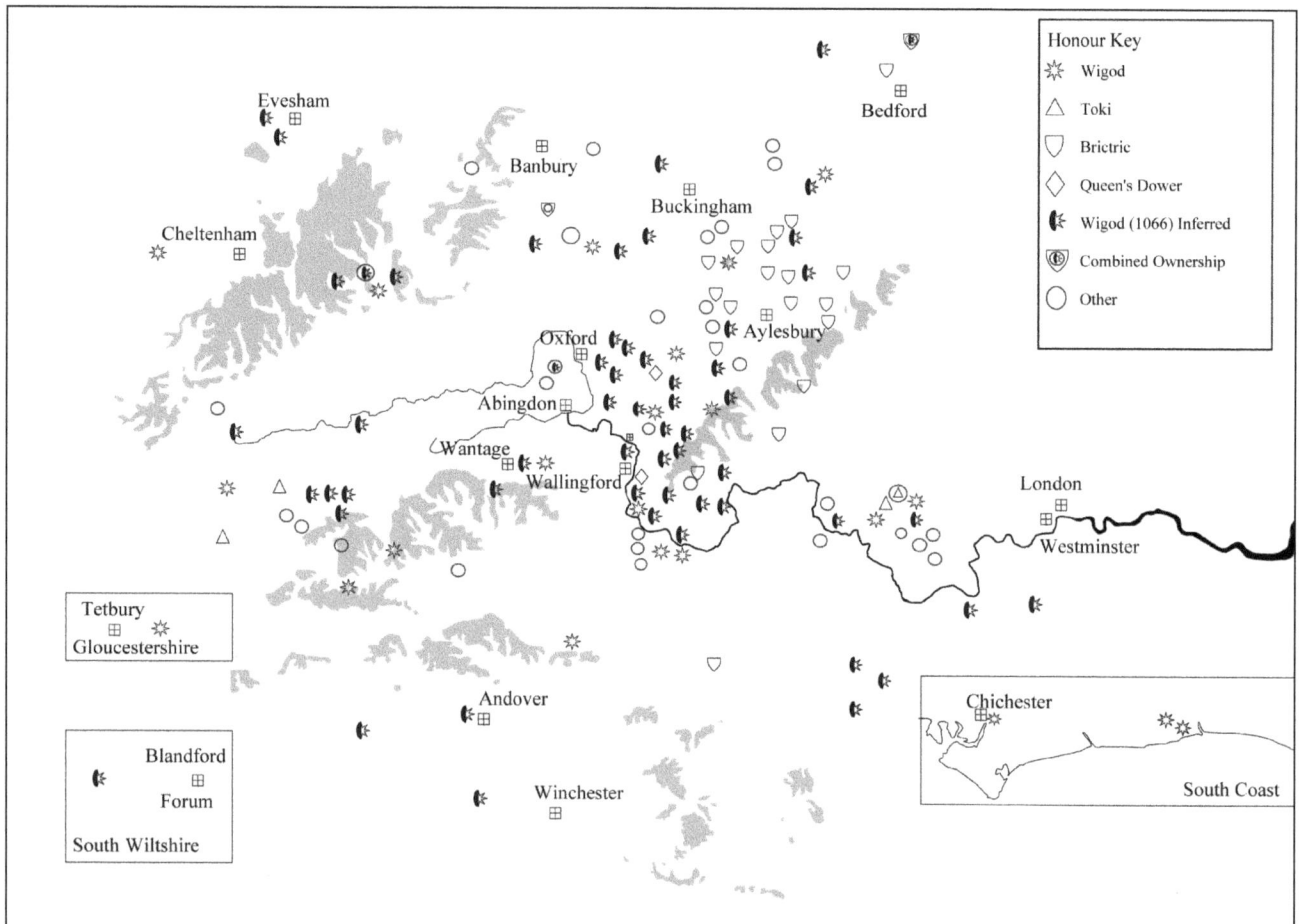

Figure 6.2 Location by predecessor 1066 of the manors of the honour of Wallingford *c.*1129.

Honour and proto-shire

Although so far we have seen no more than tantalizing hints of Wigod's background, cumulatively they add up to a clear picture of a man of influence and status as a royal servant and quite probably a royal kinsman, in the reigns of Edward, Harold and William. The distribution of his holdings shows a man actively connected with the king's service in Wallingford and its vicinity, and with a number of holdings within easy reach of other royal centres such as Westminster, Windsor, Oxford and Gloucester. In its association with queenly dower lands, something of the significance of Wallingford as a royal *burh* and borough has begun to emerge. In 1066 Wallingford was the chief town of Berkshire, which had formed part of the earldom of Wessex, held after 1052 by Harold Godwinesson. Earl Harold had held a relatively modest 11 manors, including the great complex at Faringdon, which straddled the borders of Wiltshire and Oxfordshire (Hooper 1988, 8–9; GDB, 58: *DB Berks*, 1,44). Unlike many other shires, the pre-eminence of royal rather than comital authority in Berkshire was a marked feature of the 11th century. As we have suggested, the bulk of what made up the lands held by Wigod and his family and successors was probably royal bookland (land granted hereditarily but indivisibly) or loanland, i.e. given for a fixed term of perhaps three lives, with reversion to royal control firmly envisaged. We should now look again at the distribution of Wallingford lands, this time in relation to both royal power and the function of Wallingford as a military and administrative base.

To start with we shall look at Wallingford holdings along the Thames, starting below the episcopal town of Dorchester at Shillingford. At this date and probably long before, the rich agricultural area between the river at Shillingford and the northern defences of Wallingford comprised the area known as Clapcot, which occurs as two manors held as one by Miles Crispin as of the honour of Wallingford. The link between Clapcot and the castle precinct was probably ancient, going back at least to the founding of the *burh*, if not earlier: the 'cot' element suggests a small settlement dependent upon a larger one. The area contained the borough or hundred moot hall, according to a fourteenth-century charter (*Boarstal Cartulary*, 248, no. 708), but is generally poorly understood. The recent discovery of a monumental earthwork running across it, discussed in this book by Matthew Edgeworth (pp. 83–4), potentially offers a key to understanding the topography of the *burh* and any precursor in this area. It may also provide an explanation for the name Clapcot, or 'cottages by the hill', which has puzzled philologists on topographical grounds (Gelling 1974, 536–7). Late thirteenth-century documents refer to it as the hamlet attached to the castle (*CIPM* 3, 465, no. 604). Its rich farmland was used to support knights of the honour attached to the castle (eg. Bodleian, Berks Charter, 2). Five sergeanties relating to service at the castle pertained to the honour in 1212 (*BF*, 120), including that of Robert de Basinges who held 3 virgates in return for his services as a chef; in 1292 his successor John de Basinges and his heirs were amongst those who sold their holding (60 acres) in Clapcot to William de Bereford, favourite of the earls of Cornwall, then lords of the honour (*Boarstall Cartulary*, no. 734). As we have seen, it lay within the parish of All Saints, the church of which was sited within the borough of Wallingford, outside the walls of the castle on its western flank (Dewey above, p. 25). The castle itself was extra parochial and was served by its own royal free chapel of St Nicholas. On the opposite bank, on the Oxfordshire side, Warborough was then represented by Watcombe, held partly by Miles Crispin and partly by Robert d'Oilly (GDB, 159v, 161: *DB Oxon*, 35,39;59,4).

Moving south, Benson in Oxfordshire and Cholsey in Berkshire, were both substantial royal manors. Newnham belonged to Wallingford, as did North Stoke. Crowmarsh was then held by a major tenant-in-chief, Walter Giffard (GDB, 157v, 159v: *DB Oxon*, 20,3;35,10–11), who also held Long Wittenham, part of which included tenements in Wallingford (GDB, 56, 60: *DB Berks*, B1;20,3). Streatley was held by Geoffrey de Mandeville, constable of London, who had been given the lands and ministry of Esger the staller (GDB, 62: *DB Berks*, 38,6). Wigod, doubtless also a staller, had held a large manor of 30 hides at Goring on the opposite bank, held still by Robert d'Oilly in 1086 but after 1091 by the honour of Wallingford. It included also Gatehampton, held by Miles Crispin (GDB, 158, 159: *DB Oxon*, 28,2;35,1). The king held Basildon, whilst both the king and Miles Crispin had manors at Pangbourne (GDB, 157v, 158: *DB Berks*, 1,28,44;33,1). Miles also held Whitchurch and Mapledurham, and a hide in Tilehurst (GDB, 159, 61v: *DB Oxon*, 35,8–9; *DB Berks*, 33,9). Purley and Fulscot were manors held in 1086 by Ralph fitzSeifrid which were soon afterwards joined to the honour of Wallingford, as discussed above. One of Ralph's holdings was Clewer, of which half a hide had been subtracted for the building of a royal castle at Windsor, a day's ride from London, moving away from the Saxon palace site of Old Windsor (GDB, 62v: *DB Berks*, 49,1).

The borough of Reading was held by the king. On the opposite bank lay Walter Giffard's manor of Caversham, which included three tenements in the borough of Wallingford (GDB, 56, 58, 157v: *DB Berks*, B9;1,41; *DB Oxon*, 20,1). Apart from a handful of manors in Surrey and Middlesex offering easy access to Westminster and Southwark, this was the furthest reach of the honour of Wallingford along the banks of the Thames, except for a single acre and 11 dwellings at Bray, just above Windsor at the foot of another great angle in the river (GDB, 56, 57: *DB Berks*, B2;1,22). This angle takes in the important royal minster town of Cookham, just outside which another of the Alfredan *burhs* was situated on the island of Shaftesy (now called Sashes).

In looking at these maps we notice in general a strong concentration of Wallingford lands in Oxfordshire, rather than in the county of which it was the county town in 1086. The pattern of holdings stretching from what is now Shillingford Bridge down to Reading is very marked. If we now map (Figure 6.3) the holdings of the king in Berkshire we see what has so far been wanting to make a coherent picture of the honour of Wallingford. Berkshire was indeed a peculiarly royal county, but as a borough Wallingford appears most closely connected with West Berkshire (with

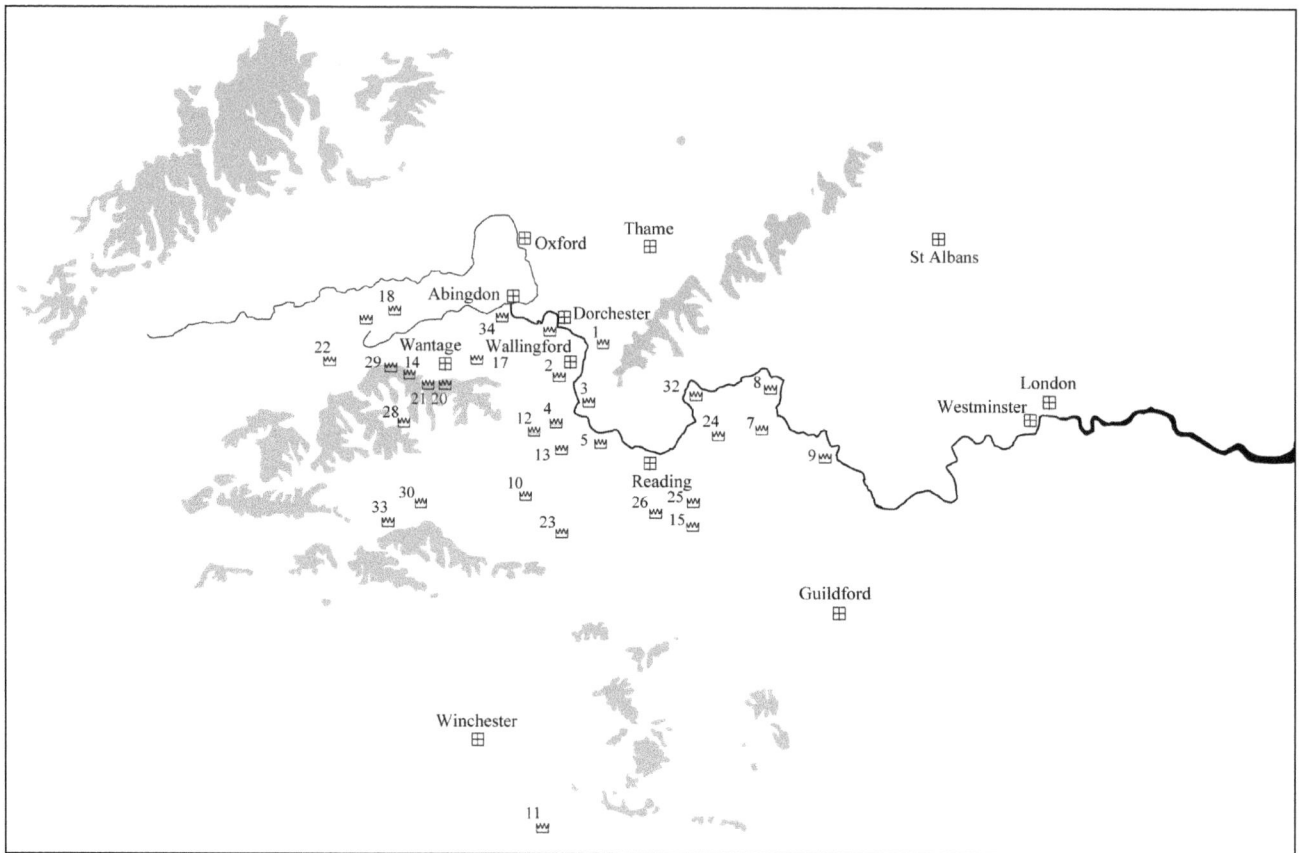

Figure 6.3 Royal manors in Berkshire and vicinity of Wallingford in 1086.

estates that straddled the border with Wiltshire in the west) and a part of Oxfordshire across the boundary formed by the Thames, rather than a unified west and east Berkshire. The area reflects in some sense the 'territory' of Wallingford. The strong connexion of the constituent manors of this territory and the later honour with the king, the queen and certain close and powerful kin such as Earl Harold is thus all the more striking. The east-west split in the shire has been noted before, for example by Margaret Gelling (1974) in her discussion of Berkshire place names, and by John Blair, who sees east Berkshire, dominated by Sonning and Reading, as once having formed part of a lost sub-kingdom which included Surrey (Blair 1989, 100). David Roffe (above pp. 42–4) has already discussed the possible origins of this striking configuration in terms of the provisions of the Burghal Hidage system at a time before the final shape of the shires had been fixed, at some point in the 10th or early 11th century, and suggested that the three key *burhs* defended the Middle Thames, probably each of them with attached territories that straddled both sides of the river.

The burghal system had its origins in the need to defend a key strategic area, dominating an important point on one of the major river systems in the kingdom of Wessex and subsequently that of England. The same strategic importance was as evident to the Danish Cnut in the early 11th century, as it was to his stepson Edward and then to William in 1066. Surprisingly, perhaps, the origin of the post-Conquest honour of Wallingford should be sought in the territory, dominated by royal holdings, that had surrounded it since its inception as a *burh* in the late 9th century. Wigod was claimed as a royal kinsman in a writ of King Edward, as

presumably his father also had been. Although the succession from Robert to Miles was effected through the marriage links between first Robert and Wigod's daughter, and then Miles and Wigod's granddaughter, the honour of Wigod and that of his successors was less a family inheritance than a deliberately created eleventh-century Anglo-Danish 'castlery' placed under the command of trustworthy kinsmen, possibly one that formalized an existing arrangement, originally based in defence and communication, that went back to the founding of the *burh*. Although the term 'castlery' is strictly accurate only after the castle was built, it aptly describes the function of Wallingford and its territory from the beginning. A parallel example is afforded by the royal borough of Nottingham. In an earlier work Roffe suggested that the post-Conquest honour at first sight has the look of a deliberated created Norman 'castlery' formed from the lands surrounding the city previously held by the disgraced Earl Tostig (brother of Harold) and held after 1066 by William Peverel, but which in fact appears to be a typical grant based on the holdings of Earl Tostig and his thegns, with the accompanying rights of sake and soke. Before the conquest of the East Midlands from the Danes by Alfred's son Edward the Elder, Nottingham was something of a backwater of little significance. Thereafter it became an important frontier town, a role it retained throughout the Middle Ages (Roffe 1997). Nottingham, like Wallingford, was in a key strategic location that formed a crucial link between Yorkshire and the North and the heart of Mercia. The major reorganization of the 960s also saw its territory extended to include Derby and its shire, as well as Rutland, where much of the English queens' dower lands were located. Its territory was bolstered by its union with the neighbouring county of Derbyshire; although they remained distinct entities they were administered by a single sheriff. Stamford provides another interesting parallel (Roffe 1997; Roffe and Mahany 1986).

The parallels do not end there. After the death of Miles Crispin in 1107, his widow Matilda was remarried to Henry I's favourite Brien fitzCount (at least according to the account of the burgesses in an inquest of 1212 [*BF*, 116], though she must have been somewhat older than Brien and unlikely, as proved to be the case, to have been able to bear him a child). Brien was fabulously wealthy at the king's death in 1135, having been pardoned many of the customs owed on his lands, especially Danegeld, and having received further grants such as the honour of Abergavenny. A colourful and quixotic character of evident charisma, he was fiercely loyal to Henry's daughter and intended successor, the Empress Matilda, giving away his honour of Abergavenny to Miles of Gloucester in gratitude for the aid Miles had extended in helping to defeat one of the usurper King Stephen's attacks on Wallingford. Eventually, either injured, terminally ill or simply weary, he retired to a monastery, very probably nearby Reading Abbey, founded by Henry I and where that king's heart was interred. His wife retired to the vicinity of Bec soon afterwards. They surrendered the honour of Wallingford, together with the castle, to the Empress's son Henry duke of Normandy (*BF*, 116), who finally raised the siege of the castle in 1153 and was accepted as his successor by King Stephen. After his succession in 1154 Henry took several major baronial castles into his own hands, and ordered the destruction of those thrown up during Stephen's reign (Brown 1989, 90–121). Wallingford, both castle and honour, had already been re-absorbed into crown lands. Nottingham castle was taken back into royal custody, and its former constable, William Peverel II, declared forfeit of his honour for his poisoning of Ranulf earl of Chester, in 1155. When Henry's son and successor Richard I left for the Third Crusade in 1191, he granted the honours of Wallingford and Peverel to his younger brother John, but he deliberately withheld the grant of the castles, since these would have given him too much power.

By the time of the inquests that led to the writing of the Hundred Rolls between 1255 and 1279/80, both honours clearly emerge as important liberties; Wallingford was *libertas honoris Warengefordie* (e.g., *Rot. Hund.* i, 9, 33, 42–3; ii, 6, 31, 777). A liberty was a collection of franchises, each of which represented a concession of some sort, whether freedom from certain dues and customs, other franchises associated with sake and soke such as the assize of bread and ale, or view of frankpledge. Rather more impressive was the liberty known as return of writs (*retornum brevium*), which entitled a baron to charge his own men with the execution of the king's writs, rather than admit the king's sheriff to his lands. Wallingford, then held by the king's brother Richard earl of Cornwall and king of Germany, and Peverel were among the few honours (others being Leicester and Warenne) to hold this franchise. The lists of the franchises that made up the liberty of the honour of Wallingford in the Hundred Rolls are indeed impressive. Even more impressive is the appearance of the honour, then

still in the hands of Henry II himself, in the Assize of Clarendon of 1164 (*EHD*, 440–43). This was a piece of legislation of the law and order sort; it established a routine circuit of justices in eyre and initiated trial by jury; it demanded that all communities and jurisdictions should cooperate with the king's officials in the pursuit of wrongdoers, and that this should apply 'even in the honour of Wallingford', a phrase twice repeated in the document. No other honour was mentioned. Bearing in mind that the king himself held the honour, this twice-repeated clause is telling evidence of the scale of the liberty that already attached to the honour, and that it was probably already of some antiquity, perhaps even going back before 1066. It is worth noting that whenever the honour was granted after Henry II's time it was always granted as the honour of Wallingford and its castle, followed by a separate grant of the royal borough. This may have been the case when the honour and castle were granted to Brien fitzCount, since he accounted for the farm of the borough in the Pipe Roll of 31 Henry I (p.139) for 1129–30. The burgesses had suffered greatly during the civil war of Stephen's reign since the castle that so dominated the town and all their lives, was several times besieged. In recognition of their great support for his pursuit of his inheritance, Henry II granted them an extensive charter of liberties in 1155. Among the franchises granted was the right to have the town reeves render account for the farm of the borough, rather than the king's sheriff, a right they claimed to have enjoyed since the time of King Edward. Quite possibly they did have privileges going back to that time: Tait pointed out in 1936 that the Domesday texts showing that the reeve was forbidden to provide food out of the king's *census* for burgesses doing carrying services to royal manors suggests that the reeve was farming the borough; moreover, as soon as the Pipe Roll series begin (with 31 Henry I), the borough was farmed separately from the county; though the farmers varied – it was Brien fitzCount who answered for the farm in 1129/30 – it was normally never farmed by the sheriff (Tait 1936, 148). Liberties relating to freedom from dues and privileged trading conditions were compared in the charter text to those enjoyed by the king's burgesses of Winchester. At the time only London had a wider range of privileges than those granted to Wallingford (Tait 1936, 227–8; cf. *EHD*, pp. 1012–1045).

Conclusion

In conclusion, then, the Norman honour of Wallingford looked both to the past and to the future. Its origins seem clearly to have lain in a territory composed of royal lands assembled for defensive purposes at the time of the *burh*'s creation. Its links with royalty continued throughout its existence. The fate of the town or borough of Wallingford and its people was for centuries intimately bound up with the castle and hence with the honour. Surviving the horrors of the Black Death of 1348, the town's real nadir was reached in the 16th century when Henry VIII, who disliked the then unfashionable and ruinous castle, demoted Wallingford and its honour to become an appendage of the manor of Ewelme, not to mention the vandalism of the Dissolution which saw the destruction of Holy Trinity Priory.

Acknowledgements

I am grateful to Judy Dewey and David Roffe for many stimulating discussions of Wallingford's early history, and to June Strong for producing Figures 6.2 and 6.3.

Appendix. Analysis of honour of Wallingford holdings 1066–*c*.1129

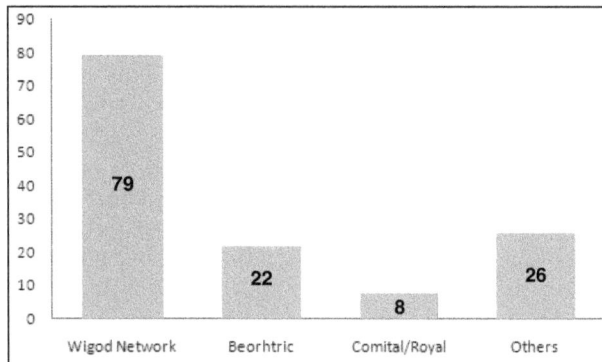

Figure 6.4 Analysis by predecessor in 1066 of the principal holdings of the honour *c*.1129.

Breakdown of honour holdings: abbreviations used

ER   Earl Roger
MC   Miles Crispin
RO   Robert d'Oilly
TIC Tenant-in-chief
+   standard county abbreviations

The tables are primarily concerned with the holdings known or likely to have been held by Wigod or members of his family. They illustrate the Latin of the Domesday text, showing where the 1066 holder's privileges associated with sake and soke can be clearly seen in the simple *X tenuit [de rege]* formula. The names of the holders in 1066 are sometimes omitted in Domesday Book, as in 14 entries in Table 3.

Table 1. Manors Held by Wigod in 1066 (* manors that did not pass to the honour).

DB Ref	Manor	TIC 1086	Wigot 1066	Tenant 1086
GDB, 26v: DB Ss 12,21	Aldrington*	William de Warenne	Wigot tenuit de rege	Godfrey
GDB, 28v: DB Ss 11,15	Bepton + site in Chichester*	ER	Wigot tenuit de rege	Geoffrey
GDB, 129: DB Mx 7,4	Harlington	ER	Wigot tenuit	Alfred/Olaf
GDB, 129: DB Mx 7,5	Colham	ER	Wigot tenuit de rege	ER
GDB, 71: DB Wl 28,12	Manton	MC	Wigod tenuit	Rainald
GDB, 71: DB Wl 28,9	Rodbourne Cheney	MC	Wigod tenuit	Rainald
GDB, 150: DB Bu 23,12	Quainton	MC	Wigot de Walingeford tenuit	MC
GDB, 150: DB Bu 23,7	Shabbington	MC	Wigot de Walingeford tenuit	MC
GDB , 169v: DB Gl 64,3	Alderley	MC	Wigot tenuit	MC
GDB , 169v: DB Gl 64, 1	Brawn	MC	Wigot tenuit	MC
GDB, 159v: DB Ox 35,18	Chesterton	MC	Wigot tenuit	William
GDB, 159v: DB Ox 35,31	Cuxham	MC	Wigot tenuit	Alfred
GDB, 159: DB Ox 35,1	Gatehampton in Goring	MC	Wigot tenuit	MC
GDB, 61v: DB Bk 33,9	Langley in Tilehurst	MC	Leuuard et non potuit ire quolibet absque licentia Wigoti	Leofweard
GDB,62: DB Bk 41,2	Letcombe Basset	RO	Wigot de rege	RO
GDB, 158: DB Ox 28,2	Goring	RO	Wigot tenuit	
GDB, 23v: DB Ss 11,15	Broadwater*	William of Braose	Wigot tenuit de rege	Robert

Table 2. Manors held in 1066 by Toki.

DB ref	Manor	TIC 1086	Toki 1966	Holder 1086
GDB, 129: DB Middlx, 7,8	Ickenham	ER	Tochi Huscarl Edwardi	various
GDB, 149: DB Bucks, 19,1	Iver	RO	Tochi teignus regis tenuit	RO of his wife's fee
GDB, 71: DB Wilts, 28,8	Brinkworth	MC	Tochi tenuit	Humphrey
GDB, 73: DB Wilts, 62,1	Chippenham	Rainald Canute	Toki	Rainald Canute

Table 3. Manors having clear or inferable connection with Wigod in 1066 (* manors that did not pass to the honour).

DB ref	Manor	TIC 1086	Holder 1066	Holder 1086
GDB, 150: DB Bucks, 23,8	Ickford	MC		Richard
GDB 159v: DB Oxon 35,32	Alkerton	MC		MC
GDB, 159v: DB Oxon, 35,27	Kingston Blount	MC		Humphrey
GDB, 159: DB Oxon, 35,4	Kingston Blount	MC		MC
GDB, 159v: DB Oxon, 35,28	Nethercote	MC		Tovi
GDB, 159v: DB Oxon, 35,30	Watcombe	MC		Geoffrey
GDB, 159v: DB Oxon, 35,26	Harpsden	MC		Alfred
GDB, 159v: DB Oxon, 35,16	Draycot	MC		Richard
GDB, 159v: DB Oxon, 35,5	Nethercote	MC		MC
GDB, 159v: DB Oxon, 35,8	Mapledurham	MC		MC
GDB, 159v: DB Oxon, 35,15	Thomley	MC		Roger
GDB, 159v: DB Oxon, 35,33	Swyncombe	MC		monks Bec
GDB, 159v: DB Oxon, 35,29	Garsington	MC		Toli
GDB, 158: DB Oxon, 28,17	Stratton Audley	RO		Alward
GDB, 158: DB Oxon, 28,12	Heyford	RO		Roger
GDB, 158v: DB Oxon, 28,23	Rousham	RO		Rainald
GDB, 158: DB Oxon, 41,10	Wheatfield	RO		Peter
GDB, 158: DB Oxon, 28,5	Bicester	RO		RO
GDB, 212: DB Bd, 19,2	Milton Earnest	MC	duo liberi	MC
GDB, 71: DB Wl, 28,6	Walcot	MC	Alnod tenuit et Leuenot tenuit	Rainbald
GDB, 159: DB Oxon, 35,3	Aston Rowant	MC	Aluric et uoluit ire potuit	MC
GDB, 129: DB Mx, 7,3	Harmondsworth	ER	Aluuin homo Wigot	ER
GDB, 50v: DB Hm 69,40	Clere Privet	MC	Aluuinus tenuit sub Wigoto pro tuitione	Aluuinus sub Milone
GDB, 225: DB Nth, 28,2	Thenford	RO	Azor tenuit libere	Roger
GDB, 71: DB Wl, 28,10	Chedglow	MC	duo taini tenuerunt	Siward
GDB, 159: DB Oxon, 35,10	North Stoke	MC	Eduin tenuit	MC
GDB, 62: DB Bk, 41,4	Ardington	RO	Edwin liber homo	RO
GDB, 129: DB Mx, 7,7	Dawley	ER	Godwin Alfit homo Wigoti tenuit	Alnoth
GDB, 71: DB Wl, 28,10	Walcot	MC	Leofnoth	
GDB, 166v: DB Gl, 27,1	Hampton Meysey	ER	Leofnoth tenuit	Turold nepos Wigot
GDB, 61v: DB Bk, 33,5	Betterton	MC	Leofric monachus [Wigod usurped -Ab Chron]	William
GDB, 71: DB Wl, 28,1	Wootton Basset	MC	Leuenod tenuit	MC
GDB, 71: DB Wl, 28,13	Draycot Foliat	MC	Leuenot tenuit	Rainald
GDB, 71: DB Wl, 28,1	Hazelbury	MC	Leuenot tenuit	Rainald
GDB, 159v: DB Oxon, 35,20	Henton	MC	Leuenot tenuit	William
GDB, 159: DB Oxon, 35,9	Whitchurch	MC	Leuric et Aluuinus libere tenuerunt	MC
GDB, 150: DB Bucks, 23,11	Hollingdon	MC	non uendere	Nigel
GDB, 159: DB Oxon, 35,24	Berrick Salome	MC	Ordgar et pater suus et auunculus tenuerunt libere	Ordgar
GDB, 159: DB Oxon, 35,25	Gangsdown in Nuffield	MC	Ordgar et pater suus et auunculus tenuerunt libere	Ordgar
GDB, 150: DB Bucks, 23,33	Wavendon	MC	Ordwig	Almar of Wootton
GDB, 34v: DB Sr, 18,4	Loseley*	ER	Osmund tenuit de rege	Turold [nepos Wigoti]
GDB, 34v: DB Sr, 18,3	Worplesdon*	ER	Osmund tenuit de rege	Turold [nepos Wigoti]
GDB, 34v: DB Sr, 18,2	Burpham *	ER	Osmund tenuit de rege	Turold [nepos Wigoti], Godric
GDB, 44v: DB Hm, 21,5	Houghton*	ER	Osmund tenuit de rege	Turold [nepos Wigoti]
GDB 68v: DB Wl 21,2	Milston	ER	Osmundus |tainus| tenuit TRE	Turold [nepos Wigoti]
GDB 68v: DB Wl 21,1	Castle Easton	ER	Osmundus |tainus| tenuit TRE	Turold [nepos Wigoti]
GDB 44c: DB Hm 21,3	Penton Mewsey	ER	Osmundus tenuit in alodium de rege Edwardo pro manerio	Turold [nepos Wigoti]
GDB, 218: DB Bd, 19,3	Thurleigh	RO	Ouiet teignus regis et uendere potuit	Richard Basset
GDB, 61v: DB Bk, 33,4	Clapcot	MC	Safford liber homo	Harold
GDB, 62: DB Bk, 41,5	Ardington	RO	Sauuinus liber homo	RO
GDB, 159: DB Oxon, 35,13	Cowley	MC	Toli libere tenuit	Toli
GDB, 159: DB Oxon, 35,6	Chalgrove	MC	Turchil libere tenuit	MC
GDB, 129: DB Mx, 7,6	Hillingdon	ER	Vlf et potuit de eo facere quod uoluit	ER
GDB, 159: DB Oxon, 35,3	Aston Rowant	MC	Vlstan libere tenuit	MC
GDB, 159: DB Oxon, 35,7	Rotherfield Peppard	MC	Vluric libere tenuit	MC
GDB, 159: DB Oxon, 35,22	Britwell Salome	MC	Wlstanus libere tenuit	Amalric
GDB, 61v: DB Bk, 33,3	Clapcot	MC	Wulfnoth liber homo	MC
GDB, 159: DB Oxon, 35,21	Adwell	MC	Wulstanus libere tenuit	William

Table 4. Manors held by Beorhtric or his men in 1066.

DB ref	Manor	TiC 1086	Beorhtric or his men 1066
GDB, 137v: DB Herts, 19,1	Tiscott	RO	duo homines Brictrici
GDB, 150: DB Bucks 23,18	Soulbury	MC	Almar homo Brictrici non potuit uendere
GDB, 149: DB Bucks, 23,22	Wingrave	MC	Almarus homo Brictric et uendere potuit
GDB, 149: DB Bucks, 19,20	Wycombe	RO	Brictric tenuit de regina
GDB, 150: DB Bucks 23,21	Wingrave	MC	Brictric homo regine uendere potuit
GDB, 150: DB Bucks 23,14	Waddesdon	MC	Brictric homo regina tenuit
GDB 149v: DB Bucks 19, 4	Marsworth	RO	Brictric tainus regis tenuit uendere potuit
GDB, 150v: DB Bucks 23,29	Stewkley	MC	Brictric teignus regis tenuit et uendere potuit
GDB 159v: DB Oxon 35,14	Somerton	MC	Brictric tenuit
GDB 159v: DB Oxon 35,12	Wainhill	MC	Brictric tenuit
GDB 150: DB Bucks 23,23	Littlecote	MC	Herch homo Brictrici et uendere potuit
GDB 150: DB Bucks 23,13	Beachendon	MC	homo Brictric et homo Azoris et uendere potuerunt
GDB, 150: DB Bucks 23,21	Wingrave	MC	Lemar homo Brictric et uendere potuit
GDB, 212: DB Beds 19,3	Thurleigh	MC	Leofric homo Brixtrici et uendere potuit
GDB, 151: DB Bucks 35,3	Burston	MC	Leofsi homo Brictrici
GDB 150v: DB Bucks 23,28	Horton	MC	Leofsi homo Brictrici et uendere potuit
GDB, 150: DB Bucks 23,26	Pitstone	MC	Leofsi homo Brictrici et uendere potuit
GDB, 150: DB Bucks 23,27	Pitstone	MC	Leofsi homo Brictrici et uendere potuit
GDB, 150: DB Bucks 23,24	Hardwick	MC	Osulf homo Brictric et uendere potuit
GDB, 150: DB Bucks 23, 17	Marston	MC	Seric homo Brictrici et uendere potuit
GDB, 150: DB Bucks 23, 11	Shortley	MC	teigni homines Brictrici et uendere potuerunt
GDB, 150: DB Bucks 23, 06	Aston	MC	Vluric et Coleman homines Brictrici tenuerunt et uendere potuerunt

Table 5. Comital or royal manors 1066

DB ref	Manor	TIC 1086	Tenant 1066	Tenant 1086
GDB, 129v: DB Bu, 23,2	Dorney	MC	Aldred homo Morcari comitis tenuit et uendere potuit	Ralph
GDB, 129v: DB Bu, 23,5	Saunderton	MC	Alric homo Heraldi comitis tenuit	Osbert
GDB, 129v: DB Bu, 23,1	Upton	MC	Alricus teignus tenuit	Alric
GDB, 71: DB Wl 28,1	Clyffe Pypard	MC	Harold [comes] tenuit	Humphrey
GDB, 150: DB Bu, 23,10	Chearsley	MC	tenuit Alden homo Haraldi et uendere potuit	Richard
GDB, 71: DB Wl 28,2	Chilton Foliat	MC	Heraldus comes tenuit	Rainald
GDB, 71: DB Wl, 28,11	Ogbourne	MC	Heraldus comes tenuit	MC
GDB, 159: DB Ox, 28,11	Haseley	MC	Edith regina	MC

Table 6. Manors held by thegns not known to be connected with Wigod's family

DB Ref	Manor Name	TIC 1086	Tenant 1066	Tenant 1086
GDB, 129: DB, Middx 7,1	Hatton	ER	duo sochemanni Alberti Lothariensis	ER
GDB, 129: DB, Middx 7,8	Ickenham	ER	Aluuinus homo Vlsi filius Manni	3 men and an Englishman
GDB, 218: DB Bd, 28,2	Thurleigh	RO	Aluuinus homo Wluui episcopi et uendere potuit	Salomon priest
GBD 159v: DB Oxon 35,17	Marsh Baldon	MC	Azur tenuit	Geoffrey
GDB 61v: DB Berks 33.2	Sulham	MC	Baldwin de rege	William
GDB 61v: DB Berks 33.1	Pangbourne	MC	Baldwin de rege	William
GBD 159v: DB Oxon 35,19	Heyford	MC	Besi libere tenuit	Ralph
GDB 150v: DB Bucks 23,32	Stantonbury	MC	Bisi teignus regis tenuit et uendere potuit	Ralph
GDB 61v: DB Berks 33.7	Eaton	MC	Bosi tenuit de rege	Alfred
GDB 71: DB Wiltss 28,2	Littlecott	MC	Godric tenuit	Turchetil
GDB 61v: DB Berks 33.6	Appleton	MC	Halden tenuit	Richard
GDB 61v: DB Berks 33.8	Eaton	MC	Halden tenuit de rege	Richard
GDB 169v: DB Glocs 64,2	Cherington	MC	Haminc tenuit de rege	Geoffrey
GDB 149v: DB Bucks 23,3	Hitcham	MC	Haming teignus tenuit et uendere potuit	Ralph and Roger
GDB 150: DB Bucks 23,15	E Claydon	MC	duo homines Haming et uendere potuerunt	same
GBD 159v: DB Oxon 35,11	Newnham Murren	MC	Ingelri tenuit	MC
GBD 159v: DB Oxon 35,34	Somerton	MC	Ketel tenuit	Rainald
GDB 150v: DB Bucks 23,30	Addington	MC	Leofwin homo Edwini tenuit et uendere potuit	Edwulf

DB Ref	Manor Name	TIC 1086	Tenant 1066	Tenant 1086
GDB 36v: DB Surry 29,2	Chessington	MC	Magnus Swarthy	MC
GDB 150v: DB Bucks 23,31	Bradwell	MC	Sibi et Goduin homines Alrici filii Goding et uendere potuerunt	William [fitz Turold]
GDB 168v: DB Gloucs 48,1	Little Rissington	RO	Siuuardus tenuit	RO
GDB 168v: DB Gloucs 48,2	Upper Turkdean	RO	Siuuardus tenuit	RO
GDB 36v: DB Surrey 29,1	Beddington	MC	Vlf tenuit de rege	William fitz Turold
GDB 129: DB Middx 7,8	Ickenham	ER	duo liberi Vluuardi	
GDB 150: DB Bucks 23,9	Ashendon	MC	Wichinus vendere potuit	Viking

NEW DIRECTIONS IN TRACING THE ORIGINS AND DEVELOPMENT OF WALLINGFORD:
Targets and Results of the Wallingford Burh to Borough Research Project

Oliver Creighton, Neil Christie, Matt Edgeworth and *Helena Hamerow*

Abstract

Combining new fieldwork and excavation with re-analysis of the archives of past archaeological investigations, the Wallingford *Burh* to Borough Research Project is shedding new light on the origins and evolving townscape of medieval Wallingford. With the current programme of fieldwork scheduled to end in 2011, this paper introduces the key issues and research questions that are being tackled. How much is really known about Wallingford's evolution and how big are the gaps in archaeological knowledge? What are the challenges of unravelling the archaeology of a small town such as Wallingford? The methodologies used are also explained and some preliminary findings discussed.

Keywords

Anglo-Saxon; Anglo-Norman; Berkshire; Wallingford; urbanism; *burh*.

Introduction

Since 2002, the Wallingford *Burh* to Borough Research Project has been addressing the rich archaeology of Wallingford with the aim of developing a major case study of the transformation of a medieval townscape. While the fieldwork is focused on Wallingford and its immediate hinterland, the qualities of Wallingford's archaeology are such that the project aims ultimately to use this case-study as a platform for modelling urban processes more generally in the key period *c.* 800–1300 AD, thus spanning the Saxo-Norman transition. While scholarship has tended to divide the archaeology of this period into watertight pre- and post-Conquest categories, the project aims to look at processes of urban transformation across this supposed divide. Furthermore, the work is intended as a testing ground to pioneer and refine methodologies for unravelling the development of medieval small towns, which represent something of a lacuna in our overall understanding of the urban process.

The project has grown from relatively small-scale beginnings, involving archival work alongside keyhole excavations and limited topographical and geophysical survey (Creighton *et al.* 2002; Christie *et al.* 2003; 2004a; 2004b), to a major endeavour, funded by the Arts and Humanities Research Council, which involves university researchers and professional archaeologists working in tandem with local stakeholders, including historical, archaeological and conservation bodies. Running from 2008 through to 2011, the project will integrate the findings of several phases of archaeological survey, excavation and buildings analysis within the town alongside more selective fieldwork in its hinterland. This short paper sets out the key issues and research questions that the project is tackling through fieldwork and excavation, and outlines some of the preliminary findings (for 2008 work, see http://www2.le.ac.uk/projects/wallingford_dig_2008).

The Archaeological Context

Wallingford has long been regarded as a 'classic' site by medieval archaeologists. Aerial views of the town that show the familiar rectangular plan of the embanked and ditched medieval defences – their perimeter especially visible because of the large open spaces immediately inside – have appeared frequently in general books on medieval British archaeology (see, for example, Beresford and St Joseph 1958, 195–7). The town is portrayed as a classic late Saxon *burh*, founded on a highly strategic location next to a crossing of the Thames near the border between Wessex and Mercia, its rectangular defences comparable to Wareham in Dorset and Cricklade in Wiltshire and embracing an area second in size only to the great former Roman centre of Winchester. The earliest defences of Wallingford have traditionally been seen as Alfredian, that is late 9th century, in date and the gridded street network also the product of a *de novo* foundation that provided a bubble of stability, commerce and defence in the face of Viking threats in the late 9th century (Biddle 1976, 126–30). The Domesday reference to a compact royal estate notionally equivalent to eight yardlands is taken as a further indication of a deliberate foundation of the king like that at Oxford (Stenton 1947, 522). Yet despite Wallingford's apparently high profile in Anglo-Saxon studies, there are surprisingly few hard published archaeological data to support and sustain this well-known story.

Wallingford may be unique in its potential to illuminate our understanding of urban form and growth in the late Saxon period. The late-medieval and post-medieval fortunes of the town have left a settlement whose present-day topography is punctuated by substantial open spaces, meaning that the historic core within the defences is not entirely urban in character but broken up by zones of recreational and park land and rough grazing. Unlike its neighbour Oxford, this historical accident means that quite large areas within the town defences are amenable to archaeological investigation. Sub-surface geophysical survey has massive potential to reveal 'lost' features such as buildings and roads, while the absence of post-medieval development ensures that earlier archaeological deposits are likely to survive well. The findings of a series of important but largely unpublished excavations in and around the urban area in the 1960s and 70s have enormous value in this regard (Brooks 1965; 1966; 1968). Further, an important fifth- and sixth-century Anglo-Saxon cemetery, examined in some detail in the 1930s, lies on the south-west urban fringe, just outside the line of the ramparts (Leeds 1938; see also Hamerow, *passim*). The distinct impression of pre-*burh* occupation in the vicinity is heightened by a striking array of stray archaeological finds. The remarkable volume of Roman coins recovered from the town has been long recognized (Field 1925, 5). A search of the Oxfordshire Historic Environment Record reveals a plethora of records for Roman antiquities recovered principally from gardens and the River Thames; they include figurines, lamps and keys alongside coins, pottery and tiles, as well as Bronze Age and Iron Age finds. Furthermore, the fine quality of documentation and the survival of a good stock of historic urban and ecclesiastical buildings combine to single out Wallingford as a superb testing ground for debates on the nature of medieval urban growth and decline more generally.

Collating and re-analysing the archives of past excavations that are invariably imperfectly recorded and employ different systems and conventions brings one set of challenges to a project such as this. A recent synthesis of unpublished archaeological sites in Oxford (Dodd 2003) shows how the collation of such information can feed into our wider appreciation of medieval urbanism. Another key challenge here is to realize the cumulative research potential of numerous smaller scale archaeological interventions that have occurred across the town. This is an issue of particular importance to the archaeology of small towns such as Wallingford: the dramatic growth of competitive tendering in commercial archaeology following the introduction of PPG16 (Planning Policy Guidance 16: Archaeology and Planning) in 1990 means that urban environments have been pockmarked with archaeological evaluations and watching briefs that are often small in scale, creating a fragmented archaeological picture. Archaeological interventions in the town were sporadic through the 1960s, 70s and 80s but intensified dramatically through the 1990s, with a proliferation of recorded evaluations whose results can be problematic to collate and whose findings can be difficult to assess as most remain unpublished (beyond archival 'grey' literature). Only occasionally does development-led archaeology in a small town such as Wallingford provide opportunities for the sort of relatively large-scale excavation witnessed prior to the construction of the new Waitrose in the town centre in 2004, which involved the discovery and the exhumation of more than 200 medieval burials. Sufficient evaluations have been carried out to confirm that early and later medieval stratigraphy often survives particularly well across the town's historic core, with scores of interventions recording significant occupation deposits within one metre of the surface (for good examples recovering evidence of late Saxon and Saxo-Norman features and activity, see Ford 1992 on the Harris Garage Site; Hull and Pine 2001 on the Lamb Garage Site; and Moore 2002 on 16 St George's Road). Yet while isolated trenches on sites

cleared for development may individually reveal relatively little information, collectively these can provide useful windows into the archaeological record more generally; realising this research potential is essential to the wider study of medieval small towns (see Dyer 2003, 86).

The location of those archaeological evaluations that occur as part and parcel of the planning process is obviously determined by the location of development itself. The methodology of digging small-scale archaeological 'test pits' in private gardens and other open areas has been applied to good effect in medieval rural settlement studies in order to help unravel the chronologies of currently occupied settlements (Lewis 2007). The *Burh* to Borough Research Project is piloting the method in an urban context. Through the recovery of dateable ceramic assemblages, it has exciting potential to indicate chronologies of occupation as well as showing the patterning of archaeological features, layers and natural deposits in order to inform excavation strategies.

Urban Space and Defence: Evolutions

Wallingford's earthen defences are physically the most impressive of the burghal period anywhere in England: in places the base of the enormous town ditch is more than eight metres beneath the height of the surviving internal rampart (Figure 7.1). Wareham is the closest parallel, although the integrity of its circuit here is compromised by the re-use of the western part of the town bank as anti-tank defences during the Second World War (Figure 7.2). The plan of Wallingford's circuit is not as regular as it first appears. While the west line of the circuit appears ruler-straight, detailed survey shows that the southern line deflects southwards on the east side of the town gate, while the northern defences projected slightly outwards in the centre, although reconstruction of their exact line is difficult because of the superimposition of the castle in this area.

An excavation in 1971 across the Kinecroft rampart confirmed a later Saxon construction here, with a primary turf bank built over a ploughsoil later supplemented with a bank of sandy loam behind it (Durham *et al.* 1973). The overall width of the bank (*c.* 11m) was exactly comparable to a section through the northern defences cut in the late 1960s, although here the turf bank was strengthened with vertical timbers and later topped with a stone wall (Brooks 1965–70). It is misleading to think of Wallingford's defences as comprising earthworks alone, however. Water would have been an essential element to these fortifications. Their effectiveness depended on a sophisticated scheme of engineering that involved the diversion of two natural brooks as well as sluices and an outflow system that were apparently still traceable in the first years of the 20th century (Field 1925, 5–6; Gould 1906; *VCH Berks*, iii, 517). In terms of countering the military threats of the late 9th and 10th centuries, Wallingford's defences may well have looked to the River Thames rather than the *burh*'s rural hinterland: in the late 9th century, along with the rather more obscure island *burh* site of Sashes, it defended the upper reaches of the Thames against a ship-borne enemy (Haslam 2006, 130–1). At Oxford, archaeological excavation in the Shire Lake area, on the south side of the city, has revealed evidence for

Figure 7.1 The town defences of Wallingford, showing part of the northern rampart and ditch (photo: Oliver Creighton).

Figure 7.2   Wareham town bank, showing the Saxon *burh* defences adapted as an anti-tank barrier in the Second World War (photo: Oliver Creighton).

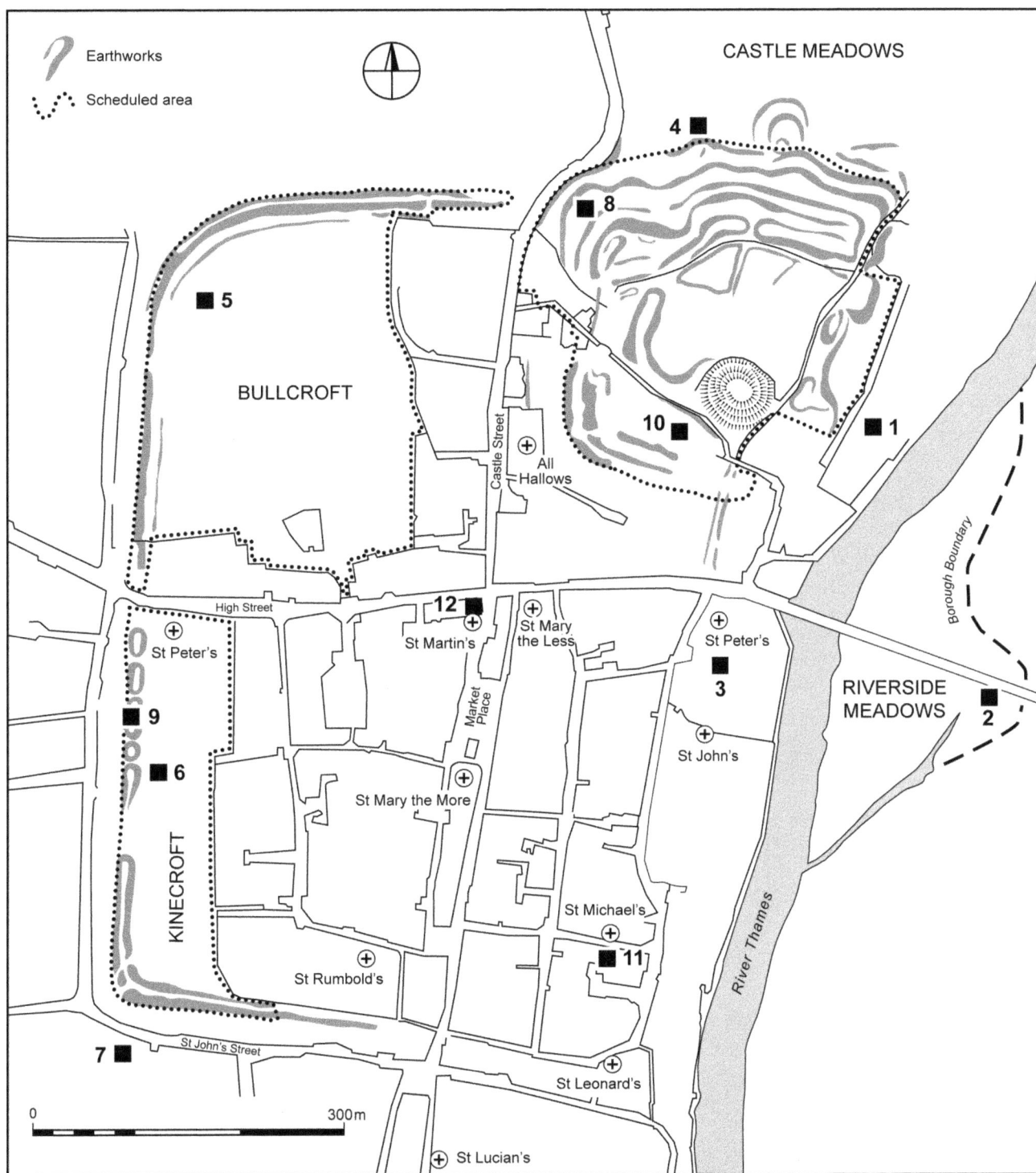

Legend:
- Earthworks
- Scheduled area

CASTLE MEADOWS

4

8

5

BULLCROFT

10

All Hallows

1

Borough Boundary

Castle Street

High Street

12
St Martin's

St Mary the Less

St Peter's

St Peter's

3

RIVERSIDE MEADOWS

2

9

6

St John's

KINECROFT

Market Place

St Mary the More

St Michael's

11

St Rumbold's

River Thames

7

St John's Street

St Leonard's

0   300m

St Lucian's

Burh to borough project excavations	**Other excavations**
1 Queen's Arbour (2003)	7 Anglo-Saxon cemetery (1930s)
2 Riverside Meadows (2005)	8 Wallingford castle (1965-8)
3 Coach House (2005)	9 Kinecroft defences (1971)
4 Castle Meadows (2008, Trench 1)	10 Wallingford castle (1972)
5 Bullcroft (2008, Trench 2)	11 St Michael's Cemetery (1974)
6 Kinecroft (2008, Trench 3)	12 Waitrose (2004)

Figure 7.3 Plan of Wallingford, showing key elements within the town plan and the location of the archaeological interventions mentioned in the text (illustration by Mike Rouillard).

middle and later Saxon civil engineering operations focused on a channel of the Thames that may have had a partly defensive function, associated with a potentially fortified bridgehead (Dodd 2003; see also Blair 1994, 101).

Within this defensive framework, central to our understanding of Wallingford's evolution is development (or its absence) in the largely open Bullcroft and Kinecroft areas that occupy a great swathe of space on the west side of the *burh* (Figure 7.3). Both place-names relate to the presence of cattle. The 'kine' in Kinecroft simply means 'cows'. However, this is apparently an early modern usage: in the mid 13th century *Kanecroft* and *Canecroft* are found and the first element may be the personal name *Cana* (Gelling 1974, 537). The name Bullcroft is also a relatively recent coinage, developed as a counterpart to the Kinecroft. In the early 15th century a seven-acre plot between the west and north gates that was the subject of a dispute between the priory and the town was the *Bodecroft* or *Bothecroft*, the first element probably referring to the temporary presence of 'booths' (*VCH Berks*, iii, 518–9).

Within the Bullcroft the site of the pre-Conquest church of the Holy Trinity (Roffe above, pp. 36–7) and the layout of the Benedictine Priory of the same dedication (founded within the church in the late 11th century and systematically demolished in the 1520s) remain matters for conjecture. Geophysical results have not shown any clear evidence of a claustral complex in the central zone, and the only likely traces of the monastic complex comprising a series of likely fishponds in the southern part of the area; the most tangible surface archaeology comprises a large surviving area of ridge and furrow, oriented north-south, in the northern part of the space (Creighton *et al.* 2002, 43–6). Excavations near the north-west corner of the Bullcroft in the summer of 2008 found a relatively sterile buried land surface at a depth of *c.* 0.8m, but little or no humanly created features. Antiquarian records and more recent findings from service trenches may instead support the theory of the core of the priory, as the earlier church, being located in the south, close to the High Street.

Occupying a rather smaller space, the longer and narrower Kinecroft, in the south-west quarter of the burghal defences, presents a rather different set of archaeological challenges. Medieval documents provide no hint that the Kinecroft area was ever permanently occupied and it remains to archaeology to unravel its place within the town's evolution. New resistivity and magnetometry surveys in the summer of 2003 proved disappointing, with the modern service trenches that criss-cross the area ensuring that a clear view of any sub-surface archaeology was impossible. The clearest archaeological anomalies related to First World War practice trenches, in the southern part of the area, with their characteristic zigzag pattern. Enigmatic traces of a potential road line were, however, apparent in the form of a linear anomaly running west south west from the line of the dead-end lane (Kinecroft) at right-angles to Goldsmith's Lane. The relative success of further geophysical survey in spring 2008 (Figure 7.4) showed the benefit of re-surveying in different conditions, with slightly wetter weather bringing out features more clearly. Excavation of a rectangular trench in the south-west part of the Kinecroft

in the summer of 2008 was targeted on a possible barrow-like geophysical anomaly but turned up quite unanticipated but highly valuable results. Painstaking excavation of a series of timber beam slots and post-holes revealed the ground-plan of a building or a row of buildings (Figure 7.4). Within the context of Wallingford's overall development several things are striking about this. First, the buildings comprised a single phase of construction, with no evidence of re-alignment, growth or contraction; they seem to relate to a single generation of development, some time between the 11th and 12th centuries. Second, the structures were on the same rectilinear alignment not only as the burghal defences, but also the likely line of an east-west hollow-way, perhaps a continuation of the feature picked up in the geophysical surveys. The regularity of the building plans is striking, but this development was not sustained. It could represent a short-term expansion in a period of prosperity and expansion. The structures may represent a work-force associated with the construction of the castle. Or the development could just possibly relate to a French borough. Domesday (GDB, 56) records that 22 houses (*masurae*) were held by Frenchmen (*francigenae*) who may be comparable with French immigrants who founded new boroughs at places such as Northampton, Norwich and Nottingham (Creighton 2005, 146). However, the Cornmarket outside the south gate is, perhaps, a more likely site for such an institution (Roffe above, p. 40).

Evidence for the transformation of the north-east quarter of the *burh* is more extensive, both in terms of surviving earthworks and a more intensive history of archaeological intervention than any other area of the town. Detailed topographical survey using differential GPS (Global Positioning System) technology alongside geophysical work is highlighting the complexity of the zone's development. Elements of the *burh* defences were incorporated into the plan of the first Norman castle, although the present earthworks owe much to a late-thirteenth-century enlargement and remodelling of the castle complex, probably by Richard, Earl of Cornwall. Including the large-scale manipulation of water features and re-planning of the street network, this transformed the entire northern-eastern part of the town into a more visibly elite quarter that showcased the symbols of lordship (the castle and the royal free chapel of St Nicholas) against the backdrop of the ancient borough. Despite the impact of this transformation on the zone, the area preserves excellent late Saxon archaeological stratigraphy. Extensive open area excavations in the north-west part of the Castle Meadows in the mid- to late 1960s revealed not just the town's medieval north gate (built in the mid 13th century as a rectangular stone structure, replacing an earlier timber gate), but also the remarkable preservation of one side of a medieval street frontage buried beneath the castle's outer earthworks, showing town houses and ancillary features to have re-planned on more than one occasion between the Saxo-Norman period and the 13th century (Brooks 1965–70, plus unpublished notes for 1965, 1966, 1968). Excavation within the eastern part of the castle's southern bailey in 1972 recovered quite remarkable evidence for mid-twelfth-century cob-built structures, surviving to a height of *c.*1.8m and probably relating to the castle

Figure 7.4 Excavations in the Kinecroft in summer 2008, showing evidence of medieval timber buildings (photo: Oliver Creighton).

kitchens. Earlier features including gullies, post-holes and pits were also encountered, some of them in a narrow extension of the trench into the bailey rampart demonstrably relating to pre-castle phases and providing glimpses of occupation layers, but forming no coherent pattern (Carr 1976). There are lessons here, of course: cob-built structures would probably not show up through geophysical survey, and open area excavation is necessary to make sense of such ephemeral underlying features.

For an urban castle the conditions of earthwork preservation in Castle Meadows are unmatched in England, thus marking the need for fuller, future study of its potentially rich data. A key question, of course, regards whether the Norman castle signalled a new high-status presence or whether it perpetuated a site of prior significance. Outwardly, the peripheral positions of urban castles located in the corners of extant defensive circuits might seem to argue against longer-term high-status continuity stretching back into the late Saxon period (Creighton 2005, 133–51). However, there is an intriguing reference in Domesday Book that King Edward had held 15 acres (*acras*) on which the housecarls (*huscarles*) were settled; 20 years later the same acres were held by Miles Crispin (GDB, 56). As these assets almost certainly lay within the area to be occupied by the Norman castle, in the north-east corner of the *burh*, a tantalising and indeed quite real possibility exists that its construction was one phase in a longer-term continuum of activity that extended back into the pre-Conquest period, with the area forming the core of a royal estate focused on

a hall or palace. Might the collegiate church and royal free chapel of St Nicholas even represent a re-foundation on an earlier Saxon site, as seems likely at Leicester, for instance (Roffe above, p. 36; Radford 1955, 156)? The presence of a high-status pre-Conquest complex in this quarter of the town may also explain the otherwise curiously low figure of eight properties destroyed to make way for the evidently substantial castle in a populous town. Within the *burh* of Stamford, the Domesday figure of five houses which were wasted on account of the castle is explicable because it lay within a former Saxon royal estate, and here there is evidence to show that the Norman fortress overlay a later Saxon elite residence (Roffe and Mahany 1986, 6).

The perception of *burhs* as 'communal' fortifications – their defences being succeeded and perpetuated by town walls – should not disguise the fact that they accommodated the assets of elite stakeholders in late Saxon society. Wallingford is one of several late Saxon *burhs* where documentary evidence makes quite clear that aristocrats held houses and land within the defended zone; in other contexts thegns and earls demonstrably owned churches, mints and mills (Fleming 1993, 8–12; Roffe above, p. 30). An intriguing possibility is that one or more of Wallingford's churches on the line of the *burh* defences, especially those adjacent to gates, represented the seats of Anglo-Saxon thegns. In Oxford, the late Anglo-Saxon tower of St Michael at the Northgate, lying on the line of the burghal defences, provided a lookout point but was also potentially part of an aristocratic or official residence; on the west side of the city

73

St George's Tower is another likely candidate (Dodd 2003, 49–50, 152–64; see also Renn 1993, 179–81). Both examples are relatively late – perhaps of the 11th century – but gate-churches and chapels are widely known from other *burhs* (Creighton and Higham 2005, 175–8). Being highly visible markers of the urban limits, gate churches had a special symbolic as well as defensive significance, forming in effect a moral cordon around the population The two churches of St Peter were positioned directly inside two of the town gates: St Peter-in-the-West lay in the north-west corner of the Kinecroft; while another medieval foundation (now heavily rebuilt and restored) overlooked the bridge from an eminence that may well be partly artificial. Both were 'holy protectors' (St Peter being the gatekeeper of heaven). St John-super-Aquam's and St Michael's stood on or near the defensive perimeter (Morris 1985, 198; see also Field 1925, 10–22). St Leonard's and St Rumbold's were similarly situated but, by way of contrast, may have had somewhat different origins. The composite parish of St Leonard's, taking in a large area to the south and west of the *burh* ramparts (Dewey above, pp. 20–1), has the appearance of an earlier entity and the site of the church itself, located on the south-east angle of the ramparts is a prime candidate for an important ecclesiastical foundation. Featuring Anglo-Saxon architectural fabric including windows and herringbone work, the building is on a different alignment to the defences, which jut out on an angle southwards from the south gate (parallel to the line of St Leonard's Lane), almost as if to incorporate an antecedent feature. St Rumbold's and St Lucian's to the south, an equally important church, were closely associated with St Leonard's from an early period (Roffe above, pp. 37–8).

A rather smaller open space in the central part of Wallingford's Thames-side frontage was investigated in 2004 and 2005, comprising a survey in the gardens of The Lodge, the Bridge House and the Coach House (all fronting onto Thames Street), followed up with a small excavation. The opening of a trench within this area revealed a substantial chalk-built riverside wall up to *c.* 1m wide, set into the natural clay and running parallel with the line of the Thames immediately south of the church of St Peter's. Although the wall is itself not securely dateable, associated pits yielded tenth- and eleventh-century pottery including St Neots type ware and early medieval Oxford Ware; the wall may be a later stone facing or revetment. Whether this represents a genuinely defensive riverside feature or merely a property boundary, the idea of a bridgehead *burh* on the opposite (east) bank of the Thames remains active. It has long been recognized that one potential explanation for the disparity between the 2400 hides needed to defend Wallingford and the apparently shorter length of the burghal defences is the existence of a fortified bridgehead on the opposite bank of the Thames in Crowmarsh Gifford, where the historic borough boundary deviates to take in a triangular wedge of land, its line partly marked by a substantial ditch (see, for example, Hinton 1977, 37; Roffe above, p. 42). Geophysical survey and small-scale excavation here has revealed no compelling late Saxon evidence, although the archaeology of the zone is complicated by alignments of palaeo-channels as well as episodes of dumping and silting

as it lies directly on the floodplain. Overall, the strong likelihood is that the area was devoid of permanent occupation, with late Saxon Wallingford certainly not resembling a 'double *burh*' after the manner of London and Southwark, although physical possession of a secure bridgehead would have been essential for the defensive functioning of the place. Nonetheless, archaeological survey in the area did locate a tantalising geophysical anomaly amounting to what may be a temporary siege castle of the Anarchy, one of at least two built in the period 1139–53 (Christie *et al.* 2004a, 98–101; 2004b, 12–13).

Explaining Space

Open spaces within medieval towns need not signify evidence of settlement contraction, nor that a settlement failed to reach its planned potential. A great medieval city such as Norwich embraced substantial areas of open meadowland because the line of its defences took a long curving line for reasons of economy, eliminating any awkward angles, while the medieval walls of places such as Canterbury, Exeter and Winchester embraced open spaces as well as built development (Creighton and Higham 2005, 95–6). These open areas could be integral to the functions of urban centres, hosting fairs and accommodating animals being bought to market as well as those owned and grazed by town dwellers. It can be contended that open spaces such as these were as essential to the everyday functions of ninth- and tenth-century *burhs* as areas of 'urban' occupation containing houses and intensively developed plots. Open zones might periodically accommodate refugee populations from the hinterland as well as offering secure central places to muster armies; they might provide storage space for campaigns but also after harvests; in certain other contexts they might comprise the estates of aristocratic families. Spaces could, of course, also signify urban population expansion potential. The plan of Cricklade, in Wiltshire, bears some comparison to that of Wallingford. Here too the *burh* seems to have incorporated large areas of open space. Excavation within the south-west corner of the defences in 1975 revealed much of the area to have been open ground and the 'planned' zone of development probably only ever took up a central strip between the north and south gates, leaving perhaps the majority of the fortified zone undeveloped (Haslam 1984, 106–10).

The development of late Saxon London shows exactly this variety and represents several interesting points of comparison with Wallingford (Figure 7.5). Since the late 1980s, archaeology has shown conclusively that *Lundenburh*, the settlement planned in the reign of Alfred following his re-establishment of London as a fortified town in 886, was effectively an 'intra-mural city' (Clark 2000, 210–11). Laid out as a series of narrow lanes at right angles to the River Thames, dividing the *burh* into regular *insulae*, it was bounded to the north by Cheapside, to the east by Billingsgate and to the west by Queenhithe, where the Saxon kings invested in new dock facilities; it was thus surrounded on three sides by a large envelope of open space, between the *burh* and the ancient part-decayed walls of *Londinium* (Tatton-Brown 1986, 25–6; Milne 2003, 41–7). Much of the area within the walls by *c.* 900, indeed perhaps

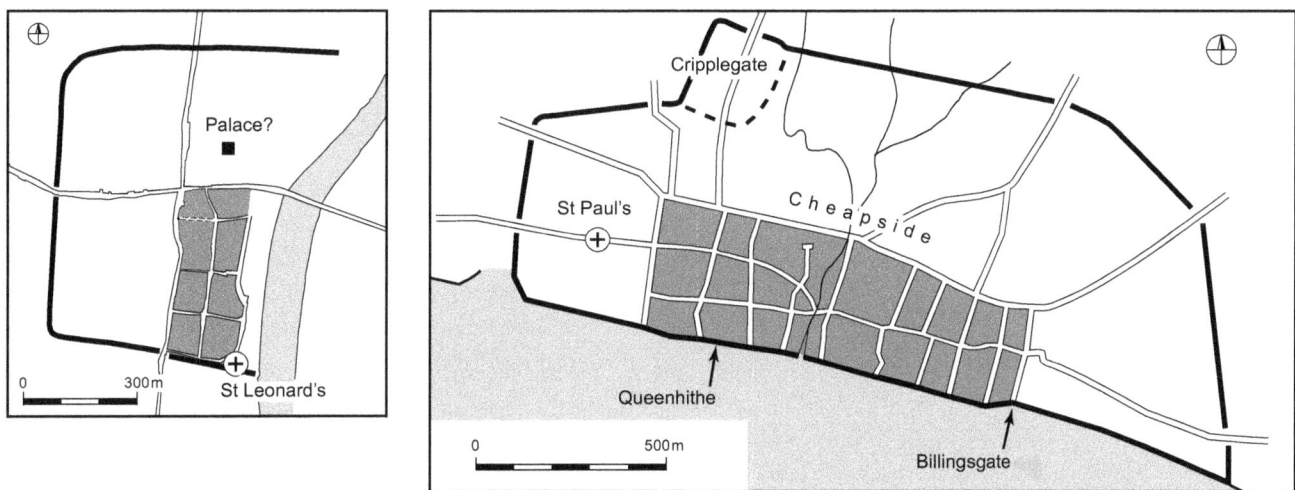

Figure 7.5 Comparative plans of the *burhs* of London and Wallingford by *c*. 900 AD (illustration by Mike Rouillard).

the majority of it, was open, while other zones quite separate from the *burh* had more specific high-status functions, including a likely Saxon palace or hall in the Cripplegate area (perhaps near Aldermanbury – 'enclosure of the earldorman'), and the ecclesiastical focus of St Paul's (*Paulesbyri*) (Vince 1990, 20). While the origins of Wallingford's earthen circuit are obviously quite different to London's defences, there may be a degree of comparability in the town's overall layout: a gridded commercial focus planned against a river using a grid based on parallel lanes (the core of the modern town, in the south-east corner of the defences, where the majority of the town's 11 parish churches lie); a high-status unit (the presumed royal palace in the vicinity of the castle); a possible episcopal zone around the church of the Holy Trinity in the north west (Roffe above, p. 37); an earlier ecclesiastical focus lying semi-detached from the gridded *burh* (St Leonard's or St Lucian's); and dedicated open spaces for marshalling troops and tethering animals (the Kinecroft and Bullcroft). The area outside the *burh* of London but within the old Roman walls features the street-names Milk Street, Hoggen Lane and Addle Street (Addle meaning the 'driving of cattle'), as well as Seething ('threshing') and Cornhill, while excavation has revealed layers of grey silts equating to intra-mural agricultural zones (Milne 2001, 120–22). These spaces were thus integral to these young, late Saxon towns – still demonstrating, arguably, the direct urban-rural bond, or else signifying an urbanism borne in a period of insecurity and requiring spaces for safety (human and animal).

Conclusion: A Town and Its Context

While the subject of this volume is the origins of Wallingford, the Wallingford *Burh* to Borough Research Project is investigating the evolution of Wallingford's townscape across a broader chronological range, from pre-*burh* antecedents through to late medieval decline. This covers a series of origins: of the settlement's roots, of settlement concentration, of *burh* growth, of Norman imposition and of medieval definition. What is important to remember is that the construction of Wallingford's first defences and earliest 'urban' occupation on the site did not necessarily occur

simultaneously. We should also be careful not to make uncritical assumptions that episodes of planning apparent in the physical fabric of the townscape relate to known and discrete historical contexts. For example, Alfred's military investments of the 880s and 890s, the aftermath of the devastating Viking attack of 1006 and the period around the castle's foundation in the wake of the Norman Conquest all present tempting chronological pegs on which to hang arguments about the town's evolution, but only exceptionally can archaeological evidence hope to provide the sort of dating evidence that could prove a direct link.

Another crucial part of the project, to be developed in the later phases, is to explore the dynamic relationship between Wallingford and its hinterland. The obvious significance of Wallingford on the late Saxon military landscape was as a fortification positioned at a critical junction of communications routes. Yet early medieval archaeologists are beginning to appreciate that *burhs* were often just component parts in wider militarized landscapes that might include 'civil defence' installations such as beacons, thegnly (or aristocratic) residences with their own fortifications and bell-towers, and were criss-crossed by military highways (Reynolds 1999, 92–6). How might Wallingford fit into such a system? In Domesday several properties within the town belonged to rural manors, perhaps reflecting the vestiges of a garrison territory (GDB, 56, 56b; Blair 1994, 117–9; Roffe above, pp. 39–40). That the links between Wallingford and its rural hinterland at Domesday not only crossed shire boundaries but also overlapped with those of Oxford tells us that these territories were not mutually exclusive nor fixed, but dynamic and evolving. Also key to Wallingford's role as a central place within its locality was its position at the junction of two contrasting types of rural landscape, between two distinctive *pays* with their own characteristic settlement patterns and economies in existence well before the 11th century. On Roberts and Wrathmell's mapping of historic settlement patterns in England, Wallingford is on the boundary between the 'Central Province' running through England and the 'South-East Province', at the interface of two countrysides (Roberts and Wrathmell 2000; 2002). To the west, north Berkshire

75

and the Vale of the White Horse were well settled at Domesday, with numerous villages and with relative development highlighted by good numbers of plough-teams and buoyant population levels, while to the east the landscape rising up to the Chiltern escarpment was far more heavily wooded (Darby and Campbell 1962, 236–7, 282–3). Wallingford's success as a market centre may have been as a point of exchange between these two regions. How far back in time did this distinction exist and what was its importance to Wallingford's early and developed economic role? Understanding these issues is thus also crucial in helping define Wallingford's roots and relative success across the periods AD 800–1200. Our project, its archaeologies and methodologies, combined with the fruits of local documentary analysis, provide the opportunity to give voice to the structures and peoples of historic Wallingford.

Acknowledgements

We would like to express thanks for all the local support we have received in Wallingford throughout the project, in particular The Wallingford Archaeological and Historical Society (TWHAS) and Members of Wallingford Museum for their unstinting help. Thanks are also due to Paul Smith, County Archaeologist for Oxfordshire, as well as various landowners, including the Northmoor Trust, South Oxfordshire District Council and Wallingford Town Council. In addition to research funding provided by the Arts and Humanities Research Council, the project has received financial assistance from the Royal Archaeological Institute, the British Academy, the Medieval Settlement Research Group and the Marc Fitch Fund.

COMPARING *BURHS*: A WALLINGFORD – BEDFORD CASE STUDY

Matt Edgeworth

Abstract

This paper examines the layout and topography of Wallingford and Bedford, with a particular focus on the defensive boundaries of the late Saxon period and on the influence these had on trajectories of development. Bedford has long appeared to be an archetypal late Saxon borough, founded and planned at a single point in time. Recent archaeological research, however, has shown that the apparently integrated plan was in reality an outgrowth from an earlier and smaller defended area. The evolution of Bedford is best described by what is called here 'the expanding town' model. This insight is used to re-examine the topography of Wallingford and suggest new lines of enquiry.

Keywords

Anglo-Saxon; Anglo-Norman; Berkshire; Bedfordsire; Bedford; Wallingford; urbanism; *burh*.

Introduction

Wallingford is justly famous for the impressive earthen ramparts that have enclosed the historic core of the town for over a thousand years. Usually Wallingford is compared with the other Wessex *burhs* listed in the Burghal Hidage which are thought to have been built or fortified by Alfred the Great (871–99) during the late 9th century and completed under Edward the Elder (899–924) in the early 10th century. Accordingly, comparisons tend to be with West Saxon boroughs. This paper, however, turns in a different direction. Looking towards the north east, it draws a comparison with the lesser known Mercian town of Bedford – a *burh* very different from Wallingford in some respects and yet strikingly similar in others.

Lack of comparison between the towns is partly due to the fact that Bedford is not one of the *burhs* listed in the Burghal Hidage (it was under viking control during the early years of Edward's reign, when the list is thought to have been compiled). But another factor is the situation of the two towns in different river valleys, Wallingford on the River Thames and Bedford on the River Great Ouse. Connections between Wallingford and other towns located within the linear corridor of the Thames are covered, for example, in Booth *et al* (2007), but links across the watershed are rarely explored: only Buckingham, a Burghal Hidage *burh*, is regularly considered (Haslam 2005). Not entirely unrelated to the physical topography of river valleys and watersheds is the organization of England (and indeed English archaeology) into regions, almost none of which group the two towns together. Thus, while Wallingford falls within the Thames Valley or Southern England, Bedford tends to be counted as part of the East Midlands or even East Anglia. Research frameworks reproduce such divisions. All of these factors unite to give the impression that Bedford and Wallingford are a considerable distance apart. But actually the distance between the towns is only 74km (46 miles).

The paper will examine the general layout and basic topography of Wallingford and Bedford, with a particular focus on the defensive boundaries of the late Saxon period and on the influence these had on trajectories of subsequent development. In recounting recent discoveries of an early defensive boundary running right through the middle of what was once thought to be the original Saxon *burh* of Bedford (Edgeworth 2004), it will ask whether this evidence can shed any light or suggest new lines of investigation for the origins and development of Wallingford.

Differences and similarities

Wallingford today is a relatively small town, fairly untouched by the great expansion of urban centres that took place in the post-medieval and industrial periods. Indeed, the historic core forms a large part of the present town. Bedford, in contrast, has grown exponentially in the last 200 years, with the historic core now forming only a small part of the sprawling whole (Edgeworth 2006). Its original form has been swallowed up, many of its earthworks flattened, and its archaeology covered over or taken out by post-medieval development.

Some minor stretches of medieval rampart do survive in Bedford, but there is nothing like the highly visible medieval ramparts of Wallingford. Straightaway, then, a brief walk around the boundaries of Wallingford can give an idea of the scale of just how much has been lost in Bedford and similar towns to later development, and conversely how much standing and visible archaeology Wallingford has retained by virtue of not being extensively redeveloped.

The plan of Bedford's historic core reveals the shape of a double-*burh*: that is, a *burh* with two parts, built on both sides of the river (Figure 8.1). In this sense too it is quite different from Wallingford which – apart from the supposed bridgehead on the east bank of the Thames – was built on one side of the river only. However, it is known from the Anglo-Saxon Chronicle (*ASC*, 63–4, *s.a.* 914) that the southern part of Bedford was constructed opposite an already existing northern *burh*. It is the earlier northern *burh* which can be usefully compared to Wallingford and which will be examined in more detail in this paper. This northern *burh* seems to have existed as an urban or proto-urban settlement as early as the 8th century. It is reputed to have been the burial place of King Offa and to have possessed an

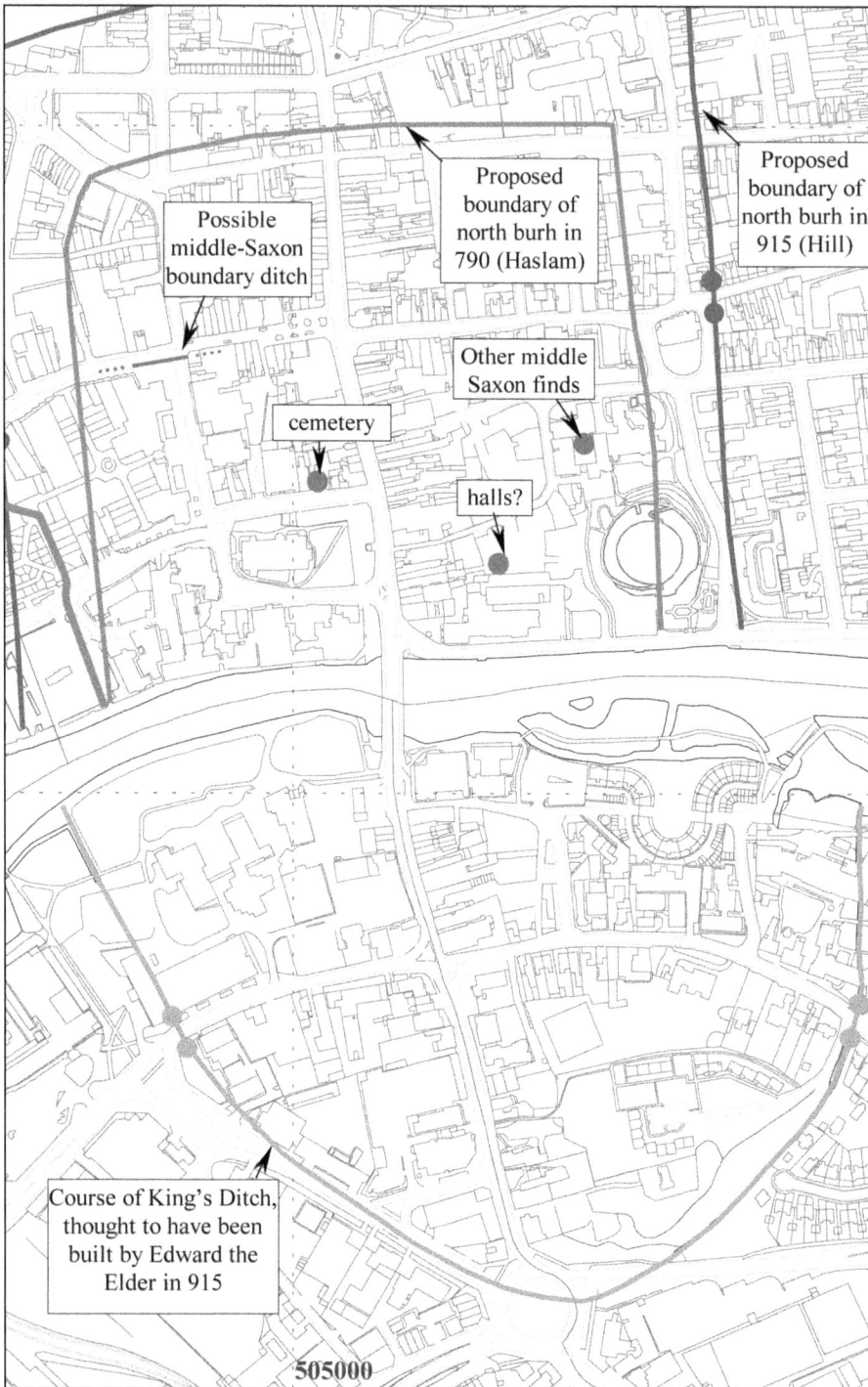

Figure 8.1 Bedford and its defences (reproduced with the permission of Bedfordshire Borough Council).

Labels on figure:
Possible middle-Saxon boundary ditch
Proposed boundary of north burh in 790 (Haslam)
Proposed boundary of north burh in 915 (Hill)
Other middle Saxon finds
cemetery
halls?
Course of King's Ditch, thought to have been built by Edward the Elder in 915
505000

abbey under the rule of Offa's queen, Cynethrith (Lapidge *et al.* 1999, 133). It was captured and held by the Danes in the 870s and held as a viking town on the very edge of the Danelaw for 30 or 40 years, before being recaptured and probably refortified by King Edward the Elder in AD 914, at the time the southern *burh* was built (Edgeworth 2004; Haslam 1983).

Had Wallingford been in the frontier zone between the West Saxons and the vikings at that time, the same technique of transforming the town into a double- *burh* would probably have been employed there too. In effect, southern Bedford is what Crowmarsh might have looked like if history had worked out slightly differently. At the same time, the V-shaped bridgehead at Wallingford on the

east bank (if a bridgehead is indeed what it is, and this has yet to be proven archaeologically) gives some idea of what a Bedford bridgehead could have been like before the southern *burh* was built (Creighton *et al.* above, pp. 71, 74).

However this may be, if we take the conventional view that Wallingford was constructed in a single planning and building event in the late 9th century – a view, incidentally, that this paper will go on to challenge – Bedford is both older (the northern part) and younger (the southern part).

Immediately significant parallels between the plans of the two settlements can be observed.

• Both are located on major rivers, at or near the limits of navigation. Rivers, of course, provided transport of

78

materials and enabled the economic functions of towns to be developed (Blair 2007). The rivers are also likely to have served as boundaries between different territories, with the settlements on their banks having the character of frontier towns (though see Roffe above, p. 74, for the late 9th and 10th centuries). In each case the river forms a principal axis of orientation for town development.

- Both are located on fords, later to be replaced by bridges. Indeed, both towns derive their names from their fords (Dewey above, p. 18). Again, in each case the road which crosses the ford at right angles to the river forms the second principal axis of town development.
- Both have a roughly rectangular shape, and are of comparable size, though Bedford is slightly smaller. There is some evidence in both towns of a boundary ditch or rampart running along the river side of the *burh* (Creighton *et al.* above, p. 74), giving protection from river-borne attack.
- Both have a rectangular street grid and show clear evidence of planning, whether such planning took place at the time of *burh* construction or later. In both towns a feature of the grid is the central crossroads. Both show more extensive development in the half of the town that is nearer to the river.
- Both Bedford and Wallingford have a Norman castle set in the most strategic position next to the river, close to and defending the river crossing and major routeways. In each case the castle was placed over the town boundary on one side, perhaps on already existing high status sites, and took up the best part of a quarter of the overall space within the town.

An important point to note here is that not all the similarities we observe necessarily relate to the same time. Rather the similarities noted seem to arise from *a common pattern of development through time*. It is these patterns of development that we need to try to understand.

Expanding and shrinking towns

Just as Wallingford is often said to have been built by Alfred the Great in the late 9th century, in (northern) Bedford too it has been the practice to try to pin down the origin of the urban defensive boundaries and the internal street grid to a specific moment in time and a particular founder – to say, for example, that the street grid and boundaries were laid out in the time of King Offa (757–96) or Edward the Elder, in a single foundational moment or planning event. Various theories of that kind have been put forward. Two examples are models by Jeremy Haslam (1983) and David Hill (1970) illustrated in Figure 8.1. In both scenarios, the early plan of northern Bedford is thought to be based around a central crossroads.

This is where archaeology put a spanner in the works, as it often does for models based entirely on topographical observations. In the late 1990s, an unexpected 70m stretch of ninth-century defensive ditch (with some indications of an internal bank) was found to underlie one of the main roads leading up to the crossroads. The 3–4m wide ditch, truncated by later development, clearly carried on in both directions. When records of other excavations nearby were

checked, it was realized that a probable continuation of the ditch had been picked up in an earlier unpublished watching brief, giving it a total length of at least 120m, with every indication that it continued even further eastwards along the line of present roads (Edgeworth 2004).

A good stratigraphic sequence was found in which the earliest road surface, dated to the early 13th century, was shown to overlay the upper layers of the filled-in ditch. This road surface was comprised of compacted limestone rubble, and may well have been laid at the time of the demolition of Bedford castle in 1224. But one thing is certain: the central road and crossroads could not be original features of the earliest *burh*, as postulated by both Haslam and Hill, because these had an earlier feature – the ditch – running directly underneath. The ditch could be an original feature, and indeed it is almost certainly an early northern boundary of Bedford; the central crossroads is actually where the gateway once was.

This does not mean that the Haslam and Hill models are wrong; rather, it shows that the boundaries they identified, and the fully extended street grid with its central crossroads, relate to later phases of town development, probably developing in the late Saxon and early Norman periods. At least in Bedford, what we seem to have is an *expanding town* whose boundaries shift through time. The street grid is added too in *modular fashion* as the town grows in size. There is no one originating moment as such, because the town was always based on something that was there before. Even the earliest *burh* shown here may in fact be an expansion from a previous, smaller, fortified settlement. Substantial early-middle Saxon structures have been found to underly the Norman castle, both in the 1970s investigations (Baker *et al.* 1979) and in more recent Bedford castle excavations (Christiane Meckseper, pers. comm.). Figure 8.2 shows a simplified 'expanding town' model, combining the models of Haslam and Hill with the more recent archaeological evidence for the early development of Bedford.

Recent archaeological investigation inside the *burh* at Stafford provides another useful comparison. There appears to be an earlier circuit of town boundaries within the circuit of the medieval town walls marked on later maps. These earlier boundaries may themselves enclose a still earlier, smaller defensive circuit (Cuttler *et al.* 2008). A model of an expanding town, then, could well be applicable to Stafford too. I suggest it could also apply to many other *burhs*, formerly thought to have been founded all in one go.

In Wallingford it is often taken as axiomatic that Alfred built the town more or less from scratch. Here I only ask whether that is necessarily the case. If he re-fortified an already existing defended settlement, which is quite likely, what would it have looked like? And did Wallingford expand outwards, as other towns seem to have done, in the post-Alfred late Saxon period? Could a model of an expanding town, of the kind that might explain the layout of northern Bedford, apply to Wallingford too? If so, earlier boundaries might be hidden within, and possibly be reflected by, the internal street layout, perhaps not noticed because not looked for and awaiting chance discovery through watching brief or evaluation. As highlighted above,

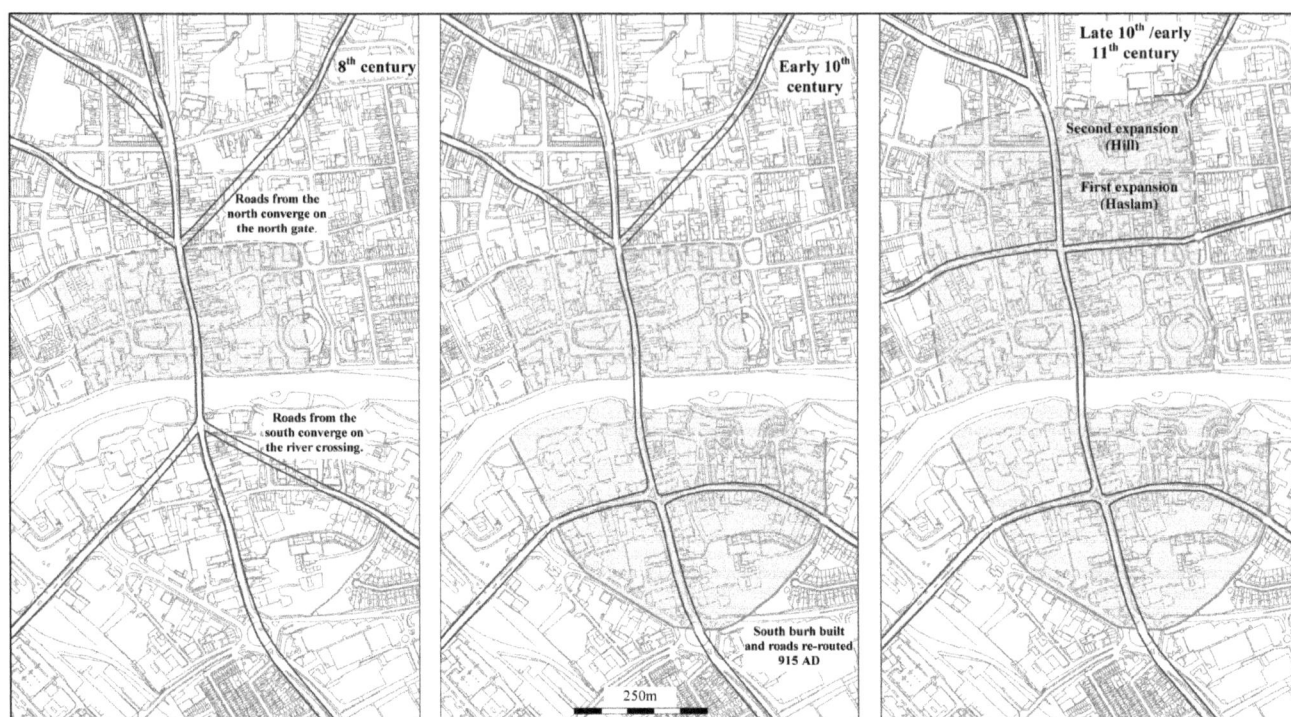

Figure 8.2 Bedford: the Expanding Town Model (reproduced with the permission of Bedfordshire Borough Council).

experience in Bedford shows that roads may reproduce (and mask) the course of earlier boundaries.

Arguably, there is already some suggestion of later expansion of Wallingford with the possible addition of a suburb on the southern side, outside the *burh* on the other side of the Millbrook. In a paper on local water systems, Grayson (2004) suggests the cutting of the present course of Bradford's Brook was undertaken to form the southern boundary of a new parish of St Lucian's, possibly in the early 12th century. It seems clear, however, that St Lucian is a pre-Conquest church and it is perhaps more likely the suburb is a pre-burh nucleus (Dewey above, pp. 20–1; Roffe above, pp. 37–8).

Any discussion of possible town expansion should be balanced by consideration of town shrinkage. Both towns have (or had until recently, in the case of Bedford) large areas of open space within the town interiors, as exemplified by the Kinecroft and the Bullcroft in Wallingford. Such open spaces may have originally been intensively occupied, with the street grid extending right up to the town boundaries. Economic decline and internal settlement shrinkage, it is argued, might have caused these spaces to revert to agricultural or other use. Alternatively, early towns may have been planned from the outset with large areas of open space, perhaps even with some notion of their potential as spaces for internal expansion built into their design (see Creighton *et al.* above, p. 74).

These possibilities were tested to some extent by the 2008 excavation trenches of the Wallingford *Burh* to Borough Research Project. A trench in the north of the Bullcroft found no trace of occupation of any date. Another trench in the central part of the Kinecroft found evidence of a single phase of occupation dating from the 11th–12th century, comprising substantial buildings adjacent to a possible street (which does indeed line up with the street

grid in the rest of the town). The evidence still requires full analysis, but it seems that this part of the Kinecroft was not built on in late Saxon times. It was, however, subject to a temporary phase of intensive occupation in the early Norman period, followed by a reversion back to open space, with the street going out of use shortly after the buildings were abandoned. Further excavation in 2009 may clarify this interpretation.

The general picture to emerge from towns like Bedford and Wallingford is that the area of settlement could expand and contract within town boundaries according to economic and demographic fluctuations, without boundaries ever needing to be brought back in. While there is evidence (at least in Bedford) for boundaries being pushed out as towns expand, there is no evidence for boundaries being pulled in as settlement contracts.

Fluid boundaries

Supply of water is an important factor in considering both the layout of early towns and their later development. *Burhs* like Bedford and Wallingford were enclosed not only by earthen banks but also by flowing water. It is easy to focus attention on the solidity of banks and walls while neglecting the more fluid aspects of earthworks. Flow is crucial: water had to flow in order for it to be controlled and utilized. It may have initially had a primary defensive function but it had a power and energy that could also be used to drive mills, to perform other industrial functions, to supply water to fishponds, and so on. The Saxon fort-builders were brilliant water engineers, willing and able to go to great lengths to acquire the necessary supply of flowing water. Grayson (2004) shows how a whole system of streams was artificially modified, ditched and diverted through a series of sluices and channels in order to bring a flow of water into the boundary ditches around Wallingford.

80

There was a similar arrangement at Bedford. In this case a stream called the Saffron Ditch was incorporated into the *burh* defences on the western side, providing a flow of water that could also be partially diverted along the northern and eastern sides. Today the ditch is culverted and runs under concrete. It is shown in Figure 8.3 as it was in 1610, on the earliest map of Bedford

The Saffron Ditch formed the western boundary of the smaller, earlier *burh* (other watercourses were utilized to provide water for the ditches of the expanded *burh*). It was most probably artificially diverted from an original natural course to feed into the north-west corner of the defences, with water re-directed from there to run along the boundary both eastwards and southwards. The course of the ditch was no doubt modified again for various purposes many times throughout the medieval period. In one case a long rectangular fishpond – excavated in the 1970s (Hassall 1983) – was constructed on the course of the ditch, with the ditch itself diverted around the fishpond in dog-leg fashion. Although the fishpond was filled in by the time the map was surveyed in 1610, the diversion of the ditch around its former location can be clearly seen on Speed's map. This is just one of many possible examples of how the flow of water in boundary ditches was made use of and modified in later centuries.

In Wallingford, as Grayson (2004) has shown, the military engineers directed a flow of water into the ditch on the western side of the Kinecroft. From this point of entry the water was divided into two – one current heading northwards into the Black Ditch and the other southwards along Millbrook, with both subsequently taken eastwards to flow into the River Thames. While the term 'Black Ditch' may imply stagnant water, it is important to recognize that a series of sluices along the course of the ditch would have enabled water to be dammed and retained, then released into stretches downstream whenever required. Water from Millbrook was used to drive a mill. During the 600 years that Wallingford castle was standing, water from the Black Ditch would have been used to fill the castle moats. It is also likely to have provided a water supply for the fishponds belonging to the Benedictine priory of Holy Trinity, which occupied part of the Bullcroft in the north-western sector of Wallingford throughout much of the medieval period.

Other activities afforded by the water-filled ditches, not only in late Saxon times but in subsequent periods too, would have included washing, bathing, fishing, drainage, small-scale transport of goods by boat, supply of water for agricultural and industrial purposes, and so on. In Bedford there is ample later map evidence of boundary ditches being forded wherever intersected by roads. Characteristically, a ford was situated alongside a small bridge, and this may have been the case in Wallingford too. The existence of fords is itself a good indication of flowing water. Carts and other traffic would simply sink supinely into the mud if

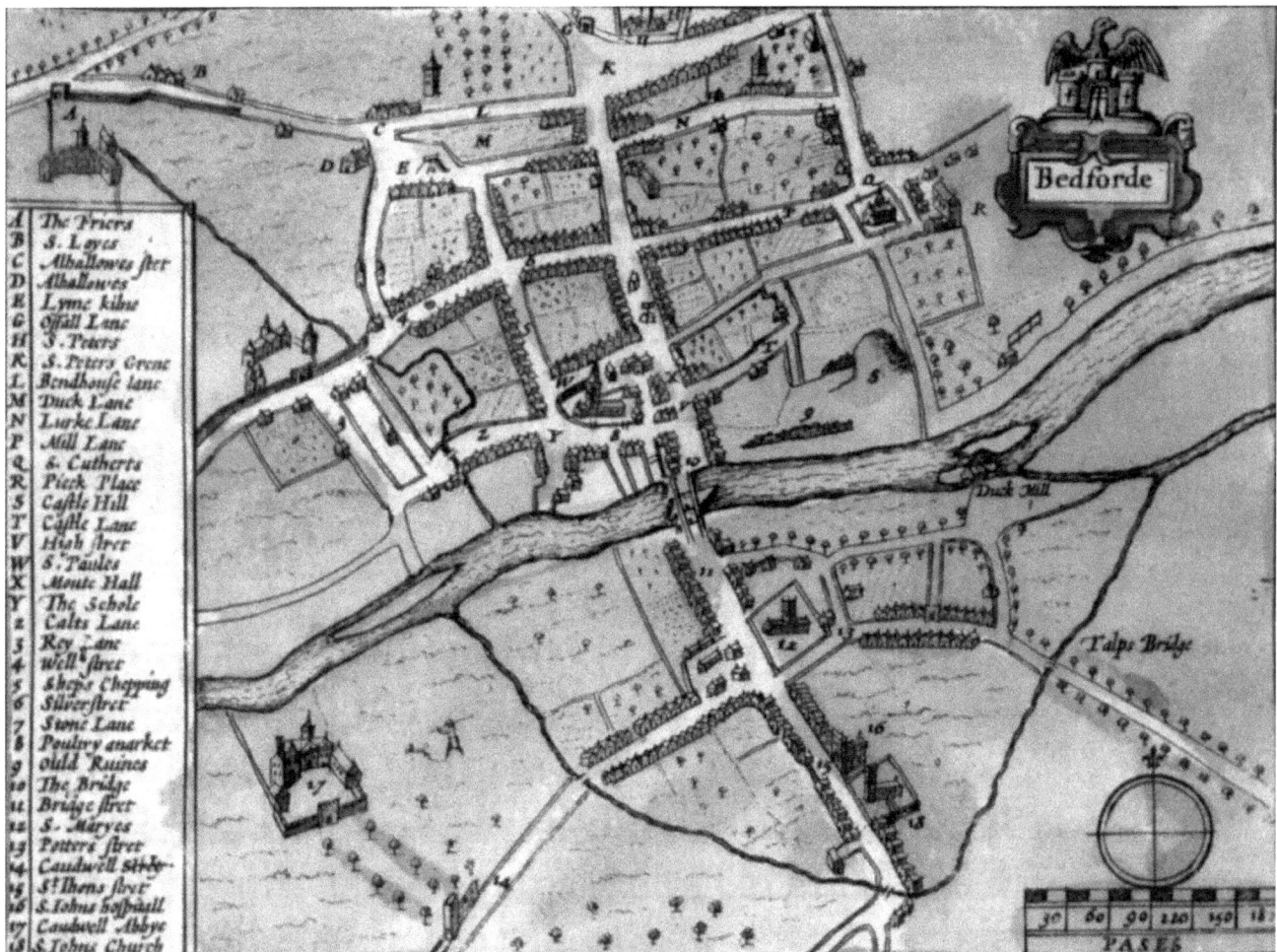

Figure 8.3 Speed's map of Bedford, 1610.

81

attempting to cross a stagnant ditch; flow is required to maintain a usable crossing-point.

The first important point about the earthworks surrounding both Bedford and Wallingford, then, is that they were designed from the outset to be dynamic, working monuments. Immense effort was put into their construction, not merely to pile up an impressive heap of earth but also, and especially, to make the flow of water possible. Any given terrain would have presented topographical obstacles to water flow which had to be overcome through ingenuity and thought on the part of military engineers – taking the ditch deeper here, or re-directing it there – to make use of the natural fall of the land. The building of the earthworks was so much more than can be quantified by the man-hours that it would take to build a given length of earthen rampart (as if all an earthwork consists of is the massing together of earth, the physical boundary itself). Considerations of flow were extremely significant when it came to the siting, depth, orientation and shape of boundary earthworks, and thus to the overall form of towns themselves.

The second important point is that the boundary earthworks surrounding Wallingford and other *burhs* are multi-period monuments. They may have been originally constructed in the late Saxon period, but they owe their preservation to the carrying out of regular maintenance throughout the medieval and much of the post-medieval periods. The fact that some earthworks really did 'work' and that they continued to perform useful functions for successive generations over hundreds of years goes some way to explaining why they endured so successfully over long periods of time, long enough to become embedded in the landscape as symbolic and territorial boundaries. Each generation had the incentive to properly look after the earthwork. By contrast, linear earthworks which performed no 'work' as such – for example those from the English Civil War in the 17th century – rarely survive. While often just as massive, they were literally of no use to subsequent generations, were not maintained, and thus largely disappeared from the landscape. Likewise, as we have seen, early town boundaries which were overtaken by settlement expansion and superseded by later boundaries – like the early ditch running beneath the roads of Bedford town centre discussed earlier in this paper – could rapidly be filled in and covered over, effectively vanishing from the evolving urban landscape.

Redirected roads

The construction of a *burh* like Bedford or Wallingford entailed re-routing of major roads. In an insightful paper, Crawley and Freeman (1988) showed that when the southern *burh* of Bedford was built by King Edward the Elder in AD 915, roads from the south east and south west that originally headed for a ford across the river were re-directed at the very point they crossed the boundary of the *burh*, with traffic diverted along the lines and right angles of a newly constructed internal street grid towards a central crossroads. In other words, the orientation of these re-directed roads points to the position of the ford or bridge *prior* to *burh* construction.

One landscape/townscape archaeology technique which might be applicable to Wallingford, then, is to look for early roads that originally headed for a river crossing but were subsequently diverted to the central crossroads at the point where they reach the *burh* defences. Such roads might indicate, for example, the position of early fords. Using this technique, one road stands out straight away and demands attention. Sometimes called the Portway, it takes a more or less direct course from Reading to Wallingford. David Pedgley (pers.comm.) has provided numerous references to the Portway in medieval times, the earliest of which is 1250. Of great interest is the fact that it not only points towards the present river crossing but also seems to have a continuation on the other side of the river, heading towards the ford at Shillingford on a line that would take it on to Dorchester (Figure 8.4).

If one now considers the line of the road as it heads in the other direction, from Shillingford through Wallingford and towards Reading, it can be observed that it once headed straight for the river crossing. But it has been diverted at the point where it reached the *burh* defences towards a central crossroads (in the manner of the roads of southern Bedford). This diversion would have taken it through the old north gate examined by Nicholas Brooks in the 1960s excavations (the archives of which are currently being worked on by the Wallingford *Burh* to Borough Research Project, leading to publication of the results of these important early investigations). As Brooks (1966) showed, this road was later diverted again when the outer defences of the castle were built in the 13th century, pushing it westwards to become Castle Street as it is now. This goes some way towards explaining why the road has such a marked kink in it.

The fact that a projection of the course of the road appears to run diagonally through not only the medieval castle but also the Saxon *burh* itself, and to be cut by both of these features, makes it worthy of further investigation. Could it have existed before the *burh* was constructed? 'Portway' is an ancient term applied to roads that led to 'ports' or market towns, though these were often re-uses of prehistoric tracks or Roman roads (Hindle 1998, 9). This particular portway is fairly straight but is not recorded as a Roman road (the nearest known Roman road runs north-south from Dorchester to Silchester, passing 2km to the west of Wallingford). The exact alignment of the two stretches of road either side of the *burh* could be a coincidence. Even so, the example shows how archaeological insights developed in connection with one *burh* can open up new avenues of investigation in another.

There are other aspects of the roads coming into and out of Wallingford which present archaeologists with difficult puzzles. St Martin's Street and St Mary's Street may together represent what was once a single broad market road, which has subsequently been largely filled in with buildings. The odd thing is that this hypothetical broad street seems to extend beyond the southern town boundaries in the form of Reading Road and Squires Walk. Does this pattern indicate the existence of a broad north-south running road, roughly parallel to the river, prior to the construction of the *burh* ramparts? Or is the extension of the two roads a later development of the St Lucian's area, possibly as a

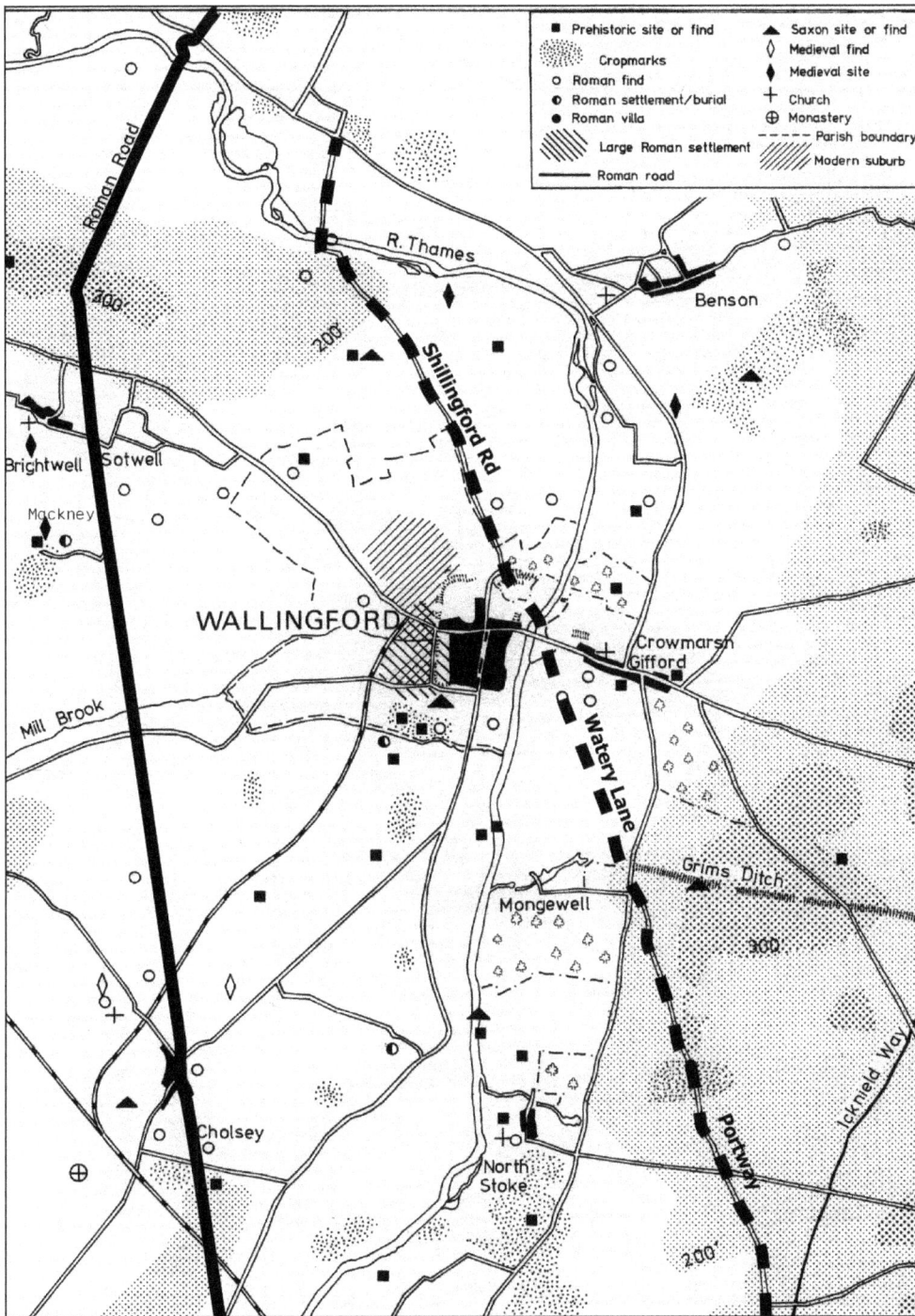

Figure 8.4 The Portway.

French borough (Roffe above, p. 40), with a deliberate broadening out of the existing road to create its own market street?

Another puzzle concerns the same road (now reduced to Castle Street) as it leaves the *burh* through the northern ramparts. The kink in the road has already been mentioned, and some explanation put forward to account for it. But if one projects the line of the road northwards straight on past the kink and into the countryside, it lines up exactly with one of a pair of parallel banks. These banks were first spotted on a LIDAR image (Figure 8.5). They show up on the ground as low, wide banks about 1m high and 15m wide, 140m apart.

These banks (or associated ditches) also show up on Google Earth aerial photos, the whole complex of features extending for about 1.5 km from near Shillingford Hill to the very outskirts of Wallingford. A projected continuation of the two banks southwards would enclose nearly all of the most densely settled half of the historic core of Wallingford, between the lines of St Martin's Street/Castle Street and Thames Street.

Perhaps the most obvious explanation is that the two parallel banks are medieval or post-medieval features, field boundaries running along the edges of river terraces, for example. But such an interpretation does not explain why they seem to link up so well with the lines of the roads of the town, nor why they appear to be earlier than all other visible landscape features. An alternative explanation of the

83

Figure 8.5
LIDAR image of
parallel banks north of
Wallingford.
Reproduced with the
permission of the
Environment Agency
and English Heritage.

banks is that they are prehistoric in origin, influencing later urban development by virtue of being present as major features in the landscape when the town was constructed. They could possibly be Iron Age in date like the Grim's Ditch just to the south east of Wallingford, though the form of that earthwork is very different. An even earlier date is possible. The idea that the banks could represent a previously unknown Neolithic cursus monument, similar to numerous others in the Upper Thames region (Barclay *et al.* 2003), is supported by the way they each mirror the slightest change in direction made by the other – a typical cursus characteristic – but is offset by the sheer distance between the banks. At 140m wide, it might be argued that the banks are too far apart to comprise a cursus. In general the width of cursus monuments rarely exceeds 100m (though the Stonehenge cursus reaches up to 150m at its widest point). Whatever the answer to the riddle posed by the parallel banks, it is clear that the study of the development of urban space needs to go hand-in-hand with the study of the surrounding landscape.

Conclusion

This paper has tried to show how comparing *burhs* in different regions can be a useful exercise. Although different in many respects, towns like Wallingford and Bedford have remarkable similarities in their basic plans and patterns of development which need to be explained. A programme of cross-comparison is especially necessary given the recent and ongoing work being carried out in Wallingford, Bedford, Stafford and other *burhs*. Up to now these places have not figured prominently in the debate on urban origins. That, crucially, is about to change.

Acknowledgements

This paper was first presented at the CBA South Midlands Archaeology Conference held in Wallingford in May 2008. The CBA South Midlands region is probably the only regional unit to include both Bedford and Wallingford. Thanks to Colin Clarke for organizing the conference, to Neil Christie for commenting on a draft version of the paper, and to Christiane Meckseper for discussions on recent work in Bedford.

A WALLINGFORD BIBLIOGRAPHY

Abingdon. Historia Ecclesie Abbendonensis: the History of the Church of Abingdon, ed. J. Hudson. Oxford, Oxford University Press, 2002–7.

Airs, M., Rodwell, K. and Turner, H. 1975. Wallingford. In K. Rodwell (ed.), *Historic Towns in Oxfordshire: A Survey of the New County*, 155–162. Oxford, Oxford Archaeological Unit.

Allen, T. 1995. *Lithics and Landscape: Archaeological Discoveries on the Thames Water Pipeline at Gatehampton Farm, Goring, Oxfordshire 1985–92.* Thames Valley Landscapes Monograph 7. Oxford, Oxford Archaeological Unit.

Allen, T. 2000. The Iron Age background. In M. Henig and P. Booth, *Roman Oxfordshire*, 1–33. Stroud, Alan Sutton.

Allen, T. G., Cramp, K., Lamdin-Whymark, H. and Webley, L. forthcoming. *Archaeological Investigations at Castle Hill and the Surrounding Landscape, Little Wittenham, Oxfordshire, 2002–2006*, Thames Valley Landscapes Monograph. Oxford, Oxford Archaeology.

Allen, T., Miles, D. and Palmer, S. 1984. Iron Age buildings in the Upper Thames region. In B. Cunliffe and D. Miles (eds), *Aspects of the Iron Age in Central Southern Britain*, 89–101. Oxford University Committee for Archaeology Monograph 2. Oxford, Oxford University Committee for Archaeology.

Allnatt, W. 1873. *Rambles in the Neighborhood of Wallingford: also Some Account Relative to its Ancient, Mediaeval and Modern Conditions*. Wallingford, S. Bradford.

Annells, P. 2006. *The Berkshire Dunches*. Wallingford, self published.

Anon. 1910. An old relic in Wallingford. *Berkshire, Buckinghamshire and Oxfordshire Archaeological Journal* 16, 116.

Anon. 1916a. A survey of Wallingford in 1550. Part 1. *Berkshire, Buckinghamshire and Oxfordshire Archaeological Journal* 21, 11–113.

Anon. 1916b. A survey of Wallingford in 1550. Part 2. *Berkshire, Buckinghamshire and Oxfordshire Archaeological Journal* 22, 21–25.

Anon. 1916c. A survey of Wallingford in 1550. Part 3. *Berkshire, Buckinghamshire and Oxfordshire Archaeological Journal* 22, 46–49.

Anon. 1916d. A survey of Wallingford in 1550. Part 4. *Berkshire, Buckinghamshire and Oxfordshire Archaeological Journal* 22, 82–84.

Anon. 1917a. A survey of Wallingford in 1550. Part 5. *Berkshire, Buckinghamshire and Oxfordshire Archaeological Journal* 23, 26–29.

Anon. 1917b. A survey of Wallingford in 1550. Part 6. *Berkshire, Buckinghamshire and Oxfordshire Archaeological Journal* 23, 66–66.

Anon. 1920. A survey of Wallingford in 1550. Part 7. *Berkshire, Buckinghamshire and Oxfordshire Archaeological Journal* 25, 70–73.

Anon. 1940. The covenant of the Baptist church at Wallingford. *Transactions of the Congregational Historical Society* 14, 25–7.

Anthony, S. and Ford, S 2006. *An Early Anglo-Saxon Urned Cremation Burial and Medieval Ditch from St John's Primary School, Wallingford, Oxfordshire*. Unpublished client report. Reading, Thames Valley Archaeological Services.

Arkell, W. J. 1944. Palaeoliths from the Wallingford fan-Gravels. *Oxoniensia* 8–9, 1–19.

Arkell, W.J. 1946. More Palaeoliths from the Wallingford fan-gravels. *Oxoniensia* 11–12, 173–5.

ASC. The Anglo-Saxon Chronicle: A Revised Translation, eds D. Whitelock, D. C. Douglas, and S. I. Tucker, 2nd ed. London, Eyre and Spottiswoode, 1963.

Astill, G. 1984. The towns of Berkshire. In J. Haslam (ed.), *Anglo-Saxon Towns in Southern England*, 53–86. Chichester, Phillimore.

Astill, G. 2000. General survey, 600–1300. In D. Palliser (ed.), *The Cambridge Urban History of Britain, Vol.1, 600–1540*, 27–49. Cambridge, Cambridge University Press.

Atkinson, D. 1916. *The Romano-British Site on Lowbury Hill in Berkshire*. Reading, University College.

Atkinson, R. J. C., Piggott, S. M. and Sandars, N. K. 1951. *Excavations at Dorchester, Oxon*. Oxford, Ashmolean Museum.

Bailey, K. A. 1992. The hidation of Buckinghamshire: Part 2 before Domesday. *Records of Buckinghamshire* 34, 87–96.

Baker, D., Baker, E., Hassall, J. and Simco, A. 1979. Excavations in Bedford 1967–1977. *Bedfordshire Archaeological Journal* 13, 7–307.

Baker, S. 2002. Prehistoric and Romano-British landscapes at Little Wittenham and Long Wittenham, Oxfordshire. *Oxoniensia* 67, 1–28.

Ballard, A. 1904. *The Domesday Boroughs*. Oxford, Oxford University Press.

Barclay, A., Bradley, R., Hey, G. and Lambrick, G. 1996. The earlier prehistory of the Oxford region in the light of recent research (the Tom Hassall lecture for 1995). *Oxoniensia* 66, 105–62.

Barclay, A., Lambrick, G., Moore, J. and Robinson, M. 2003. *Lines in the Landscape. Cursus Monuments in the Upper Thames Valley: Excavations at the Drayton and Lechlade Cursuses*. Thames Valley Landscapes Monograph 15. Oxford, Oxford Archaeology.

Barlow, F. 1976. *The English Church, 1000–1066: a History of the Later Anglo-Saxon Church*, 2nd ed. London, Longman.

Barlow, F. 1979. The Winton Domesday. In M. Biddle (ed.), *Winchester in the Early Middle Ages: an Edition and Discussion of the Winton Domesday*, 1–141. Winchester Studies 1. Oxford, Oxford University Press.

Barton, N. 1995. The long blade assemblage. In T. Allen (ed.), *Lithics and Landscape: Archaeological Discoveries on the Thames Water Pipeline at Gatehampton Farm, Goring, Oxfordshire 1985–92*, 54–64. Thames Valley Landscapes Monograph 7. Oxford, Oxford Archaeological Unit.

Bean, S. C. 2000. *The Coinage of the Atrebates and Regni*. School of Archaeology Monograph 50, Oxford, Oxford University.

Beasley, D. 1994. *Around Wallingford in Old Photographs*. Britain in Old Photographs. Stroud, Sutton Publishing.

Beasley, D. 1998. *Around Wallingford*. The Archive Photographs Series. Stroud, The Chalford Publishing Company.

Beasley, D. 2004. *Wallingford: the Twentieth Century*. Britain in Old Photographs. Stroud, Sutton Publishing.

Bec. Select Documents of the English Lands of the Abbey of Bec, ed. M. Chibnall. Camden Society, 3rd ser. 73, 1951.

Benson, D., Miles, D., Balkwill, C. J., Clayton, N. 1974. *The Upper Thames Valley. An Archaeological Survey of the River Gravels*. Survey No. 2. Oxordd, Oxfordshire Archaeological Unit.

Beresford, M. W. and St. Joseph, K. 1958. *Medieval Britain: an Aerial Survey*. Cambridge, Cambridge University Press.

Berk, C. J. 2008. Saxon fortifications in the Cookham area and Sashes Island http://www.arcserv.org/Ck%20Saxon%20Rev/Text.htm.

BF. The Book of Fees, Public Record Office, 2 vols in 3. London, 1920–31.

Biddle, M. 1976. Towns. In D. M. Wilson (ed.)*, The Archaeology of Anglo-Saxon England*, 99–150. London, Methuen.

Biddle, M. and Hill, D. 1971. Late Saxon planned towns. *Antiquities Journal* 51, 70–85.

Blair, J. 1989. Frithuwold's kingdom and the origins of Surrey. In S. Basset (ed.), *The Origins of the Anglo-Saxon Kingdoms*, 97–107. Leicester, Leicester University Press.

Blair, J. 1990. An introduction to the Oxfordshire Domesday. In A. Williams and R. H. W. Erskine (eds), *The Oxfordshire Domesday*, 1–19. London, Alecto Historical Editions.

Blair, J. 1994. *Anglo-Saxon Oxfordshire*. Stroud, Alan Sutton.

Blair, J. 2005. *The Church in Anglo-Saxon Society*. Oxford, Oxford University Press.

Blair, J (ed). 2007. *Waterways and Canal-Building in Medieval England*. Oxford, Oxford University Press.

Boarstall Cartulary. The Boarstall Cartulary, H. E. Salter and A. H. Cooke (eds), Oxford Historical Society 88, 1930.

Bodleian Library. Oxford, Bodleian Library.

Böhme, H. 1974. *Germanische Grabfunde des 4. bis 5. Jahrhunderts zwischen Elbe und Loire*. Munich, C. H. Beck'sche Verlags.

Booth, P. 2001. Late Roman cemeteries in Oxfordshire: a review. *Oxoniensia* 66, 13–42.

Booth, P., Dodd, A., Robinson, M. and Smith, A. 2007. *The Thames Through Time; the Archaeology of the Gravel Terraces of the Upper and Middle Thames. The Early Historical Period: AD 1–1000*. Thames Valley Landscapes Monograph 27. Oxford, Oxford Archaeology.

Booth, P. and Simmonds, A. forthcoming. *Appleford's Earliest Farmers: Excavation at Appleford Sidings, 1993–2000*. Oxford Archaeology Occasional Paper. Oxford, Oxford Archaeology.

Boyle, A., Dodd, A., Miles, D. and Mudd, A. 1995. *Two Oxfordshire Anglo-Saxon Cemeteries: Berinsfield and Didcot*.

Thames Valley Landscapes Monograph 8. Oxford, Oxford Archaeological Unit.

Bracton's Notebook. Bracton's Note Book. A Collection of Cases Decided in the King's Courts During the Reign of Henry the Third, Annotated by a Lawyer of that Time, Seemingly by Henry of Bracton, ed. F. W. Maitland. London, C. J. Clay and Sons, 1887.

Bradbury, J. 1996. *Stephen and Matilda: the Civil War of 1139–1153*. Stroud, Sutton Publishing.

Bradley, R. 1978. Rescue excavation in Dorchester-on-Thames 1972. *Oxoniensia* 43, 17–39.

Bradley, R. and Chambers, R. 1988. A new study of the cursus complex at Dorchester-on-Thames. *Oxford Journal of Archaeology* 7, 271–289.

Bradley, T. and Armitage, P. 2002. A partial cow skeleton of the Middle Bronze Age at Wallingford, Oxfordshire. *Oxoniensia* 67, 359–363.

Briggs, G., Cook, J and Rowley, T. (eds) 1986. *The Archaeology of the Oxford Region*. Oxford, Oxford University Department of External Studies.

BRO Berkshire Record Office.

Brooks, N. P. 1964. The unidentified forts of the Burghal Hidage. *Medieval Archaeology* 8, 74–90.

Brooks, N. 1965a. *Wallingford Castle Excavations from the 9th to 31st August, 1965*. Unpublished notes. Wallingford, Wallingford Museum.

Brooks, N. P. 1965b. Excavations at Wallingford Castle 1965: an interim report. *Berkshire Archaeological Journal* 62, 17–21.

Brooks, N. P. 1966. Wallingford Castle Excavations August 1st to 27th 1966. Unpublished notes. Wallingford, Wallingford Museum.

Brooks, N. P. 1968. Wallingford Castle Excavations 1968 August 13th to September 7th. Unpublished notes. Wallingford, Wallingford Museum.

Brooks, N. P. 1996. The administrative background to the Burghal Hidage. In D. Hill and A. R. Rumble (eds), *The Defence of Wessex: the Burghal Hidage and Anglo-Saxon Fortification*, 128–50. Manchester, Manchester University Press.

Brown, R. A. 1959. A list of castles, 1154–1216. *English Historical Review* 74, 249–80.

Bullen, L. 1989. The poor man's guide to the history of Wallingford. 2nd ed, Wallingford Magazine.

Burnham, B. C. and Wacher, J. S. 1990. *The 'Small Towns' of Roman Britain*. London, Batsford.

CA. Current Archaeology.

Cam, H. 1963. *Liberties and Communities in Medieval England*. New York, Barnes and Noble.

Campbell, J. 2000. Power and authority, 600–1300. In D. Palliser (ed.), *The Cambridge Urban History of Britain, Vol. 1, 600–1540*, 51–78. Cambridge, Cambridge University Press.

Carmen. The Carmen de Hastingae Proelio of Guy, Bishop of Amiens, ed. and trans. F. Barlow. Oxford Medieval Texts. Oxford, Oxford University Press, 1999.

Carr, R. D. 1976. Excavations at Wallingford Castle: an Interim Report. Unpublished notes. Wallingford, Wallingford Museum.

Case, H. J. 1982. The linear ditches and southern enclosure, North Stoke. In H. J. Case and A. W. R. Whittle (eds), *Settlement Patterns in the Oxford Region: Excavations at the Abingdon Causewayed Enclosure and Other Sites*, 60–75. Research Report 44, London, Council for British Archaeology.

CChR. Calendar of Charter Rolls Preserved in the Public Record Office,. 6 vols, Public Record Office, 1903.

Chadwick, H. M. 1905. *Studies on Anglo-Saxon Institutions*. Cambridge, Cambridge University Press.

Chalkley Gould, I. 1906. The walls of Wallingford. *Journal of the British Archaeological Association* 12, 119–124.

Chambers, R. A. 1986. A Roman timber bridge at Ivy Farm, Fencott with Murcott, Oxon. *Oxoniensia* 51, 31–36.

Chambers, R. A. 1987. The late- and sub-Roman cemetery at Queenford Farm, Dorchester-on-Thames, Oxon. *Oxoniensia* 52, 35–69.

Chambers, R. A. and McAdam, E. 2007. *Excavations at Barrow Hills, Radley, Oxfordshire, 1983–5. Vol. 2: The Romano-British Cemetery and Anglo-Saxon Settlement.* Thames Valley Landscapes Monograph 25. Oxford, Oxford Archaeology.

Cheetham, C. J. 1995. Some Roman and pre-Roman settlements and roads by the confluence of the Cherwell and the Ray near Otmoor. *Oxoniensia* 60, 419–26.

Cholsey 1695. A survey of the manor of Cholsey in the County of Berks, comprehending Cholsey Town and Farm with ye Tenements, Enclosures and Craut-Lands... Truly and Faithfully made and taken in Sept. 1695 and Apr. 1696. By Edward Bostock Fuller. Scale 1:3,168. Manuscript on parchment (R), MS C17:13 (41). Oxford, Bodleian Library.

Christie, N. J., Creighton, O. H. and O'Sullivan, D. 2003. Wallingford *Burh* to Borough Research Project: first interim report, 2002. *South Midlands Archaeology* 33, 105–113.

Christie, N. J., O'Sullivan, D., Browning, J., Butler, A., Creighton, O., Hamerow, H. (2003). The Wallingford Burgh to Borough Research Project. *South Midlands Archaeology* **34**, 94–103.

Christie, N. J., O'Sullivan, D., Creighton, O. H. and Hamerow, H. 2004a. The Wallingford *Burh* to Borough Research Project: 2003 interim report. *South Midlands Archaeology* 34, 94–102.

Christie, N. J., O'Sullivan, D., Creighton, O. H. and Hamerow, H. 2004b. The Wallingford *Burh* to Borough Research Project: 2003 fieldwork. *Medieval Settlement Research Group Annual Report* 18, 9–13.

CI. Calendar of Inquisitions Post Mortem and Other Analogous Documents Preserved in the Public Record Office, Public Record Office, Public Record Office, 1904 and in progress.

CIPM. Calendar of Inquisitions Post Mortem. Public Record Office, 14 vols. London, HMSO, 1904–54.

Clanchy, M. T. (ed.) 1973. *Roll and Writ Files of the Berkshire Eyre of 1248*. Selden Society 90.

Clark, J. 2000. Late Saxon and Norman London: thirty years on. In I. Hayes, H. Sheldon and L. Hannigan (eds), *London Under Ground: the Archaeology of a City,* 206–222. Oxford, Oxbow.

Clarke, C. M. 1996. Excavations at Coldharbour Farm, Crowmarsh. *South Midlands Archaeology* 26, 71–76.

Clarke, C. M. 1997. *Excavations of a Roman-British Cemetery: Cold Harbour Farm, Crowmarsh.* Unpublished Wallingford Historical and Archaeological Society Report. Wallingford.

Clarke, P. A. 1994. *The English Nobility under Edward the Confessor*. Oxford, Oxford University Press.

CMF. Cartulary of the Monastery of St. Frideswide at Oxford, ed. S. R. Wigram, Oxford Historical Society 28 and 31 (1895–6).

COEL. K.S.B. Keats-Rohan, *Continental Origins of English Landholders 1066–1166 Database (COEL))*, on CD-ROM, Coel Enterprises, 2000, with regular updates.

Collins, A. E. P. 1949. Bronze and pottery from Wallingford. *Berkshire Archaeological Journal* 51, 65–66.

Collins, A. E. P. 1949. Iron Age and Romano-British finds at Wallingford. *Berkshire Archaeological Journal* 51, 65.

Compton, H. J. 1978. River tolls: Wallingford Bridge. *Journal of the Railway and Canal Historical Society* 24, 108–9.

Cook, J. and Rowley, T. (eds) 1985. *Dorchester Through the Ages.* Oxford, Oxford University Department for External Studies.

Cooke, A. H. 1927. Early mayors of Wallingford. *Berkshire, Buckinghamshire and Oxfordshire Archaeological Journal* 31, 28–29.

Crake, A. D. 1888. *Brian Fitz-Count: A Story of Wallingford Castle and Dorchester Abbey*. New York, E. and J. B. Young.

Crawford, S. 1999. *Childhood in Anglo-Saxon England*. Stroud, Alan Sutton.

Crawley, A. and Freeman, I. 1988. Bedford's oldest streets. *Bedfordshire Archaeological Journal* 18, 99–108.

Creighton, O. H. 2005: *Castles and Landscapes: Power, Community and Fortification in Medieval England*. London, Equinox.

Creighton, O. H., Christie, N. J., O'Sullivan, D. and Hamerow, H. 2002. The Wallingford *Burh* to Borough Research Project. *Medieval Settlement Research Group Annual Report* 17, 43–46.

Creighton, O. H. and Higham, R. A. 2005. *Medieval Town Walls: a Social History and Archaeology of Urban Defence*. Stroud, Tempus.

Cromarty, A. M., Barclay, A., Lambrick, G. and Robinson, M. 2006. *Late Bronze Age Ritual and Habitation on a Thames Eyot at Whitecross Farm, Wallingford: the Archaeology of the Wallingford Bypass, 1986–92*. Thames Valley Landscapes Monograph 22, Oxford, Oxford Archaeology.

Croney, A, 1998. 21b and 22 St Mary's St, Wallingford. An Archaeological watching brief. Thames Valley Archaeological services, report 98/26. Reading, Thames Valley Archaeological Services.

CRR. Curia Regis Rolls, Public Record Office, 1922 and in progress.

Cunliffe, B., and Miles, D. 1984. *Aspects of the Iron Age in Central Southern Britain,* Oxford University Committee for Archaeology Monograph 2. Oxford, Oxford University Committee for Archaeology.

Cuttler, R., Hunt, J., and Rátkai, S. 2008. *Saxon Burh and Royal Castle: Re-thinking Early Urban Space in Stafford*. Birmingham, Birmingham Archaeology.

Dalton. J. and Hiller, J. 2001. 64/65 High Street, Wallingford, Oxfordshire, NGR SU 6062 8949. Archaeological watching brief report. Oxford, Oxford Archaeological Unit.

Darby, H. C. 1977. *Domesday England*. Cambridge, Cambridge University Press.

Davies, P. 1974. *Colourful Characters of North Berkshire*. Wallingford, self published.

Davis, R. H. C. 1972. The College of St. Martin-le-Grand and the Anarchy, 1135–54. *London Topographical Record* 23, 9–26.

DB Berks. Domesday Book: Berkshire, ed. P. Morgan. Chichester, Phillimore, 1979.

DB Bucks. Domesday Book: Buckinghamshire, ed. J. Morris. Chichester, Phillimore, 1978.

DB Cambs. Domesday Book: Cambridgeshire, ed. A. Rumble. Chichester, Phillimore, 1981.

DB Derby. Domesday Book: Derbyshire, ed. P. Morgan. Chichester, Phillimore, 1978.

DB Essex. Domesday Book: Essex, ed. A. Rumble. Chichester, Phillimore, 1983.

DB Gloucs. Domesday Book: Gloucestershire, ed. J. S. Moore. Chichester, Phillimore, 1982

DB Hants. Domesday Book: Hampshire, ed. J. Mumby. Chichester, Phillimore, 1982.

DB Hunts. Domesday Book: Huntingdonshire, ed. S. Harvey. Chichester, Phillimore, 1975.

DB Leics. Domesday Book: Leicestershire, ed. P. Morgan. Chichester, Phillimore, 1979.

DB Lincs. Domesday Book: Lincolnshire, ed. P. Morgan and C. Thorn. Chichester, Phillimore, 1986.

DB Middx. Domesday Book: Middlesex, ed. J. Morris. Chichester, Phillimore, 1975.

DB Northants. Domesday Book: Northamptonshire, eds F. Thorn and C. Thorn. Chichester, Phillimore, 1979.

DB Notts. Domesday Book: Nottinghamshire, ed. J. Morris. Chichester, Phillimore, 1977.

DB Oxon. Domesday Book: Oxfordshire, ed. J. Morris. Chichester, Phillimore, 1978.

DB Surrey. Domesday Book: Surrey, ed. J. Morris. Chichester, Phillimore, 1975.

DB Sussex. Domesday Book: Sussex, ed. J. Morris. Chichester, Phillimore, 1976.

DB Warks. Domesday Book: Warwickshire, ed. J. Morris. Chichester, Phillimore, 1976.

DB Wilts. Domesday Book: Wiltshire, ed. C. and F. Thorn. Chichester, Phillimore, 1979.

DB Worcs. Domesday Book: Worcestershire, eds F. and C. Thorn. Chichester, Phillimore, 1982.

DB Yorks. Domesday Book: Yorkshire, eds M. L. Faull and M. Stinson. Chichester, Phillimore, 1986.

Dean, M. 1977. Lead tokens from the River Thames at Windsor and Wallingford. *Numismatic Chronicle* 137, 137–47.

Denton. J. H. 1970. *English Royal Free Chapels, 1100–1300: a Constitutional Study*. Manchester, Manchester University Press.

Dewey, J. and Dewey, S. 1977. *The Book of Wallingford, a Historical Portrait*. Chesham, Barracuda Books.

Dewey, J. and Dewey, S. 1990. *Payne and Son - Two Centuries of a Family Firm*. Cholsey, Pie Powder Press.

Dewey, J. and Dewey, S. 1996. *Historic Wallingford: Walk-round Guide*. Wallingford, The Wallingford Historical and Archaeological Society in association with Pie Powder Press.

Dewey, J. and Dewey, S. 1996. *Wallingford and the Civil War*. Cholsey, Pie Powder Press.

Dewey, J. and Dewey, S. 2005. *1155 and All That: The Story of Wallingford's 850–year old Charter*. Cholsey, Pie Powder Press.

Dewey, J. and Dewey, S. (eds) 1983. *Men of Iron*. Wallingford, The Wallingford Historical and Archaeological Society

Dewey, J., Dewey, S., Beasley, D. 1989. *Window on Wallingford: 1837–1914. Life in a Thames-side Market Town*. Cholsey, Pie Powder Press.

Dickinson, T. M. 1976. *The Anglo-Saxon Burial Sites of the Upper Thames Region, and their Bearing on the History of Wessex, circa AD 400–700'*. Unpublished PhD thesis, University of Oxford.

Dodd, A. (ed.) 2003. *Oxford Before the University: the Late Saxon and Norman Archaeology of the Thames Crossing, the Defences and the Town*. Oxford, Oxford Archaeology.

Durham, B. 1980. Wallingford, *Council for British Archaeology Group 9 Newsletter* 11, 140–142.

Durham, B, and TWHAS, 1981. Wallingford: 9–11 St Martin's Street, *South Midland Archaeology* 11, 140–2.

Durham, B. 1983a. Wallingford 9–11 St Martin's St, *South Midlands Archaeology* 13, 148–50.

Durham, B. 1983b. Wallingford, The Mill, St Mary's Street, *South Midlands Archaeology* 13, 150.

Durham, B., Hassall, T., Rowley, T. and Simpson, C. 1973. A cutting across the Saxon defences at Wallingford, Berkshire 1971. *Oxoniensia* 37, 82–85.

Durham, B. and Rowley, T. 1972. A cemetery site at Queensford Mill, Dorchester. *Oxoniensia* 37, 32–37.

Dyer, C. C. 2003. The archaeology of medieval small towns. *Medieval Archaeology* 47, 85–114.

Edgeworth, M. 2004. Recent archaeological investigations in Bedford town centre: evidence for an early northern boundary? *Bedfordshire Archaeology* 25, 190–200.

Edgeworth, M. 2006. *Extensive Urban Survey of Bedford*. Bedford, Albion Archaeology. Available online: http://ads.ahds.ac.uk/catalogue/projArch/EUS/bedsluton_eus_2006/downloads.cfm; accessed 23/06/2009.

EHD. English Historical Documents ii, 1042–1189, eds D. C. Douglas and G. W. Greenaway. London, Eyre Methuen, 2nd ed. 1981.

Eke, C. 2007. *The Story of Angier's Almshouses, Wallingford*. Wallingford, self-published.

Evison, V. I. 1968 for 1967. A sword from the Thames at Wallingford Bridge. *Archaeological Journal* 124, 160–89.

Evison, V. I. 1978. Early Anglo-Saxon applied disc brooches. *Antiquaries Journal* 58, 88–102.

Fauroux, M. 1961. *Recueil des Actes des Ducs de Normandie (911–1066)*. Mémoires de la Société des Antiquaires de Normandie 36. Caen, Société des Antiquaires de Normandie.

Fern, C. 2005. The archaeological evidence for equestrianism in early Anglo-Saxon England. In A. Pluskowski (ed), *Just Skin and Bones? New Perspectives on Human-Animal Relations in the Historical Past*, 43–71. British Archaeological Reports International Series 1410. Oxford, BAR Publishing.

Fernie, E. 1991. Anglo-Saxon lengths and the evidence of the buildings. *Medieval Archaeology* 35, 1–5.

Field, J. E. 1893. The antiquities of Wallingford, *Berks Archaeological Journal*. 3, 18–20

Field, J. E. 1895. The antiquities of Wallingford. *Berkshire Archaeological and Architectural Society* 3, 96–99, 117–122.

Field, J. E. 1906. History of Wallingford. *Journal of the British Archaeological Association* new series 12.

Field, J. E. 1917. Survey of Wallingford, 1550. *Berkshire, Buckinghamshire and Oxfordshire Archaeological Journal*, 21.

Field, J. E. 1925. *Historical Notes on the Antiquities of Wallingford*. Wallingford, Arthur Jenkins.

Fleming, R. 1991, *Kings, and Lords in Conquest England*. Cambridge, Cambridge University Press.

Fleming, R. 1993. Rural elites and urban communities in late Saxon England. *Past and Present* 141, 3–26.

Foard, G., 1995. The early topography of Northampton and its suburbs. *Northamptonshire Archaeology* 26, 109–22.

Ford, S. 1990. The archaeology of the Cleeve-Didcot Pipeline, South Oxfordshire, 1989. *Oxoniensia* 55, 1–40

Ford, S. 1992. Harris Garage Car Park, Wallingford: An Archaeological Evaluation for South Oxfordshire District Council. Unpublished client report. Reading, Thames Valley Archaeological Services.

Ford, S. 2004. 60 High St Wallingford, Oxfordshire. Archaeological watching brief. Reading, Thames Valley Archaeological Services.

Ford, S., Bowden, M., Mees, G. and Gaffney, V. 1988. The date of the 'Celtic' Field-Systems on the Berkshire Downs. *Britannia* 19, 401–404.

Ford, S. and Hazell, A. 1989. Prehistoric, Roman and Anglo-Saxon settlement patterns at North Stoke, Oxfordshire. *Oxoniensia* 54, 7–23.

Ford, S. and Hazell, A. 1990. Trial trenching of a Saxon pottery scatter at North Stoke, South Oxfordshire, 1988. *Oxoniensia* 55, 169–171.

Ford, S., Lowe, J. and Pine, J. 2006. Early Bronze Age, Roman and medieval boundaries and trackways at Howbery Park, Crowmarsh Gifford, Oxfordshire. *Oxoniensia* 71, 197–210.

Frere, S. S. 1962. Excavations at Dorchester on Thames, 1962. *Archaeological Journal* 119, 114–149.

Frere, S. S. 1984. Excavations at Dorchester on Thames, 1963. *Archaeological Journal* 141, 91–174.

Fulford, M. G. and Rippon, S. J. 1994. Lowbury Hill, Oxon: a re-assessment of the probable Romano-Celtic temples and the Anglo-Saxon barrow. *Archaeological Journal* 151, 158–211.

Fulford, M. and Timby, J. 2000. *Late Iron Age and Roman Silchester: Excavations on the Site of the Forum-Basilica 1977, 1980–86*. Britannia Monograph Series 15. London, Society for the Promotion of Roman Studies.

Gaffney, V. and Tingle, M. 1989. *The Maddle Farm Project: an Integrated Survey of Prehistoric and Roman Landscapes on the Berkshire Downs*. British Archaeological Reports British Series 200. Oxford, BAR Publishing.

Garrod, H. W. 1926. Richard of Wallingford's connection with Merton College, Oxford. *Transactions of the St Albans and Hertfordshire Architectural and Archaeological Society*, 230–1.

Gasquet, F. A. 1912. *Abbot Wallingford: an Inquiry into the Charges made against Him and his Monks*. London, Sands and Co.

GDB. *Great Domesday*, ed. R. W. H. Erskine. London, Alecto Historical Editions, 1986.

Gelling, M. 1974. *The Place-Names of Berkshire*. English Place-Name Society 49, 50, and 51.

Gelling, M. 1979. *The Early Charters of the Thames Valley*. Studies in Early English History 7. Leicester, Leicester University Press.

Gelling, M. and Cole, A. 2000. *The Landscape of Place names*. Stamford, Shaun Tyas.

Gesta Stephani. Gesta Stephani. ed. K. R. Potter, 2nd edition. with a new introduction and notes by R. H. C. Davis. Oxford, Oxford University Press, 1976.

Gesta Willelmi. The Gesta Guillelmi of William of Poitiers, eds R. H. C. Davis and M. Chibnall. Oxford, Oxford University Press (1998).

Ginsberg, L. B. 1964. Wallingford: the archaeological argument. *Architects' Journal* 163, 22.

Gould, I. C. 1906. The walls of Wallingford. *Journal of the British Archaeological Association* 12, 2–8.

Grayson, A. 2004 (2005). Bradford's Brook, Wallingford. *Oxoniensia* 69, 29–44.

Green, A. 1964. Borough records of Wallingford. *Journal of the Society of Archivists* 2, 10, 476–479.

Green, J. A. 1990. *English Sheriffs to 1154*. Public Record Office handbook 24. London, HMSO.

Griffin, S. 2000. *Wallingford in the English Civil War, 1642–1646*. Bristol, Stuart Press.

Grove, L. R. A. 1938. Norman pottery from Wallingford Market Place. *Berkshire Archaeological Journal* 42, 67–70.

Gunther, R. T. 1926. Wallingford's scientific instruments. *St Albans and Hertfordshire Architectural and Archaeological Society Transactions*. 235–43

Haggar. M. 2008. The Gesta Abbatum Monasterii Sancti Albani: litigation and history at St. Albans. *Historical Research* 81, 373–398.

Halpin, C. 1983. Wallingford: John Wilder's, Goldsmith's Lane. *South Midlands Archaeology* 13. Council For British Archaeology Group 9, 148–9.

Hamerow, H. 1999. Anglo-Saxon Oxfordshire, 400–700. *Oxoniensia* 64, 23–38.

Hamerow, H., Hayden, C. and Hey, G. 2007. Anglo-Saxon and earlier settlement near Drayton Road, Sutton Courtenay, Berkshire. *Archaeological Journal* 164, 109–196.

Harden, D. B. 1936. Two Romano-British potters'-fields near Oxford. *Oxoniensia* 1, 81–102.

Harden, D. B. 1940. Wallingford, Berks. *Oxoniensia* 5, 164.

Hardman, J. S. 1994. *Wallingford, a History of an English Market Town*. Lambourn.

Harman, M., Lambrick, G., Miles, D. and Rowley, T. 1978. Roman burials around Dorchester-on-Thames. *Oxoniensia* 43, 1–16.

Harrison, J. P. 1890. Notes on St Leonard's church, Wallingford

Harrison, J. P. 1892. St. Leonard's Church, Wallingford. *Journal of the British Archaeological Association* 47, 135–138.

Hart. C. R. 1992. *The Danelaw*. London, Hambledon Press.

Harvey, S. P. J. 1971. Domesday Book and its predecessors. *English Historical Review* 86, 753–73.

Haslam, J. 1983. The origin and plan of Bedford. *Bedfordshire Archaeology* 16, 29–36.

Haslam, J. 2005. King Alfred and the vikings - strategies and tactics, 876–886 AD. *Anglo-Saxon Studies in Archaeology and History* 13, 121–53.

Hassall, J. 1983. Excavations in Bedford 1977 and 1978. *Bedfordshire Archaeology* 16, 37–64.

Haslam. J. 1984. The towns of Wiltshire. In J. Haslam (ed.), *Anglo-Saxon Towns in Southern England*, 87–147. Chichester, Phillimore.

Hassall, T. 1986. The Oxford region from the conversion to the Conquest. In G. Briggs, J. Cook, and T. Rowley (eds), *The Archaeology of the Oxford Region*, 109–114. Oxford, Oxford University Department of External Studies.

Hassall, T. G. and Airs, M. 1978. Wallingford. *Archaeological Journal* 135, 291–4.

Haverfield, F. 1901. Romano-British remains in the Upper Thames Valley near Wallingford, Dorchester, Oxford and Eynsham. *Proceedings of the Society of Antiquaries of London* 2nd ser. 18.

Hedges, J. K. 1881. *The History of Wallingford from the Invasion of Caesar to the Present Time*. London, William Clowes and Sons.

Hedges, J. K. 1892. Wallingford. *Journal of the British Archaeological Association* 47, 124–131.

Henig, M. and Booth, P. 2000. *Roman Oxfordshire*. Stroud, Alan Sutton.

Herbert, N. M. 1969. *The Borough of Wallingford, 1155–1400*. Unpublished PhD thesis, Reading University.

Herbert, N. M. 1969. The family of De Stallis at Wallingford in the 13th century. *Berkshire Archaeological Journal* 64, 21–33.

Hill, D. 1970. Late Saxon Bedford. *Bedfordshire Archaeological Journal* 5, 96–8

Hill, D. 1996. The nature of the figures. In D. Hill and A. R. Rumble (eds), *The Defence of Wessex: the Burghal Hidage and Anglo-Saxon Fortification*, 74–86. Manchester, Manchester University Press.

Hill, D. and Rumble, A. R. (eds) 1996. *The Defence of Wessex: the Burghal Hidage and Anglo-Saxon Fortification*. Manchester, Manchester University Press.

Hinchliffe, J. 1975. Excavations at Grim's Ditch, Mongewell, 1974. *Oxoniensia* 40, 122–135

Hinchliffe, J. and Thomas, R. 1980. Archaeological investigations at Appleford. *Oxoniensia* 45, 9–111.

Hindle, P. 1998. *Medieval Roads and Tracks*. Oxford, Shire Publications.

Hingley, R. 1980. Excavations by R A Rutland on an Iron Age site at Wittenham Clumps. *Berkshire Archaelogical Journal* 70, 21–55.

Hingley, R. and Miles, D. 1984. Aspects of Iron Age settlement in the Upper Thames Valley. In B. Cunliffe and D. Miles (eds), *Aspects of the Iron Age in Central Southern Britain*, 52–71. Oxford University Committee for Archaeology Monograph 2. Oxford, Oxford University Committee for Archaeology.

Hinton, D. 1977. *Alfred's Kingdom: Wessex and the South, 800–1500*. London, Dent.

Hirst, S. 1985. *An Anglo-Saxon Cemetery at Sewerby, East Yorkshire*. York University Archaeological Publications 4, 62–85.

Hooper, N. 1984. The housecarls in England in the eleventh century. *Anglo-Norman Studies* 7, 161–76.

Hooper, N. 1988. An introduction to the Berkshire Domesday. In A. Williams and R. H. W. Erskine (eds), *The Berkshire Domesday*, 1–28. London, Alecto Historical Editions.

Hooper, N. 1989. An introduction to the Wiltshire Domesday. In A. Williams and R. H. W. Erskine (eds), *The Berkshire Domesday*, 1–30. London, Alecto Historical Editions.

Howgrave-Graham, R. P. 1926. Early clocks and horologies: Richard of Wallingford's clock. *St Albans and Hertfordshire Architectural and Archaeological Society Transactions*, 231–5.

Huggins, P. J. 1991. Anglo-Saxon timber building measurements: recent results. *Medieval Archaeology* 35, 6–28.

Hull. G. 1999. The Masonic Centre, Goldsmiths Lane, Wallingford, Oxfordshire. An archaeological watching brief, report 99/31. Reading, Thames Valley Archaeological Services.

Hull, G. and Pine, J. 2001. The Lamb Garage Site, Castle Street, Wallingford, Oxfordshire: An Archaeological Evaluation for Grace Hotels Ltd. Unpublished client report. Reading, Thames Valley Archaeological Services.

Hunter, J. 1995. *A History of Berkshire*. Darwen County History. Chichester, Phillimore.

Keats-Rohan, K. S. B. 1989. The devolution of the honour of Wallingford, 1066–1148. *Oxoniensia* 54, 311–18.

Keats-Rohan, K. S. B. 1999. *Domesday People. A Prosopography of Persons Occurring in English Documents 1066–1166. Volume I. Domesday Book*. Woodbridge, Boydell Press.

Keats-Rohan, K. S. B. 2001. *Domesday Descendants. A Prosopography of Persons Occurring in English Documents 1066–1166. Volume II. Pipe Rolls to Cartae Baronum*. Woodbridge, Boydell Press.

Keevil, G. 1995. The Town Hall, Wallingford, Oxfordshire, SU 60728936. Record of Archaeological Monitoring Visit Site Code WATH 94. Oxford, Oxford Archaeological Unit.

Keevill, G. D. 2004. Archaeological investigations in 2001 at the Abbey Church of St Peter and St Paul, Dorchester-on-Thames, Oxfordshire. *Oxoniensia* 68, 313–362.

Kelly, S. E. 2007. King Æthelwulf's decimation. *Anglo-Saxon* 1, 285–317.

Keynes, S. 1987. Regenbald the chancellor (sic). *Anglo-Norman Studies* 10, 185–222.

Keyser, C. E. 1907. Note on a carved Norman stone from the museum of Wallingford Castle. *Proceedings of the Society of Antiquaries* 21, 118–123.

Kirk, J. R. and Leeds, E. T. 1952/53. Three early Saxon graves from Dorchester, Oxon. *Oxoniensia* 17/18, 63–76.

Knowles, D. 1952. The case of St. Albans abbey in 1490. *Journal of Ecclesiastical History* 3, 144–58.

Lamborn, E. A. G. 1948. The medieval archives of Wallingford. *Notes and Queries* 193, 68–9.

Lambrick, G. 1998. Frontier territory along the Thames. *British Archaeology* 33, April.

Lambrick, G. 1990. Farmers and shepherds in the Bronze Age and Iron Age. *Current Archaeology* 11, 14–18.

Lambrick, G., 1992. The development of prehistoric and Roman farming on the Thames gravels. In M. Fulford and E. Nichols (eds), *Developing Landscapes of Lowland Britain. The Archaeology of the British Gravels: A Review*, 78–105. Society of Antiquaries London Occasional Papers 14. London, Society of Antiquaries.

Lambrick, G., forthcoming a. *The Thames Through Time; the Archaeology of the Gravel Terraces of the Upper and Middle Thames. Volume 2: the Foundation of Modern Society in the Thames Valley 1500 BC-AD 50*. Thames Valley Landscapes Monograph. Oxford, Oxford Archaeology.

Lambrick, G. forthcoming b. *Neolithic to Saxon Social and Environmental Change at Mount Farm, Berinsfield, Dorchester on Thames*. Occasional Paper. Oxford, Oxford Archaeology.

Lambrick, G., More, J., Wardle, P. 1992. Grim's Ditch and the Wallingford bypass. *Oxford Archaeological Unit Annual Report 1991–1992*, 11–12.

Lapidge, M., Blair, J,. Keynes, S., and Scragg, D (eds) 1999. *The Blackwell Encyclopaedia of Anglo-Saxon England*. Oxford, Blackwell.

Lawson, M. K. 1993. *Cnut: the Danes in England in the Early Eleventh Century*. London, Longman.

Laycock, S. and Marshall, C. 2005. Late Roman buckles in Britain 6 – horsehead. Web, http://www.laycokinfo. co.uk/rombuckles/pages/horsehead_buckles.htm (accessed September 2008).

Le Breton, M. E. 1928. *A History of Wallingford (Berkshire)*. London, The Acorn Press.

Leeds, E. T 1910. The Wallingford sword. *Antiquary* 46, 348.

Leeds, E. T. 1923. A Saxon village near Sutton Courtenay, Berkshire. *Archaeologia* 73, 147–192.

Leeds, E. T. 1927. A Saxon village at Sutton Courtenay, Berkshire, second report. *Archaeologia* 76, 59–80.

Leeds, E. T. 1938. An Anglo-Saxon cemetery at Wallingford, Berkshire. *Berkshire Archaeological Journal* 42, 93–101.

Leeds, E. T. 1947. A Saxon village at Sutton Courtenay, Berkshire, third report. *Archaeologia* 92, 79–93.

Leland. The Itinerary of John Leland in or about the Years 1535–1543, ed. L. Toulmin-Smith. London, George Bell and Sons (1908–10).

Lemaire, K. 1988. *Wallingford: a bibliography*.

Lewis, C. 2007. New avenues for the investigation of currently occupied medieval rural settlement: preliminary observations from the Higher Education Field Academy. *Medieval Archaeology* 51, 133–163.

Mack, K. 1984. Changing thegns: Cnut's conquest and the English aristocracy. *Albion* 16, 375–87.

Maitland, F. W. 1897. *Domesday Book and Beyond*. Cambridge, Cambridge University Press.

Malpas, F. J. 1987. Roman roads south and east of Dorchester-on-Thames. *Oxoniensia* 52, 23–33.

Martin, G. H. 1985. Domesday Book and the boroughs. In P. H. Sawyer (ed.), *Domesday Book: a Reassessment*, 143–63. London, Arnold.

McKisack, M. 1948. The mediaeval records of the Corporation of Wallingford. *Oxoniensia* 13, 84–142.

Miles, D. 1986 (ed.). Miles, D. *Archaeology at Barton Court Farm, Abingdon, Oxon: an Investigation of Late Neolithic, Iron Age, Romano-British and Saxon Settlements*. Research Report 50. London, Council for British Archaeology.

Miles, D. 1997. Conflict and complexity: the later prehistory of the Oxford region. *Oxoniensia* 62, 1–19

Milne, G. 2001. *Excavations at Medieval Cripplegate, London: Archaeology after the Blitz, 1946–68*. London, English Heritage.

Milne, G. 2003. *The Port of Medieval London*. Stroud, Tempus.

Milne, J. G. 1940. Muniments of Holy Trinity Priory, Wallingford. *Oxoniensia* 5, 50–77.

Mon. Ang. Monasticon Anglicanum, eds J. Caley, H. Ellis, and B. Bandinel, 6 vols in 8. London, Longman, Hurst, Rees, Orme and Brown (1817–30).

Montagu, H. 1892. Find of groats at Wallingford. *Numismatic Chronicle* 12, 220–226.

Moore, J. 2002. *An Archaeological Watching Brief at 16 St George's Road, Wallingford*. Unpublished client report. Oxford, John Moore Heritage Services.

Moore, J. 2004. 16 St George's Road, Wallingford, *South Midlands Archaeology* 32, 81.

Moorey, P. R. S. 1982. A Neolithic ring-ditch and Iron Age enclosure at Newnham Murren, near Wallingford. In P. H. J. Case and A. W. R. Whittle (eds), *Settlement Patterns in the Oxford Region: Excavations at the Abingdon Causewayed Enclosure and Other Sites*, 55–9. Research Report 44. London, Council for British Archaeology.

Morris, R. 1986. Alcuin, York, and the *Alma Sophia*. In L. A. S. Butler and R. K. Morris (eds), *The Anglo-Saxon Church: Papers on History, Architecture, and Archaeology in Honour of Dr H. M. Taylor*. London, Council for British Archaeology.

Morris, R. 1989. *Churches in the Landscape*. London, Dent.

Mortimer, I. (ed.) 1995. *Berkshire Glebe Terriers 1634*. Berkshire Record Society 2.

NA. London, National Archives

Nairn, I. 1968. Remarkably crude and boorish new building. *Architectural Review* 143, 247.

Network Archaeology 2004. Chalgrove to East Ilsley Natural Gas Pipeline, archaeological excavations and watching brief, post-excavation assessment of potential for analysis and updated project design. Unpublished client report for TRANSCO. Lincoln, Network Archaeology.

NI. Nonarum Inquisitiones in Curia Scaccarii temp. Edwardi III, Record Commission, 1807.

North, J. D. (ed.) 1976. *Richard of Wallingford. An edition of his writings with Introduction, English Translation, and Commentary*. Oxford, Oxford University Press.

North, J. D. 2004. *God's Clockmaker: Richard of Wallingford and the Invention of Time*. Oxford, Oxbow Books.

OHER. *Oxfordshire Historic Environment Record*, accessible at http://www.oxfordshire.gov.uk/wps/portal/publicsite/doitonline/finditonline/heritage

Orme, N. and Webster, M. 1995. *The English Hospital, 1070–1570*. New Haven, Yale University Press.

Oseney Cartulary. Cartulary of Oseney Abbey, ed. H. E. Salter, 6 vols, Oxford Historical Society, 89, 90, 91, 97, 98, and 101, 1929–36.

Oxford Archaeology in preparation. *The Thames Through Time; the Archaeology of the Upper and Middle Thames. Volume 1: the Formation and Changing Environment of the Thames Valley and Early Human Occupation to 1500 BC*. Thames Valley Landscapes Monograph. Oxford, Oxford Archaeology.

Pagan, H. E. 1984. A die-linked group of coins of Wallingford. *Spink Numismatic Circular* 92, 322–3.

Palliser, D. M. 1990. *Domesday York*. York, Borthwick Institute.

Palmer, J. 2007. *Electronic Edition of Domesday Book: Translation, Databases and Scholarly Commentary, 1086*. Deposited with the United Kingdom Data Archive at http://www.data-archive.ac.uk/findingdata/snDescription.asp?sn=5694, accessed on 07 November 2008.

Pedgley, B. and Pedgley, D. 1990. *Crowmarsh – a history of Crowmarsh Gifford, Newnham Murren, Mongewell and North Stoke*. Crowmarsh, Crowmarsh History Group.

Pevsner, N. 1966. *The Buildings of England: Berkshire*. London, Penguin Books.

Pine, J. 2003. 51, 52 and 53 St Mary's Street, Wallingford, Oxfordshire, An Archaeological Watching Brief and Evaluation, report 03/91. Reading, Thames Valley Archaeological Services.

Pine, J. 2005. Early Roman occupation at Jubilee Villa, 21 The Moorlands, Benson, Oxfordshire. *Oxoniensia* 70, 115–128.

Pine, J. and Ford, S. 2003. Excavation of Neolithic, late Bronze Age, early Iron Age and early Saxon features at St Helen's Avenue, Benson, Oxfordshire. *Oxoniensia* 68, 131–178.

Pipe Roll 31 Henry I. 1929. *The Pipe Roll of 31 Henry I, Michaelmas 1130. Reproduced in Facsimile from the Edition of 1833*. London, HMSO.

Pounds, N. J. G. 1990. *The Medieval Castle in England and Wales: a Social and Political History*. Cambridge, Cambridge University Press.

Prior, M. 1981. The accounts of Thomas West of Wallingford, a sixteenth century trader on the Thames. *Oxoniensia* 46, 73–93.

Radford, C. A. R. 1955. Leicester: church of St Mary de Castro. *Archaeological Journal* 112, 156–8.

Radford, C. A. R. 1971. The later pre-Conquest boroughs and their defences. *Medieval Archaeology* 14, 83–103.

Radford, C. A. R. 1980. The pre-Conquest boroughs of England, 9th-11th centuries. *Proceedings of the British Academy* 64, 131–53.

Reading Cartularies. *Reading Abbey Cartularies*, ed B. R. Kemp, Camden Society, 4th ser., 31, 33, 1986–7.

Regesta. Regesta Regum Anglo-Normanorum 1066–1154, H. W. C. Davis, C. Johnson, H. A. Cronne, and R. H. C. Davis (eds), 4 vols. Oxford, Oxford University Press, 1913–69.

Regesta Bates. *Regesta Regum Anglo-Normannorum: the Acta of Wiliam I (1066–1087)*, ed. D. Bates. Oxford, Oxford University Press, 1998.

Renn, D. 1993. Burhgeat and gonfanon: two sidelights from the Bayeux tapestry. *Anglo-Norman Studies* 16, 177–198.

Reynolds, A. 1999. *Later Anglo-Saxon England: Life and Landscape*. Stroud, Tempus.

Reynolds, S. 1977. *An Introduction to the History of English Medieval Towns*. Oxford, Oxford University Press.

Reynolds, S. 1986. Towns in Domesday. In J. C. Holt (ed.), *Domesday* Studies, 295–309. Woodbridge, The Boydell Press.

Rhodes, P. P. 1948. A Prehistoric and Roman site at Wittenham Clumps, Berks. *Oxoniensia* 13, 18–31.

Rhodes, P. P. 1950. The Celtic field-systems on the Berkshire Downs. *Oxoniensia* 15, 1–28.

Richardson, H. G. and Sayles, O. 1963. *The Governance of Medieval England from the Conquest to Magna Carta*. Edinburgh, Edinburgh University Press.

Richmond, A. 2005. Excavation of a Peterborough Ware pit at Wallingford, Oxfordshire. *Oxoniensia* 70, 79–96.

Riley, H. T. (ed.) 1873. Registra Johannis Whethamstede, Willelmi Albon, et Willelmi Walingforde, abbatum monasterii S. Albani. In H. T. Riley (ed), *Registra Quorundam Abbatum Monasterii S. Albani*. Rerum Britannicarum Medii Aevi Scriptores 28, 1–291.

Riley, H. T. 1876. *Appendix to the Sixth Report: The Corporation of Wallingford*. Historical Manuscripts Commission.

Ritchie, C. I. A. 1956. Abbot Thomas Ramryge's lost register, and the date of William Wallingford's death. *English Historical Review* 71, 434–5.

Roberts, B. K. and Wrathmell, S. 2000. *An Atlas of Rural Settlement in England*. London, English Heritage.

Roberts, B. K. and Wrathmell, S. 2002. *Region and Place: A Study of English Rural Settlement*. London, English Heritage.

Robertson, A. J. (ed.) 1956. *Anglo-Saxon Charters*. Cambridge, Cambridge University Press.

Rocque, J. 1761/1972. *County Map of Berkshire*, first published in 1761; new edition 1972. Woodbridge, Harry Margary

Rodwell, K. 1975. *Historic Towns of Oxfordshire: a Survey of the New County*. Oxford, Oxfordshire Archaeological Unit.

Roffe, D. and Mahany, C. 1986. Stamford and the Norman Conquest. *Lincolnshire History and Archaeology* 21, 5–9.

Roffe, D. R. 1990. From thegnage to barony: sake and soke, title, and tenants-in-chief. *Anglo-Norman Studies* 12, 157–76.

Roffe, D. R. 1997. Anglo-Saxon Nottingham and the Norman Conquest. In . J. V. Beckett (ed.), *A Centenary History of Nottingham*, 24–42. Manchester, Manchester University Press.

Roffe, D. R. 2000. *Domesday: the Inquest and the Book*. Oxford, Oxford University Press.

Roffe, D. R. 2007. *Decoding Domesday*. Woodbridge, The Boydell Press.

Rosevear, A. 1993. *The Wallingford, Wantage and Faringdon turnpike*. Wantage: privately published.

Ross, S. 1991. *Dress Pins from Anglo-Saxon England: their Production and Typo-chronological Development*. Unpublished PhD thesis, University of Oxford.

Rot. Chart. Rotuli Chartarum in Turri Londinensi Asservati, 1199–1216, ed. T. D. Hardy, Record Commission, 1837.

Rot. Hund. Rotuli Hundredorum, ed. W. Illingworth. Record Commission, 1812–18.

Rot. Orig. Rotulorum Originalium in Curia Scaccarii Abbreviatio, 2 vols. Record Commission, 1805–10.

Rotuli Parliamentorum. Rotuli Parliamentorum, 6 vols, Record Commission, 1783.

Rotulus de Redditibus. BRO, RTa 1.

Rowley, T. 1985. Roman Dorchester. In J. Cook and T. Rowley (eds), *Dorchester Through the Ages*, 21–28. Oxford, Oxford University Department for External Studies.

Rowley, T. and Brown, L. 1982. Excavations at Beech House Hotel, Dorchester-on-Thames 1972. *Oxoniensia* 46, 1–55.

RRH. The Register of Robert Hallum, bishop of Salisbury, 1407–17, ed. J. Horn. Canterbury and York Society 72, 1982.

RRM. The Register of Roger Martival: the Register of Presentations and Institutions to Benefices, ed. K. Edwards. Canterbury and York Society 55, 1959.

Ruben, I. and Ford, S. 1992. Archaeological excavations at Wallingford Road, Didcot, South Oxfordshire, 1991. *Oxoniensia* 57, 1–28.

Rumble, A. R. 1996. An edition and translation of the Burghal Hidage, together with recension C of the Tribal Hidage. In D. Hill and A. R. Rumble (eds), *The Defence of Wessex: the Burghal Hidage and Anglo-Saxon Fortification*, 14–35. Manchester, Manchester University Press.

Rutland, R. A. and Coghlan, H. H. 1972. Bronze Age flat axes from Berkshire. *Berkshire Archaeological Journal* 66, 45–59.

S. P. H. Sawyer, *Anglo-Saxon Charters: an Annotated List and Bibliography*, Royal Historical Society Guides and Handbooks, 8, (1968).

Salisbury Acta. English Episcopal Acta: Salisbury, 1078–1217, ed. B. R. Kemp. English Episcopal Acta 18. Oxford, Oxford University Press, 1999–2000.

Salway, P. 1999. Roman Oxfordshire. *Oxoniensia* 64, 1–22.

Sauer, E. W. 2005a. *Linear Earthwork, Tribal Boundary and Ritual Beheading: Aves Ditch from the Iron Age to the Early Middle Ages*. British Archaeological Reports British Series 402. Oxford, BAR Publishing.

Sauer, E. W. 2005b. Inscriptions from Alchester: Vespasian's base of the Second Augustan Legion(?). *Britannia* 36, 101–133.

Sayer-Milward, W. C. 1892. St. Leonard's Church, Wallingford. *Journal of the British Archaeological Association* 47, 132–134.

Sellwood, L. 1984. Tribal boundaries viewed from the perspective of numismatic evidence. In B. Cunliffe and D. Miles (eds), *Aspects of the Iron Age in Central Southern Britain*, 191–204. *Oxford University Committee for Archaeology* Monograph 2.

Oxford, Oxford, Oxford University Department for External Studies.

Sephton, R. S. 2003. William Seymour Blackstone (1809–1881) a Wallingford M.P. Self Published.

Sharpe, J. and Carter, P. 2008. A 'new' Roman road east of the Thames from Benson to Pangbourne. *South Oxfordshire Archaeological Group Bulletin* 62, 7–12.

Sherwood, G. F. T. 1906. The advowson of St Peter's, Wallingford, 1638–70. *Berkshire, Buckinghamshire and Oxfordshire Archaeological Journal* 12, 19–20.

Simpson, C. 1973. *Wallingford the Archaeological Implications of Development: a Survey*. Oxford, Oxfordshire Archaeology Unit.

Skermer, R. c1712. *Antiquities of Wallingford*. There are only six known copies in public collections: Reading Public Library: BU/D/L6867; Berkshire Record Office: D/EN/Z8; Bodleian Library: MS. Top. Berks. d.12, fols 1–15; MS.Top.Berks. d.28, pp 1–74; MS. Top. Berks. e.19 fols 1–35; 36–48; British Library: Add. MSS. 28667, fols 41–71.

Slade, C. F. 1960. Wallingford castle in the reign of Stephen. *Berkshire Archaeological Journal* 58, 33–43.

Smith, E. A. 1960. Bribery and disfranchisement: Wallingford elections, 1820–32. *English Historical Review* 75, 618–30.

Smith, R. A. 1924. Two prehistoric vessels. *Antiquaries Journal* 4, 127–30.

Speight, S. 2000. Castle Warfare in the Gesta Stephani. *Chateau Gaillard XIX: Actes du Colloque International de Graz, 1998*.

Spokes, P. S. 1949. Some notes on the domestic architecture of Wallingford, Berkshire. *Berkshire Archaeological Journal* 50, 30–48.

Spurrell, M. 1995. Containing Wallingford Castle, 1146–53. *Oxoniensia* 60, 257–270.

St. Joseph, J. K. 1965. Air reconnaissance in Britain, 1961–64. *Journal of Roman Studies* 55, 74–89.

Stafford, P. 1997. *Queen Emma and Queen Edith: Queenship and Women's Power in Eleventh-Century England*. Oxford, Blackwell Publishers.

Stenton, F. M. 1947. *Anglo-Saxon England* (2nd ed.). Oxford, Clarendon.

Stevenson, J. (ed) 1854. *Chronicles of John Wallingford*. The Church Historians of England, Volume 2 Part 2, 523–631.

Sylloge. Sylloge of Coins of the British Isles http://www.fitzmuseum.cam.ac.uk/dept/coins/emc/, accessed 08/09/2008.

Tait, J. 1936. *The Medieval English Borough*. Manchester, Manchester University Press.

Tatton-Brown. T. 1986. The topography of Anglo-Saxon London. *Antiquity* 60, 21–28.

Taylor, H. M. and Taylor, J. 1975. *Anglo-Saxon Architecture* 3. Cambridge, Cambridge University Press.

Taylor, J. 2007. *An Atlas of Roman Rural Settlement in England*. Research Report 151. York, Council for British Archaeology.

Taylor, P. 2000. Introduction. In A. Williams and G. H. Martin (eds), *Little Domesday Book: Essex*, 9–32. London, Alecto Historical Editions.

TE. Taxatio Ecclesiastica Angliae et Walliae Auctoritate P. Nicholai

IV, eds T. Astle, S. Ayscough, and J. Caley, Record Commission, 1802. Online at http://www.hrionline.ac.uk/taxatio/.

Thacker, F. S. 1968. *The Thames Highway*. Newton Abbot, David and Charles.

Thomas, R. 1985. Bronze age metalwork from the Thames at Wallingford. *Oxoniensia* 49, 9–18.

Thomas, R., Robinson, M., Barrett, J. and Wilson, B. 1986. A late Bronze Age riverside settlement at Wallingford, Oxfordshire. *Archaeological Journal* 143, 174–200.

Thorn, F. R. 1988a. Hundreds and wapentakes. In A. Williams and R. W. H. Erskine (eds), *The Berkshire Domesday*, 29–33. London, Alecto Historical Editions.

Thorn, F. R. 1988b. Hundreds and wapentakes. In A. Williams and R. W. H. Erskine (eds), *The Buckinghamshire Domesday*, 37–41. London, Alecto Historical Editions.

Thorn. F. R. 1990. Hundreds and Wapentakes. In A. Williams and R. W. H. Erskine (eds), *The Oxfordshire Domesday*, 20–29. London, Alecto Historical Editions.

Thorn, F. R. and Thorn, C. 2001. The Writing of Great Domesday Book. In E. Hallam and D. Bates (eds), *Domesday*, 37–73. Stroud, Tempus.

Timby, J., Stansbie, D., Norton, A., Welsh, K. J., Stansbie, D., Norton, A. and Welsh, K. 2005. Excavations along the Newbury Reinforcement Pipeline: Iron Age-Roman activity and a Neolithic pit group. *Oxoniensia* 70, 203–307.

Tipper, J. 2004. *The Grubenhaus in Anglo-Saxon England: an Analysis and Interpretation of the Evidence from a Most Distinctive Building Type*. Yedingham, Landscape Research Centre.

Turner, H. H. 1926. Remarks on Richard of Wallingford. *St Albans and Hertfordshire Architectural and Archaeological Society Transactions*, 223–5.

Vaughan, R. (ed.) 1958. The chronicle attributed to John of Wallingford. *Camden Miscellany* 21, Camden 3rd ser. 90.

Vaughan, R. 1958. The chronicle of John of Wallingford. *English Historical Review* 73, 66–77.

VCH Berks. Victoria County History: Berkshire, eds P. H. Ditchfield and W. Page, 4 vols (London, 1906–27).

VE. Valor Ecclesiasticus, eds J. Caley and J. Hunter, Record Commission, 6 vols, 1810–34.

Vince, A. 1990. *Saxon London: An Archaeological Investigation*. London, Batsford.

Voigts, L. E. 2004. The 'Declaracions' of Richard of Wallingford: a case study of a Middle English astrological treatise. In I. Taavitsainen and P. Pahta (eds), *Medical and Scientific Writing in Late Medieval English*, 197–208. Cambridge, Cambridge University Press.

Von den Brincken, A. 1973. Die Klimatenkarte in der Chronik des Johann von Wallingford - ein Werk des Matthaeus Parisiensis? Westfalen 51, 47–56.

Walne, P. 1961. A 'double charter' of the Empress Matilda and Henry, duke of Normandy, c.1152. *English Historical Review* 76, 649–54.

Watson, E. 1979. The St Albans clock of Richard of Wallingford. *Antiquarian Horology* 11, 372–384.

Weare, T. J. 1977. Excavations at Wallingford, 1974. *Oxoniensia* 42. 204–215.

Wells, E. T. 1892. *Wallingford and its historic facts*. Wallingford, Bradford Printer and Publisher.

Wessex Archaeology 2004. Round Hill, Wittenham Clumps, Oxfordshire: an archaeological evaluation and an assessment of the results. Unpublished client report for Video Communications Ltd, document ref. 52568.09. Salisbury, Wessex Archaeology.

Wessex Archaeology. 2009. Land west of Reading Road, Winterbrook, Wallingford. Unpublished client report, document ref: 70781.03. Salisbury, Wessex Archaeology.

Whittle, A., Atkinson, R. J. C., Chambers, R. and Thomas, N. 1992. Excavations in the Neolithic and Bronze Age complex at Dorchester-on-Thames, Oxfordshire, 1947–1952 and 1981. *Proceedings of the Prehistoric Society* 58, 143–201.

Wigram, W. A. 1926. Richard of Wallingford, the abbot. *St Albans and Hertfordshire Architectural and Archaeological Society Transactions*.

Wilder, A. 2006. *Victorian Artists of Wallingford - a Tale of Two Dynasties*. Cholsey, Pie Powder Press.

Williams, A, 1995. *The English and the Norman Conquest*. Woodbridge, Boydell Press

Wilson, T. 2008. *A Narrow View Across the Upper Thames Valley in Late Prehistoric and Roman Times: Archaeological Excavations Along the Chalgrove to East Ilsley Gas Pipeline*. British Archaeological Reports British Series 467. Oxford, BAR Publishing.

Wright, P. 2004. Time and tithes. *History Today* 54:8 22–27.

Writs. Anglo-Saxon Writs, ed. F. E. H armer. Manchester, Manchester University Press, 1952.

Yates, D. T. 1999. Bronze Age field systems in the Thames Valley. *Oxford Journal of*

Yates, D. T. 2007. *Land, Power and Prestige: Bronze Age Field Systems in Southern England*. Oxford, Oxbow.

Yorke, B. 1995. *Wessex in the Early Middle Ages*. Leicester, Leicester University Press.

Young, C. J. 1977. *The Roman Pottery Industry of the Oxford Region*. British Archaeological Reports British Series 43. Oxford, BAR Publishing.

INDEX

All places are assigned to the historic counties as they were before re-organization in 1974.

Hatton (Middlx), 66
Hazlebury (Wilts), 58, 65
Healfdene, 66
Healfdene, a thegn of Earl Harold, 59, 66
Hedsor (Bucks), 44
Hemming, 59, 66
Hemming, two men of, 66
Hendred, East (Berks), 42, 53
Hendred, West (Berks), 37
  manor, 36
Henry, 46, 47
Henry de Ferrers, 30, 32, 37, 46, 47, 32,
  39, 43, 48, 49, 54, 55
Henry I, king of England (1101–35), 20,
  22, 37, 38, 39, 56, 57, 63
Henry II, king of England (1154–89), 40,
  60, 63
Henry III, king of England (1216–72),
  55, 59
Henry of Anjou, 18, 22, 38, 63
  See Henry II
Henry the larderer, 39
Henry VIII, king of England (1509–47),
  63
Henry, duke of Normandy, 63
  See Henry II
Henton (Oxon), 58, 65
Herch, man of Beorhtric, 66
Hertfordshire, 8, 36
Heyford (Oxon), 65, 66
Hill, David, 79
Hillingdon (Middlx), 58, 65
Hinksey (Berks) 43
History of the Church of Abingdon, 56, 57
Hitcham (Bucks), 59, 66
Hollingdon (Bucks), 65
Honorius II, Pope (1124–30), 20, 37
Hook Norton (Oxon), 57
  barony of, 57
Horton (Bucks), 66
Houghton (Hants), 65
housecarl, 26, 30, 39, 40, 41, 46, 47, 56,
  58, 73
Hugh de Bolbec, 32, 36, 39, 48, 49
Hugh de Port, 38
Hugh, 48, 49
Hugh, earl of Chester, 32, 39, 48, 49
Hugh the Great of Scoca, 32, 46, 47, 48,
  49, 49 n26
Humphrey, 64, 66
Humphrey Visdeloup, 46, 47
Hundred Rolls, 63
Hungerford (Berks), manor of, 34
Huntingdon (Hunts), 32, 41
Huscarle family, 41, 56, 58
Hutchinson, Mr., 13

Ickenham (Middlx), manor of, 56, 58, 64,
  66, 67
Ickford (Bucks), 65
Icknield Way, 17, 52
Ilbert de Lacy, 48, 49
Ilsley, East and West (Berk), 7, 32, 39,
  43, 48, 49
Ingelri see Engelric
Isle of Wight, 48 n12
Iver (Bucks), 56, 59, 64
  manor, 58

John de Basinges, 61
John, king of England (1189–1216), 55,
  53
Joscelin, bishop of Salisbury (1142–
  1184), 37

Kennett, River, 52
Ketel, 66
Kingston Blount (Oxon), 65

Lambert the priest, 31, 32, 48, 49
Lambourne Downs, 52
Lanfranc, archbishop of Canterbury
  (1070–89), 37, 39, 48, 49
Langley (Berks), 64
Langtree Hundred (Oxon), 44
lawmen, 31, 32, 40
Leeds, E. T., 10, 13
  archive, 13
Leicester (Leics), 30, 36, 73
  University of, 2
Leicester, honour of, 63
Leland, John, 22
Lemar, see Leofmær
Leofflæd, 31, 32, 39, 48, 49
Leofgifu, 32, 48, 49
Leofmær, a man of Beorhtric, 66
Leofnoth, 58, 65
Leofric, 65
Leofric, a man of Beorhtric, 66
Leofric, son of Æthelwold II, 58
Leofsi, see Leofsige
Leofsige, a man of Beorhtric, 66
Leofweard, 64
Leofwig, a man of Eadwig, 66
Leofwin, see Leofwig
Letcombe Basset (Berks), 64
Leuenod, see Leofnoth
Leuric, see Leofric
Leuuard, see Leofweard
Lewknor Hundred (Oxon), 44
Lincoln (Lincs), 1, 31, 32, 35
Lincoln, bishop of, 35
  See Remigius
Little Domesday Book, 30
Littlecote (Bucks), 66
Littlecott (Wilts), 66
loanland, 55, 59, 61
London, 8, 41, 52, 57, 61, 63, 74, 75
  Addle Street, 75
  Aldermanbury, 75
  Billingsgate, 74
  Cheapside, 74
  constable of, see Geoffrey de
    Mandeville
  Cornhill, 75
  Cripplegate, 75
  Hoggen Lane, 75
  London Bridge, 52
  Lundenburh, 74
  Milk Street, 75
  Queenhithe, 74
  Seething, 75
  St Martin le Grand, 36, 59
  St Paul's (Paulesbyri), 75
Loseley (Surrey), 65
Lowbury Hill (Berks), 9
Ludric, 40

Ludwell (Oxon), 56
Lundenburh, 74

Mackney (Berks), 8, 17, 18, 19, 22, 26,
  38, 42, 53
Magnus Swarthy, 67
Maisy family, 58
Maitland, F. W., 27
Manton (Wilts), 58, 64
Mapledurham (Oxon), 61, 65
Mappleborough (Warks), 37
Marcus Varius Severus, 8
Marlborough (Wilts), 52, 58
Marlborough Downs, 52
Marston (Bucks), 66
Marsworth (Bucks), 59, 66
Matilda of Wallingford, 38, 55, 56, 57,
  58, 60, 63
Matilda, Empress, 18, 22, 38, 63
Matthew Paris, 37
Mercia, 20, 68
metalwork in the Thames, 6
Middlesex, 55
Miles Crispin, 4, 30, 31, 32, 36, 38, 39,
  40, 41, 46, 47, 55, 56, 57, 58, 59, 60,
  61, 62, 63, 64, 65, 66, 67, 73
Miles Molay, 32, 33, 48, 49
  See Miles Crispin
Miles of Gloucester, 63
Millbrook, 17, 18, 21, 22, 26, 80, 81
Milston (Wilts), 65
Milton Earnest (Wilts), 65
Mongewell (Oxon), 17, 19
Monk Sherborne Priory, 38
Morcar, see Ealdræd, man of
Moreton, North (Berks), 18, 36, 37, 39,
  41, 42, 43
  manor, 31, 36, 37
Moreton, South (Berks), 18, 42
Moulsford Road North (Oxon), 7, 10
Moulsford (Berks), 18, 37, 39, 53
  Halfpenny Lane, 7
Musgrave, Capt. C., 13, 14, 15, 16

Nakedthorn (Berks), manor of, 32
Nethercote (Oxon), 65
Newbury Reinforcement pipeline, 7
Newington (Oxon), 7, 48, 49
  Ewe Farm, 7
  manor, 33, 39, 43
Newnham Murren (Oxon), 7, 31, 36, 46,
  47, 59, 60, 61, 66
  manor, 39, 43, 59
  parish, 17
Nigel, 65
Nigel d'Aubigny, 30, 36, 37, 46, 46 n1,
  47
Nigel d'Oilly, 57, 60
North Wessex Downs, 52
Northampton Archaeology, 25
Northampton (Northants), 30, 33, 40, 72
Norwich (Norf), 30, 35, 40, 72, 74
Nottingham (Notts), 30, 40, 62, 72
  castle, 63
Nottinghamshire, 33, 54

Ock, River, 52
Offa, King (757–96), 16, 79, 77

Stratford, Fenny (Bucks), 10
Stratton Audley (Oxon), 65
Streatley (Berks), 9, 61
Sulham (Berks), 66
Surrey, 55
Sutton Courtenay (Berks), 10, 31, 46, 47,
  52, 53, 54, 59–60
  manor, 31, 39, 43
Svertingr, 37
  See Swærting
Swærting, 37, 46, 46 n1, 47
  See Svertingr
Swein, 39
Swindon (Wilts), 58
Swyncombe (Oxon), 56, 65

tenure by barony, 54
Thame (Oxon), 20
Thame Hundred (Oxon), 44
Thame, River, 3, 43, 44, 52
Thames Valley Archaeological Services,
  13 See TVAS
Thatcham (Berks), 31
theft, 31, 48, 49
Thenford (Northants), 59, 65
Third Crusade in 1191, 63
Thomley (Oxon), 65
Thorkil, 36, 39
Thurleigh (Beds), 65, 66
Tidmarsh (Berks), 59
Tilehurst (Berks), 61
Tiscott (Herts), 55, 66
Toki the housecarl, 52, 55, 56, 58, 59, 60,
  64
Toli, 65
Tostig, Earl, 62
Tovi, 36, 40
Tovi the Wend, 40
Turchetil, see Turchil
Turchil, 66
Turkdean, Lower (Gloucs), 60
Turkdean, Upper (Gloucs), 67
Turold nephew of Wigod, 57, 58, 65
TVAS, 15, 16
TWHAS, 1, 2, 4, 9

Ulf, 39, 65, 67
Ulf housecarl, 58
Ulf, thegn of King Edward, 58
Upton (Bucks), 66

Vale of the White Horse, 44, 52, 76
view of frankpledge, 4, 63
Viking, 67
Vlf, see Ulf
Vlstan, see Wulfstan
Vluric, see Wulfric
Vluuardi, see Wulfweard

Waddesdon (Bucks), 66
Wainhill (Oxon), 66
Walcot (Wilts), 58, 65
Walkelin, bishop of Winchester, 31, 39,
  46, 47
Wallingford (Berks)
  acres, 4, 30, 34, 41, 42, 46, 47, 56
  Anglo-Saxon cemetery, 3, 11, 13–16,
    20, 69

bridge, 2, 3, 17, 18, 23, 25, 26, 42, 74
bridgehead, 42, 59, 74, 77, 78
Bullcroft, 1, 2, 3, 4, 17, 23, 36, 72, 75,
  80, 81
castle, 1, 2, 3, 4, 17, 18, 23, 25, 26, 30,
  34, 36, 38, 40, 41, 46, 47, 55, 56, 60,
  61, 62, 63, 69, 72, 73, 75, 79, 81, 82
  Castle Meadows, 2, 72, 73
  chapel, see St Nicholas
  construction, 34, 38, 55
  ditches, 17
  earthworks, 17
  inner bailey, 2, 72
  kitchens, 73
  middle bailey, 1
  moats, 81
  outer defences, 82
churches and chapels, 17–26, 36–8
  All Saints, All Hallows, 2, 3, 4,
    23, 25, 26, 36, 41, 42, 60
    churchyard, 23
    parish, 17, 25, 61
  Christchurch, 37
    See Holy Trinity
  Holy Trinity, 3, 4, 23, 25, 26, 36–
    37, 38, 39, 41, 60, 63, 72, 75,
    81
    parish, 25, 36, 41
  Holy Trinity the lesser, 20, 22, 26,
    38
    See St Leonard
  St John-super-Aquam, 3, 6, 23,
    25, 36, 37, 41, 74
  St Leonard, 2, 3, 20, 21, 22, 23,
    25, 26, 37, 38, 42, 60, 74, 75
    advowson, 40
    churchyard, 17, 21
    parish, 21, 22, 23, 37–8, 74
  St Lucian, 2, 3, 20, 21, 22, 25, 26,
    34, 38, 60, 74, 75, 83
    advowson, 40
    parish, 22, 23, 36, 38, 40, 80
  St Martin, 3, 4, 23, 25, 26, 36, 37,
    41
    churchyard, 1, 25
    parish, 25
  St Mary Grace, 23
  St Mary le More, 23, 25, 26, 36,
    37, 41
    parish, 23, 25, 36
  St Mary-the-less, St Mary of the
    Stalls, 25
  St Michael, 25, 74
    churchyard, 1, 25
  St Nicholas, 4, 23, 25, 26, 36, 40,
    41, 56, 60, 61, 72, 73
    dean, 25
  St Peter in the West, 23, 25, 74
    parish, 25, 26
  St Rumbold, Ruald, 2, 21, 22, 26,
    37, 38, 42, 74
    advowson, 40
    atrium, 22, 37
    churchyard, 22, 37
    parish, 22, 23. 38
defences and gates, 32, 42, 69–72, 74,
  80–2
  east gate, 31, 38

north gate, 72, 74, 82
south gate, 2, 3, 18, 22, 23, 36, 37,
  38, 40, 42, 72, 74
west gate, 25, 41, 72
fields, 17–26
  Chalmore, 18, 22, 23, 37, 38
  Portmanfield, 22, 38
  Portmanmoor, 22
  St John's Field, 23
French borough, 22, 40, 72, 83
Holy Trinity Priory, 3, 4, 23, 25, 26,
  36–37, 38, 39, 41, 60, 63, 72, 75, 81
Hospital of St John the Baptist, 22, 23,
  38
  chapel, 23
Kinecroft, 1, 2, 3, 22, 36, 69, 72, 73,
  74, 75, 80, 81
mills, 18, 22, 36
mint, 30, 46, 47, 54
moothall and gallows, 40
palace, 4, 41, 60, 73, 75
people
  burgesses, 30, 33, 34, 39, 40, 41, 46,
    46 n1, 47, 63
  reeve, 40, 46, 47, 48, 49
  moneyers, 30, 46, 47
  smiths, 31, 32, 48, 49
streets and places
  Alms House, 21
  Boots the Chemist, 36
  Bred Streat, 22
  Bridge House, 74
  Bruttestrete, 22, 37
  Castle Priory, 17
  Castle Street, 4, 25, 31, 82, 83
  Cattle Market car-park, 25
  Coach House, 74
  Cornmarket, 22, 37, 40, 72
  Council School, 13
  Fish St, 22
  Goldsmith's Lane, 22, 37, 72
  Gospel Hall, 13
  Harris Garage, 69
  High Street, 3, 4, 23, 25, 31, 35, 36,
    38, 72
    George Hotel, 35
    no 89, 35
    St Michael's House, 35
  Kinecroft, 72
  Lamb Garage, 69
  market, 26, 48, 49, 41
  Market Place, no. 7, 36
  St Mary's Street, 22, 25, 82
    no. 14, 36
  Medical Practice, 18
  Mill Lane, 22
  New Road, 25
  Pavilion, 13
  Reading Road, 17, 21, 82
  Squires Walk, 82
  St George's Road, no 16, 69
  St John's School, 2
  St Leonard's Lane, 74
  St Martin's Street, 22, 25, 82, 83
  Thames Street, 74
  The Lodge, 74
  Town Wharf, 18, 22, 26
  Upper School, 6

www.ingramcontent.com/pod-product-compliance
Lightning Source LLC
Chambersburg PA
CBHW061008030426
42334CB00033B/3414